Information Systems for the Nontechnical Manager

Information Systems for the Nontechnical Manager

Theodore Larson and Daniel Friesen

University of North Texas at Dallas

cognella®
SAN DIEGO

Bassim Hamadeh, CEO and Publisher
John Remington, Executive Editor
Gem Rabanaera, Senior Project Editor
Alia Bales, Production Editor
Emely Villavicencio, Senior Graphic Designer
Stephanie Kohl, Licensing Coordinator
Natalie Piccotti, Director of Marketing
Kassie Graves, Vice President of Editorial
Jamie Giganti, Director of Academic Publishing

Cover image copyright © 2018 iStockphoto LP/shuoshu.

Printed in the United States of America.

3970 Sorrento Valley Blvd., Ste. 500, San Diego, CA 92121

Dedicated to Dr. Daniel Friesen,
a committed teacher, mentor, and friend

Table of Contents

Preface . . . . **xiii**

Introduction . . . . **xv**

Part I **Overview** . . . . **xix**
Look Ahead   xix

Chapter 1 **Intro to Information Systems** 1
Pre-Reading Checklist   1
Main Story: Driving Principles   1
Side Quest: Analogy   1
Main Story: Moore's Law   2
Side Quest: What Is a Transistor?   4
Side Quest: Core Competency Decay   5
Main Story: Communication Constraints   6
Side Quest: Business Communication   7
Main Story: Skill Decay   8
Bonus Loot: Business Function—Entry-Level Workers   8
Bonus Loot: Resume Builders—Known Technologies   9
Bonus Loot: Soft Skills   10
Bonus Loot: Certifications—MOS   10
References   11

Chapter 2 **Models** 13
Pre-Reading Checklist   13
Main Story: Driving Principles   13
Side Quest: Analogy   13
Main Story: Models   15
Main Story: The Seesaw Model   16
Side Quest: Seesaw Model Manipulation   17
Main Story: The Decision-Mode Ternary   19
Side Quest: Ternaries   19
Main Story: Distillation Model   20
Side Story: Distillation Model Manipulation   22
Bonus Loot: Business Function—Health Care   22

Bonus Loot: Resume Builders—Distillation   23
Bonus Loot: Soft Skills—Elevator Pitch   24
Bonus Loot: Certifications—Open Badges   24
References   25

Chapter 3   **Information Security** 27
Pre-Reading Checklist   27
Main Story: Guiding Principles   27
Side Quest: Analogy—Bank Vaults   27
Main Story: Organizational Security   29
Side Quest: Threat Sources   29
Side Quest: Threat Categories   30
Main Story: Information Security Responsibility   32
Main Story: Security Oversight   33
Side Quest: Security Outsourcing   34
Main Story: Security Plan   34
Main Story: Information Security and the Seesaw Model   36
Main Story: Security Priority   37
Bonus Loot: Business Functions—Operations   38
Bonus Loot: Resume Builders—IT Certifications   38
Bonus Loot: Soft Skills—Personal/Online Security   39
Bonus Loot: Certifications—Security Certifications   40
References   41

Part II   **The Seesaw Model** 43
Where We've Been   43
Look Ahead   43

Chapter 4   **Hardware** 45
Pre-Reading Checklist   45
Side Quest: Analogy—Fire   45
Main Story: Driving Principles   47
Main Story: The Four-Component Model   47
Side Quest: Scope   48
Main Story: Consultation   50
Main Story: Price Points   51
Bonus Loot: Business Function—Customer Support   52
Bonus Loot: Resume Builders—Technical Support   52
Bonus Loot: Soft Skills—Negotiation   53
Bonus Loot: Certifications—A+   54
References   54

Chapter 5   **Software** 55
Pre-Reading Checklist   55
Main Story: Driving Principles   55
Side Quest: Analogy—Liquor Sales   56

Main Story: Software Licensing   56
Side Quest: License Types   58
Main Story: Software Types   59
Side Quest: Software Price Points   60
Main Story: ... as a Service   62
Side Quest: The Virus Effect   62
Bonus Loot: Business Function—Accounting   63
Bonus Loot: Resume Builders—Open Source Contribution   64
Bonus Loot: Soft Skills—First Impressions   65
Authors' Note   66
Bonus Loot: Certifications—Further Microsoft   66
References   66

Chapter 6   **Communications** 67
Pre-Reading Checklist   67
Main Story: Driving Principles   67
Side Quest: Analogy—Nuclear Power Plants   67
Main Story: What Is Communication?   68
Side Quest: Networks   69
Side Quest: The Internet   71
Main Story: Information Overload   72
Side Quest: The Cloud   73
Bonus Loot: Business Function—Public Relations   74
Bonus Loot: Resume Builders—Leadership   75
Bonus Loot: Soft Skills—Online First Impressions   75
Bonus Loot: Certifications—Training Websites   76
References   77

Chapter 7   **People** 79
Pre-Reading Checklist   79
Main Story: Driving Principles   79
Side Quest: Analogy—Characters Versus NPCs   80
Main Story: Roles   80
Side Quest: Semantics   81
Main Story: Decision-Mode Ternary   82
Side Quest: Operationalization   83
Main Story: Security Vulnerability   84
Side Quest: Further Training   85
Bonus Loot: Business Function—Human Resources   85
Bonus Loot: Resume Builders—Professional Organizations   86
Bonus Loot: Soft Skills—Meetings   87
Bonus Loot: Certifications—Speech and Public Speaking   87
References   88

Chapter 8   **Process** 89
  Pre-Reading Checklist   89
  Main Story: Driving Principles   89
  Side Quest: Analogy—Carpentry   89
  Main Story: Four-Component Model   90
  Side Quest: Pseudo Code   92
  Main Story: Importance of Process   93
  Side Quest: UML   94
  Side Quest: BPMN   95
  Side Quest: ISO 9000 Certification   95
  Bonus Loot: Business Function—Industrial Engineering   96
  Bonus Loot: Resume Builders—Process Description   96
  Bonus Loot: Soft Skills—Work Ethic   97
  Bonus Loot: Certifications—Six Sigma   97
  References   98

Chapter 9   **Decisions** 99
  Pre-Reading Checklist   99
  Main Story: Driving Principles   99
  Side Quest: Analogy—Pets   99
  Main Story: Who Makes Decisions?   100
  Main Story: What's the Point of Information Systems?   101
  Side Quest: Impact   102
  Main Story: Structure of Problems   103
  Side Quest: Model Application   105
  Bonus Loot: Business Function—Customer Support   106
  Bonus Loot: Resume Builders—Personal Brand   106
  Bonus Loot: Soft Skills—Getting Employee Buy-In   107
  Bonus Loot: Certifications—SAS   108
  References   108

Chapter 10   **Data** 109
  Pre-Reading Checklist   109
  Main Story: Driving Principles   109
  Side Quest: Analogy—Wealth   109
  Main Story: What Is Data?   110
  Side Quest: Data Types   111
  Main Story: Data ETS/ETL   112
  Main Story: Data Security   113
  Side Quest: Data Scarcity   115
  Bonus Loot: Business Function—Sales   116
  Bonus Loot: Resume Builders—Academic/Professional Papers   117
  Bonus Loot: Soft Skills—Asking the Right Questions   117
  Bonus Loot: Certifications—Tableau   118
  References   118

Chapter 11   **Data Processing** **119**

Pre-Reading Checklist   119
Main Story: Driving Principles   119
Side Quest: Analogy—A House   120
Main Story: Information Utility   120
Side Quest: Data Visualization   122
Main Story: Timeliness of Data Processing   123
Main Story: Storytelling   124
Side Quest: Feature Creep   125
Main Story: Logical Fallacies   126
Bonus Loot: Business Function—Project Management   127
Bonus Loot: Resume Builders—Self-Promotion   127
Bonus Loot: Soft Skills—Elevator Pitch Follow-Up   128
Bonus Loot: Certifications—PMI   129

Chapter 12   **DSS (Decision Support Systems)** **131**

Pre-Reading Checklist   131
Main Story: Driving Principles   131
Side Quest: Analogy—Computer Sidekicks   132
Main Story: What Is a DSS?   132
Side Quest: DSS Examples   134
Main Story: Decisions and the Three-Tier Model   134
Main Story: Machine Intelligence   137
Side Quest: Data Warehouses   138
Bonus Loot: Business Function—Consulting   139
Bonus Loot: Resume Builders—Websites   140
Bonus Loot: Soft Skills—Feature Creep Mitigation   140
Bonus Loot: Certifications—College   141
References   142

Part III   **Analysis and Design** **143**

Where We've Been   143
Look Ahead   143

Chapter 13   **Systems Development Life Cycle** **145**

Pre-Reading Checklist   145
Main Story: Driving Principles   145
Side Quest: Analogy—Waterfalls (Cascades)   145
Main Story: Cascade Model and SDLC   146
Side Quest: Each Stage of the SDLC   147
Analysis   148
Design   148
Testing   149
Implementation   150
Maintenance   151
Side Quests: New or Revised Processes   151

Main Story: Time, Money, Correctness   152
Side Quest: Efficiency and Effectiveness   154
Main Story: Agile Methods   155
Side Quests: Full Circle   156
Bonus Loot: Business Function—Finance   156
Bonus Loot: Resume Builders—Community Organizations   158
Bonus Loot: Soft Skills—Assessment   159
Bonus Loot: Certifications—Process Design   159
References   160

Chapter 14   **Systems Analysis** 161
Pre-Reading Checklist   161
Main Story: Driving Principles   161
Side Quest: Analogy—Marathons   161
Main Story: Back to Basics   162
Main Story: What Is a Process?   163
Side Quest: Information Flow   164
Side Quest: Process Definition   165
Main Story: Process Concierge   166
Side Quest: Problem Solving   167
Main Story: Support Function   168
Bonus Loot: Business Function—Management   168
Bonus Loot: Resume Builders—Governance   169
Bonus Loot: Soft Skills—Admittance of Fault   169

Chapter 15   **Systems Design** 171
Pre-Reading Checklist   171
Main Story: Driving Principles   171
Side Quest: Analogy—Civilization   171
Main Story: Gantt Charts   172
Side Story: The System Process   174
Main Story: Redesigning Hardware or People   175
Side Quest: User Input   176
Side Quest: Departmental Needs   177
Bonus Loot: Business Function—Facilities and Construction   178

Part IV   **Conclusion** 179
Where We've Been   179
Look Ahead   179

Chapter 16   **Business Analytics** 181
Pre-Reading Checklist   181
Main Story: Driving Principles   181
Side Quest: Analogy   181
Main Story: Business Analytics   183
Main Story: Analytic Triangles   183

Side Quest: Data Visualization   184
Side Quest: Modeling   185
Side Quest: Data Analytics   185
Side Quest: Data Cleaning   186
Main Story: Artificial Intelligence   186
Bonus Loot: Business Function—Hospitality Management   188
Bonus Loot: Resume Builders—Online Training Sites   189
Bonus Loot: Soft Skills—Finding an Audience   190
Bonus Loot: Certifications—Khan Academy   190
References   190

Chapter 17   **Bringing It All Together** 191
Pre-Reading Checklist   191
Main Story: Driving Principles   191
Side Quest: Analogy—Megastructures   191
Side Quest: Information Silos   192
Main Story: Big Data   193
Main Story: Semantic Web   193
Main Story: Augmented Reality   194
Bonus Loot: Business Function—Information Systems   194
Bonus Loot: Resume Builders—External Review   195
Bonus Loot: Soft Skills—Summary and BLUF   195
References   196

Chapter 18   **Driving Principles** 197
Pre-Reading Checklist   197
Main Story: Driving Principles   197
Side Quest: Analogy—Blood and the Vascular System   197
Main Story: *Abstractio ad Absurdum*   198
Main Story: General Principles   200

Chapter 19   **So You Want to Work in IT?** 203
Main Story: David Alston   203

Chapter 20   **So You Want to Manage IT?** 205
Main Story: Alan Lowrie   205

Chapter 21   **So You Want to Be a CIO?** 211
Main Story: Sherry Byrnes   211

Chapter 22   **Cases** 215
Overview   215
Case 1: La Superior   215
Case 2: D'ansa Jazz Stage   218
Case 3: Management of Technical People   219
Case 4: Thoughts on Managing Technical People   220

Chapter 23   **Models** 221
Overview   221
Chapter 1 Model: Optimization   222
Chapter 2 Model: SWOT Analysis   222
Chapter 3 Model: CIA Model   223
Chapter 4 Model: Revenue Model (P = R − C)   223
Chapter 5 Model: C = VC + FC   224
Chapter 6 Model: Theory of Transportation   225
Chapter 7 Model: Classical Economics   225
Chapter 8 Model: Five Forces   226
Chapter 9 Model: Theory X Versus Theory Y (Theory Z)   227
Chapter 10 Model: Plutchik's Wheel of Emotion and Sentiment Lexicons   227
Chapter 11 Model: Ratios   228
Chapter 12 Model: Deming (PDCA) Cycle   228
Chapter 13 Model: Maslow's Hierarchy of Needs   229
Chapter 14 Model: Accounting Model (A = L + E)   230
Chapter 15 Model: Simon's Model of Decision Making   230
Chapter 16 Model: Cluster Analysis   231
Chapter 17 Model: Porter's Generic Strategies   231
Chapter 18 Model: Prisoner's Dilemma   232
References   233

Chapter 24   **Historical Figures** 235
Overview   235
Chapter 1 Figure: Herbert Simon   236
Chapter 2 Figure: Michael Porter   236
Chapter 3 Figure: Brian Krebs   236
Chapter 4 Figure: Michael Dell   237
Chapter 5 Figure: Ada Lovelace   237
Chapter 6 Figure: Vint Cerf and Tim Berners-Lee   238
Chapter 7 Figure: Richard Stallman   238
Chapter 8 Figure: Donald Knuth   239
Chapter 9 Figure: John McAfee   239
Chapter 10 Figure: Noam Chomsky   239
Chapter 11 Figure: Elon Musk   240
Chapter 12 Figure: Jack Ma and Jeff Bezos   240
Chapter 13 Figure: Linus Torvalds   241
Chapter 14 Figure: Bill Gates   242
Chapter 15 Figure: Steve Jobs   242
Chapter 16 Figure: Barack Obama and Donald Trump   243
Chapter 17 Figure: John von Neumann   243
Chapter 18 Figure: Sun Tzu   244
References   244

Conclusion **247**

Preface

If you read any part of the preface, this first paragraph is the most likely one. So please take a moment to note that the authors welcome feedback and criticism on this text. Please feel free to contact head author, Theodore Larson, at theodore.larson@untdallas.edu with your thoughts or ideas.

Introduction

"Those who fail to learn from history are doomed to repeat it" is a phrase that applies to so many areas that it's practically universal. But consider briefly what it means. Does it mean that if we fail to learn about the Civil War there will be another Battle of Little Round Top? Will we have a second War of the Roses between warring feudal lords? Obviously not. Such pithy statements, or ours at least, are rarely that literal.

Instead, the broad meaning of the statement is that we should take the principles that we see in hindsight and apply them toward the future. So, while individual events from history may be broadly important, our approach is to understand (a) the principles that caused certain events to happen and (b) how those principles can be used to encourage similar positive outcomes (peace, scientific revolution, prosperity) and discourage similar negative outcomes (war, famine, oppression).

That is the underlying theory of this book. You, the nontechnical reader, shouldn't be bogged down in a thousand technical concepts, exposed to serial numbers that may not even be valid by the time you read this book (e.g., let's take a moment to figure out a few subnet masks for our IP addresses!), or learn about how to apply the application programs produced by internet companies who are frequently fickle in their interface. Not that there's anything wrong with that, if that is your interest! As I write this, I am waiting on an IT employee to repair my office PC's software so that the material that I want to save in the cloud can be found again. Important? Very! Good use of my time to learn how to reliably fix it myself? Debatable—probably not so much. Instead, the idea is to present you with some core principles that you can use to understand how information systems affect an organization and how your area can take advantage of the benefits of thinking in terms of information systems.

Going one step further, many of the principles from information systems apply across a wide range of disciplines. Understanding how information flows through an organization is critical to understanding how to improve the effectiveness and efficiency of any business function.

THEME

Memory athletes will tell you that one of the most effective ways of making a memory linger is to make it unique, offensive, or memorable through some form of whimsy. We have chosen that last option as the most effective for a textbook and attempted to structure this book in terms of a video game. Video games start with a main story where the protagonist is given a primary task and the story develops along with that task. Typically, along the way there are side quests that can be attempted. And then there are little hidden places that have bits of extra bonus loot.

1. Main Story: These sections are intended to present themselves as a set of driving principles, and then we explore those driving principles in more detail. These are intended to build into a broad gestalt by the end of the text.
2. Side Quests: These sections are important, but if they are too much of a detour, too detailed, boring, or otherwise unhelpful, they can probably be safely ignored. That's not to say that they aren't valuable to retain, but they aren't essential to grasping the central principles.
3. Bonus Loot: One theme that will be repeated is that there's no point in anything if it doesn't return back to the real world with an action statement. These Bonus Loot sections are intended to provide a smattering of related action points by theme.

   a. Business Functions: Each chapter will explore how information systems relates to a different business function, with the understanding that information systems is simultaneously a part of every other business function and every other function is a part of information systems.
   b. Resume Builders: There are certain approaches that make sense to a seasoned information systems professional that won't necessarily be apparent to a pre-employment student or a young professional. These are intended to give options for how to make oneself stand out.
   c. Soft Skills: Employers consistently emphasize that they are not looking for applicants with more training on technical skills. Almost every company rolls their eyes at what students learn in college and then proceeds to teach them the "real" way to do something. However, students who are able to lead meetings, solve disputes, get along well with others, or even practice hygiene have the skill sets that every hiring manager doesn't feel like they see enough of.
   d. Certifications: A core part of being an information worker is having certifications. A core part of managing information workers is knowing what the certifications mean. These sections are intended to be a mélange somewhere between encouraging you to gain certain certifications and explaining what they'll mean when they appear on someone's resume.

HOW TO READ THIS BOOK

This book is intended for a survey course in management information systems. This presumes, then, that it is largely being read by business majors from a variety of nontechnical fields. This book likely also has value to technical fields, but there is a presumption that most of the material will be conveyed to those students over time and across the rest of their classes. The target student does not expect to enter a technical field but knows that having a technical department assigned or attached to them is increasingly likely over the course of their career.

This textbook assumes several things on the part of the student, specifically that they've already completed a modicum of business coursework. The target student level is junior year, which means that students will likely have already taken coursework in accounting, economics, and business statistics. There's a presumption that a general education or a lower-level "how to use computers" class has also been taken. There is a tendency in books of this level to reiterate many of the basic concepts that should have been addressed in earlier coursework. The authors make every effort to not repeat those explanations, except where the nuance plays a part in the overall pedagogical narrative.

This textbook is trying to express very simple concepts; however, like many Zen koans, the simpler the idea, the more difficult it is to put into words. Remember that there is a single, unifying narrative and that all of the words are reflections of that primary conceptualization, not the conceptualization itself. In another sense, this textbook is trying to survey a large, technically oriented field in a manner that's 1,000 miles wide and 2 inches deep, all while keeping in mind the strategic nature of the information systems function.

A NOTE ON FIGURES

In Japanese Martial Art tradition, the sensei doesn't teach stupid things. The first technique that a new student learns is packed with a number of concepts that are not immediately apparent at first. The figures in this text attempt to emulate, in as much as the product of a few months can attempt to emulate a tradition that spans millenia, that practice. To that extent, here are a few notes:

1. The figures are simple. An apt student should have no difficulty remembering the basic themes and reproducing them in a brainstorming session, consultation, or on the back of a napkin during an informal meeting to illustrate a point.
2. The figures are recognizable. The authors are not artists. And yet, they've drawn these same illustrations on whiteboards and Post-It notes a thousand times. These are the same illustrations they use to demonstrate basic business concepts, which should be readily understandable by most business graduates.
3. The figures are adaptable. Consider the difference between figures 2.2 and 2.3; the same figure can be layered with more or less information as the situation warrants, or even turned to a completely different purpose to help explain the matter at hand.

4. The figures are dynamic. Something is lost in the translation to static images. Don't underestimate the value of using the act of drawing an illustration as an expository aid for the telling of a story.

These figures are intended to encourage you to use them. Some of them are shaky and have bad handwriting. The authors could have fixed that. But if the authors are willing to show you these figures with some minor flaws, you should feel comfortable using, creating, and adapting them to situations as you see fit.

PART I

Overview

LOOK AHEAD

Clearly, the first section of this book is about information systems and the management thereof. So we can't really proceed without a definition or two.

Information systems is an academic study of systems with a specific reference to information and the complementary networks of hardware and software that people and organizations use to collect, filter, process, create, and distribute data.

The authors of that definition made information systems both (a) a type of system (found in and used by businesses everywhere, of all types) as well as (b) the study of them. Note the components: networks of hardware and software. These authors remove people from the systems; however, that point can be argued, so there is no need to consider that to be a hard-and-fast rule. How does this relate to other highly used definitions of terms in popular use?

Information technology is the study or use of systems (especially computers and telecommunications) for storing, retrieving, and sending information.

These authors focus on the devices—which consist of both hardware and software or instructions—at the expense of the data *and* people. This is not unusual for a definition of information technology.

Computer science is the study of processes that interact with data and that can be represented as data in the form of programs. It enables the use of algorithms to manipulate, store, and communicate digital information.

The authors of this definition relegate computer science to an academic study, but they also sneak in a creation aspect: People write programs to manage digital information.

These are the things that need to be covered before proper study of information systems can be made. We begin with Moore's law, the principal driving force in computers and technology.

We then move into a description of the models that will be used in this text (seesaw, ternary, and distillation), and finally we cover information security. This last item is frequently considered a side topic, but the importance of it being "baked in" to organizational and application development is a core principle of the field.

CHAPTER 1

Intro to Information Systems

VOCABULARY

> Analogy

> Communication

CONCEPTS

> Moore's law

> Skill decay

> Business communication

MAIN STORY: DRIVING PRINCIPLES

1. Information systems is the current driver of market expansion via Moore's law.
2. Constraints on the ability to communicate limit technological and, therefore, systems-oriented growth.
3. Moore's law and communication limits have disrupted the traditional view of personal and professional development.

SIDE QUEST: ANALOGY

Rather than wrestle with definitions, sometimes it's clearer to examine reality through the lens of analogy. Consider this idea: "At its peak, the Roman Empire had spread throughout the entire known world." That's a commonly encountered introduction to the ancient Roman Empire. If you look at a map, you can see that its land area was less than half that of the United States. We now know that "the entire known world" was a bit of an overzealous hyperbole on the part of the Romans. What kept them from expanding further? Why were they eventually brought down by groups of barbarians when they were one of the most sophisticated societies—including civil and military engineering—of the ancient world?

A historian might balk at giving a short and simple answer. However, we can call attention to at least one factor: communication. As long as the armies of Caesar could report to Rome or transmit his instructions in a reasonable time, things went well. But as the boundaries expanded, communications became more difficult, allowing for more autonomy by the prefects and generals at the borders.

So why grow? If Caesar had less immediate control over remote outposts as they grew further away and the technology didn't exist to support that growth, why were the legions constantly fighting to expand the Roman borders?

The impetus, again simplified to stay with this analogy, lies in the structure of the Roman economy. The maxim that "all roads lead to Rome" wasn't just about geography. Goods, services, and learning from the outlying provinces all made their way to Rome. For Rome to grow it had to do so by acquiring new territory and the goods that came along with it. As long as there was an increase in the amount of goods and services flowing into Rome, the ruling classes could grow without direct conflict. But when the rate of growth slowed, there was growth only through internal conflict. Rome could thrive only as long as it was growing.

Remember, this chapter is the first one in the book, so its ideas should form the foundation for the rest of the material. How does expansionism of the Roman Empire relate to information systems? It's a bit of a cognitive leap to go from the Roman Era of 2,500–1,500 years ago to a field that has existed for less than 25 years. But one key to fully understand a field is to see analogies from history and understand history's place within the greater context.

MAIN STORY: MOORE'S LAW

Gordon Moore was one of the founders of Intel—one of the more prominent and important computer-based corporations.

> ### BOX 1.1
>
> For those who need more history on Intel, check out *In Search of Excellence*. If you're studying business, it's difficult to go wrong with that book. The original was published in 1982, but it's been updated since.

One of the questions that is always asked of people in leadership positions is "What's going to happen next?" Relying on his observations of past products, Moore predicted that the trend that he had observed over his career would continue. His prediction was that the number of components in an integrated circuit would double every year or two. Since we are not interested in processor design, we need to extrapolate that idea a little bit.

In fact, the idea behind Moore's prediction has been popularized into Moore's law. Moore's law, from a business perspective, is now focused on the idea that the speed of processors will double every 18 months. There are a number of mitigating factors and technical extrapolations that come from this, mostly stemming from the idea that "speed" in this context is not a technical term. But what's important is that what originated as an observation of past behavior (and Moore's law has held broadly steady since about 1970) has now become a predictive metric that manufacturers in the industry try to maintain.

FIGURE 1.1 *A curve showing Moore's law.*

When we see a generic phrase that follows the pattern "a rate every time period," we're dealing with an exponential growth factor. Consider compound interest: A bank may promise a savings rate of 2% every year (and therefore a simple interest rate of 3% every 18 months). Money saved at that bank would double in 35 years ($10 invested in year 0 becomes $10.20 in year 1, etc.). How much more acceleration (growth) is there when the doubling rate happens in 18 months? The U.S. Department of Education measures graduation rates from undergraduate programs based on how many students complete their program 6 years after they started (National Center for Education Statistics, n.d.). By the time such a student finishes their degree, Moore's law suggests that processor speed will have doubled four times (that

---

BOX 1.2

Exponential growth of Y at time t is $Y(t) = a*b^{t/\tau}$ where a is the starting value of Y or Y at time 0 or Y(0). For traditional exponential growth, b = 2 (clearly, other values are available but b = 2 and b = 10 are the most commonly encountered). For Moore's law, τ = 18 months, which means that t must be time in months—we *really* don't like exponents to have units. So $Y(t) = a*2^{t/18}$. Say that a = 1. After one period has passed (e.g., t = 18 months), $Y(18 \text{ months}) = 1*2^{(18/18)} = 2$ or doubled at 18 months. $Y(36 \text{ months}) = 1*3^{(36/18)} = 4$ (i.e., quadrupled or double-doubled at time period two, or 36 months). Exponential decay is the same formula except that the exponent has a negative sign. So if a = $1,000 and we want to evaluate the year 15 value, we see $Y(t = 15 \text{ years} * 12 \text{ months} / \text{year}) = a*b^{(-t/\tau)} = $1000*2^{(-15*12/18)} = 1000*0.00098 = $ about $1.

is, 6 years / (1.5 years / period) = 4 periods). Phrased differently, processors will be 16 times faster (that is $2^4 = 16$) when these students graduate than when they started.

We can take the analogy further: Were you twice as smart halfway into your second year of study? Do you expect to be 16 times as smart when you graduate as when you started? Will you know 16 times as much? Has your social position risen 16 times over? The answer is probably no, and that's because education and people work differently than computer processors. Since information systems derives from a technological origin, it operates more like computers than people in many ways.

The corollary to the way business functions is immediate. Suppose that instead of considering how powerful new processors are, we take a certain amount of processing power and consider how much it costs. Instead of seeing a doubling, what we see is a halving. That is, to buy a processor with the same amount of power, it costs half as much every 18 months. Consider again a student who graduates in 6 years. If she bought a new laptop for $1,000 when she started her program, Moore's law suggests that she could buy a similar one for $62.50 after graduation ($1,000/16).

The industry now treats that trend as a primary guideline. Most companies expect to be around for longer than 6 years (in accounting, this idea is called a "going concern"). That is, companies don't plan to just stop; they assume they will continue indefinitely. So what happens in 15 years? That computer might cost less than a dollar (halving 10 times: 1/1,024). In 30 years? Less than a tenth of a cent (halving 20 times: 1/1,048,576).

BOX 1.3

This is easy to see, practically. Watch *Willy Wonka and the Chocolate Factory* (the good one, with Gene Wilder). There's a scene where a "supercomputer" is not even capable of producing sound. But now chips that remember and produce sound are cheap enough to be a free add-on to discount greeting cards in the grocery store. That 50-year difference reduced the size and cost of a sci-fi-level computer from impossible down to routine, mundane, and effectively free.

We've abstracted the concepts a little for this section. Computers are not just processors, and information systems are not only computers. But there are similar "laws" regarding computer storage, network speed, display technology, battery life, and most other aspects of a computer. So while the numbers aren't exact, they aren't substantially wrong.

SIDE QUEST: WHAT IS A TRANSISTOR?

A transistor is an electronic component. Before transistors, there were vacuum tubes: expensive, bulky, and somewhat fragile glass tubes that got hot when they were running. The transistor concept was patented during the late 1920s, but they weren't produced until 1948, by Bell Labs. But that bit of background doesn't begin to describe what a transistor is, what it does, or why that's important. The website How Stuff Works (Chandler, n.d.) describes a transistor as being like a water faucet, except with electricity instead of water. Electrical current can be started, stopped, strengthened (amplified), and weakened (attenuated) with great precision. Anything that can be converted to an electrical current, say, sounds captured by microphone or vibrations captured by a guitar pickup, can be manipulated before being converted again, say, to a radio signal or a speaker signal.

Transistors are smaller, cooler, more durable, and more long-lived than glass vacuum tubes. And as the technology improved, they became cheaper and more versatile. The "9-transistor" radio became pocket-sized during the 1950s (my grandmother had a vacuum tube radio—it was huge, and it took a minute to warm up too). Transistors are awesome for creating two-state or binary-state signals (i.e., the 0s and 1s of computers). Texas Instruments put them into calculators, which resulted in a pocket device vastly smaller and simultaneously more powerful than the previous "adding machines."

According to Moore's law, the transistors keep getting smaller, so more and more of them can be grouped into integrated circuits and manufactured in one operation. Transistors are made from semiconducting materials. The originals were made out of pricey rare-earth metals; today they are made from silicon. Silicon is plentiful; it's the primary component of sand.

SIDE QUEST: CORE COMPETENCY DECAY

When a company is considering something that currently costs $1,000 but will cost less than $1 in 15 years, and less than $0.001 in 30 years, it's considering something that will eventually be free. This is important, because most strategic considerations and high-level decisions center on core competencies. A core competency is the thing that a company does better than anyone else. This leads to a competitive advantage where they can offer a better product or a better value for the same product.

Consider a transportation company—let's call it Company T—that excels at calculating efficient routes for metropolitan-based delivery companies. A delivery company that uses Company T's routes is more efficient than the other delivery companies. Since their routes are more efficient, their operating costs are lower. They can offer cheaper prices for delivery because they save fuel in their highly efficient routes. Where do these efficient routes come from? Maybe they have better maps of the city. Maybe Company T has a wealth of experience. Maybe they have a proprietary algorithm that calculates routes faster and/or better. Maybe they invested heavily into technology and so they have more and faster computers than their competitors.

Regardless of the reason, Company T has only a temporary advantage. Suppose Company T is 20% better than the competition at calculating routes. If the cost to calculate those routes will drop to effectively 0 in 15 years, their competitive advantage drops to 20% of 0 (i.e., their clients don't need them anymore). This is aside from the decreasing rate of return; that is, if Company T's competitive advantage is 20% now, in 18 months it will be 10%. In 3 years, it will be 5%; in 6 years, it will be 1.25%; and so forth, since Company T's competitors are getting better.

> **BOX 1.4**
>
> Creating optimal routes for transportation systems has been a goal of managers since before computing. The problems have names like "Post Office," and "milk man," and "traveling salesman." Mathematical treatment often relies on combinatorial mathematics. These problems are classified as "NP-hard." These terms have quite technical definitions; however, the gist is that there are so many possible solutions that it takes a really long time to solve and there is no way to guarantee you have the best solution.

So what should Company T or any other organization do? How do they maintain their competitive advantage when it will always decay to 0 over time?

The key to understanding how information systems and Moore's law play into making these decisions is to understand that an organization can no longer rely on being better than its competitors. An organization has to rely on being better at being better than its competitors. This duplication of words isn't accidental—it's an emphasis on rate versus position. Consider Company T again. If their core competency stemmed from having a higher investment in computing capacity, the consideration needs to be made now for what will happen in the future. In other words, they consistently need to be planning for 5 or 10 years in the future to ensure that they are maintaining their core competency at the same rate that technology is improving. So Company T would need to be continually investing in technology at a rate that continues to result in a 20% advantage over the competition. Unfortunately for Company T, information systems have progressed to the point that no singular action will succeed but must always fall within the framework of a broader pattern of action.

MAIN STORY: COMMUNICATION CONSTRAINTS

Just like the Roman Empire had an ultimate limit on the size of their expansion based on their ability to communicate from Rome to the border, technology is limited based on communication. Now, this is an instance where the word *communication* has two denotations. The first is the concept that we have of the translation of ideas from one party to another, which is a limiter on the size of business. The other is the technical term related to the transmission of data from one point to another, which is a limiter on the capacity of technology.

Processors are about a square inch in size, depending on purpose and current technology. Why? Oreo cookies are tasty, so logically Double Stuf Oreos are tastier. In turn, Mega Stuf Oreos are even better. So if a processor can calculate a certain amount at an inch in size, wouldn't it be able to calculate four times as much if it were 2 inches squared? As we've seen from Moore's law, cramming more transistors into the same space on an integrated circuit makes it faster, so why not increase the amount of space and make it faster that way? If two inches squared, why not a foot? If a foot, why not a mile? Why not make a giant science fiction–sized processor?

This is one of the areas where the popular understanding of processor design breaks down. It's possible that no one person knows all of the details about any given processor, since they're complex and designed by large teams of engineers. There are concerns about blocking out components, power bleed, heat distribution, and so on. But we can largely abstract all of the terms by summing it up as the speed of light.

Processors don't operate in a theoretical environment. They operate in the real world. And in that real world, electricity doesn't transfer immediately. It transfers at some fraction of the speed of light. The speed of light is fast, but it's not infinite; it's still a fixed speed. So modern processors are running into a limit where the time it takes for the electrons in a processor to make it from one side of the processor to the other is too slow compared to the speed of the processor.

Consider this hard, physical limit on the size of a processor as a sort of counterbalance to Moore's law. Strictly, Moore's law is no longer true. We do not double the density of transistors on a processor every 18 months. Otherwise, we'd have a problem when the transistors got smaller than an atom in size. Instead, improvements in processor engineering, shrinking the size of the "wires" that make up the transistors, changing the materials the processor is made out of, and other areas of research take the place of the strict interpretation. So Moore's law still maintains its exponential pace, even if it's not strictly because of the observation Gordon Moore made.

But keeping up with all of the technical details of processor design is a hobby in itself (akin to train aficionados or ham radio enthusiasts—keeping skills fresh takes a lot of time and interest). A fair compromise is to consider the speed of light a general substitute for what's keeping technology from outpacing Moore's law. Researchers and engineers keep coming up with clever ways of working around that limit of the speed of light.

SIDE QUEST: BUSINESS COMMUNICATION

This leads us to a practical application. Businesses are obviously more capable of communicating over time. At one point, trains opened up the ability for slow, nationwide distribution of goods. Telephones allowed instantaneous communication of decisions and requests for consultation across the country. With the internet and modern data-sharing methods, we have the ability to communicate large amounts of data immediately and efficiently.

This is the point of almost all of what we have discussed and will discuss. Later we'll talk about data being the fulcrum of the entirety of information systems. That data leads to better, more effective communication. The speed of light is the limiter for communication on the technical side of Moore's law. But, as Moore's law continues, it allows for increasing communication on the business side (remember there are two meanings for the word communication). This communication is the continuance of the process of expanding opportunities for businesses to operate on a wide presence globally.

MAIN STORY: SKILL DECAY

Moore's law has disrupted the traditional view of professional development. Once upon a time, the idea was that accomplishing a task or learning a skill provided a backdrop for experience. But modern organizations want to know what a job seeker has done lately. Skill decay of information technology workers is a primary concern. Consider an employee at a technical support department in 1998 who is so successful at solving problems that he easily earns a certification in Windows 95. But is that certification in Windows 95 useful in 2010 when not only is Windows 95 no longer sold or supported by Microsoft but it can't even be installed or used in a modern business environment?

The individual in that situation would find that consistently maintaining a high degree of skill in the next operating system would be more beneficial than relying on his certification in Windows 95 to maintain employment. So in 2010 he won't be saying, "I was certified in a Microsoft product," but he can say, "I have demonstrated a pattern of consistently achieving certifications in Microsoft products." Of course, the implication is that the employee will continue to do so.

What that individual is really saying is that his skill set is not based on his certifications. Instead, he's saying that his skill set is based on adapting to new technologies.

In the same way, all individuals (not just employees in information technology or information systems) should be making this transition. A fashion designer can no longer say, "I made the best bell bottom jeans"; she has to be able to say, "I have a pattern of producing the best jeans in the current style, every year." A mechanical engineer can no longer say, "I designed a hinge that sold well"; she has to be able to say, "As new materials develop, I produce designs for hinges that consistently perform better and sell better than average."

People who are successful in the long term emphasize growth, learning, and adaptation to new situations.

BONUS LOOT: BUSINESS FUNCTION—ENTRY-LEVEL WORKERS

Everybody starts somewhere. Entry-level workers are a key part of almost every organization; they have neither more nor less intrinsic moral value than anybody else at the organization. These are the people who, for example, take orders at restaurants, call people and talk smoothly about political candidates, or route calls to people in a department or organization. Most organizations can't run without these people, even if for most career-oriented workers the position is a stepping-stone toward higher levels of responsibility.

But they are also a key component in the data-gathering function of an organization. Almost any piece of data can be utilized to help make decisions at various levels. But that data has to come from somewhere, and the first place it tends to come from is these entry-level positions.

This is why few large organizations have their cashiers using a point-of-sale device that isn't computer driven. The sales are all useful pieces of data that are retained in a database (analyzing how the items you've purchased relate to each other and to your demographic profile is big business). Further, you've likely seen a trend that even small retail locations use a tablet or other similar type of generic device with a similar interface to accept your payments. It's not just similar; it's likely the same interface. Larger data-collection companies are realizing the amount of sales data that is lost in retail organizations that don't have enough time or expertise to collect and analyze the data. They've offered their point-of-sale devices at an attractively low price in order to gain access to the wealth of data produced by the sales from all of the disparate retail locations.

Going a step further, if you shopped at any big-box stores, and certainly if you've been stationed at the register, you know that there is a constant pressure to have customers sign up for loyalty programs, branded credit cards, or anything that provides your information to them. This pressure is because the data that the organization collects is vastly more valuable if they can associate it with an individual. Not only do they gain personal information about you, which might be what affects your shopping habits and receptivity to advertisement, but they are now able to associate you with data produced by other retail establishments.

Entry-level workers are the cornerstone of almost all data-acquisition patterns. They are a vital part of modern information systems.

BONUS LOOT: RESUME BUILDERS—KNOWN TECHNOLOGIES

One of the strongest resume builders a nontechnology worker can add to their resume is a Known Technologies section. This is a section at the bottom of the resume that lists things like Microsoft Word, Microsoft Excel, Adobe Acrobat, or Dreamweaver. But when you say you "know" a technology, what are you saying? And when the person who's reviewing resumes sees that, how do they know you're being honest?

The reality behind the resume can be fuzzy—both what's on it and how it's used. Resumes for open positions are rarely handled by individuals anymore. They're almost always filtered through an automated system. Depending on the complexity of the system, it might only look for the presence of keywords or the answers to specific questions on the application form itself. Or it might run through a complex artificial intelligence analysis that, at its core, is comparing your resume with what it has been told (by programming!) is a "successful" resume.

Since the training process for the complex resume filter is generally proprietary, you may need to treat the process as a black box. You need to figure out how to represent all of the areas possible.

This is where application certifications come in. If the position requires expertise in Microsoft Word, you'll want to be sure that you've got the actual words "Microsoft Word" on your resume. But when a human manages to get their hands on it, you want to be able to convey to that person that you didn't just write the words, you actually have the expertise.

Microsoft, for example, offers Microsoft Office User Specialist certifications. There are no employment situations where having one or more will be harmful to how you present yourself (in general, however, there may be some situations where the benefit is not worth the time it takes to study for the test). It is a good idea to work toward some of these standard user-level certifications so that when you say, "I have gained the following certifications," your reviewer knows exactly what skill level she can expect.

Most business software applications have at least a basic level of certification to demonstrate competency. It's a good marketing move on their part, because the more people who proudly portray their experience with an application, the better/more popular the application appears to be. We've included a few certification exams that we feel are beneficial to every industry and every role.

BONUS LOOT: SOFT SKILLS

Employers are looking for a set of skills that are hard to define and measure. A typical list similar to a job posting might be

1. good oral and written communications skills;
2. dynamic;
3. self-motivated and innovative; and
4. demonstrated client-centered focus.

But what do these words mean? These aren't just fluff. Someone looked at a job posting that didn't have these vague terms and added them. Even postings for technical jobs will frequently have phrases like these. For a job applicant, how does one demonstrate experience in being "dynamic"?

Essentially, the crux of the problem is that these skills are not fixed step-by-step skills. They're trying to express the inexpressible set of skills that differentiates a confident, experienced candidate from a person who is going to be unable to perform the job.

Examples of the skills that employers are really looking for are as follows:

1. Ability to lead a group meeting with confidence and without wasting time
2. Ability to identify a customer's true problem by reading behind what they say
3. Ability to develop new solutions that address prior weaknesses
4. Cheerful and positive mien that makes the company look good

There are two extensions to this problem: (a) These skills are not necessarily "polite" to write down. Nobody wants to be told they didn't get a job because they weren't cheerful enough, but the fact is that cheerful salespeople make more sales. (b) This list can never be exhaustive, because it's really a variation on "does the right thing in the right way regarding things that are only noticed when they're done wrong."

These Soft Skills sections are an attempt to help identify some of the things that can be worked on as core business skills, even though they aren't always explicitly stated anywhere. These should be for both technical and nontechnical roles, and they are valid for both presenting oneself and for observing the way others present themselves.

BONUS LOOT: CERTIFICATIONS—MOS

One of the most straightforward and easily recognizable certifications for the average worker is the Microsoft Office Specialist. Essentially, for each of the programs in Microsoft Office, it allows a professional to demonstrate certain levels of expertise with the application. Even in an environment where Microsoft is not the primary platform, it demonstrates a level of understanding of that type of application and presumes that a similar level of skill can more easily be attained in other applications.

What good is a certification? Essentially, a certification demonstrates an objective, third-party acknowledgment of skill levels. Otherwise, what can a company use to measure the skills of an applicant? Testing each candidate on basic, utility skills like the ability to use a word processor is of limited use when there are so many basic skills that would need to be measured.

Most companies typically filter applicants based on whether they mention any skill with an application on their resume. For example, if a job requires a lot of spreadsheet use, filters might be put in place to only display applications that mention the phrase "Microsoft Excel." But how does the company know whether the person really knows how to use Excel? Maybe the applicant just wrote a bunch of tech phrases at the bottom of their resume to fill up space. How can the employer be sure the applicant is a good judge of their own skill (e.g., a person may think they know everything there is to know about Excel; however, if they've never heard of logic functions or PivotTables, they wouldn't know that they don't know everything)?

No one is going to get hired because they include a certification for a Microsoft Office app on their resume. However, having and mentioning the certification is the sort of slight boost that might elevate one resume from the rest.

Some alternatives to Microsoft Office Specialist are available for WordPerfect, Apple's iWork Suite, and Google's G Suite.

REFERENCES

Chandler, N. (n.d.). How transistors work. https://electronics.howstuffworks.com/transistor.htm

National Center for Education Statistics. (2019). Time to degree. https://nces.ed.gov/fastfacts/display.asp?id=569

CHAPTER 2

Models

VOCABULARY

- Hardware
- Software
- Communication
- People
- Process
- Decisions
- Data
- Operational
- Managerial
- Strategic
- Information

CONCEPTS

- Models
- Abstraction
- Scope
- Ternary

MAIN STORY: DRIVING PRINCIPLES

1. The seesaw model
2. Anthony's triangle, adapted to the decision-mode ternary
3. The distillation model

SIDE QUEST: ANALOGY

Everyone should remember this diagram of an atom from their grade school days. Teachers used this diagram to explain the parts of an atom in simple terms. Likely, there was a two-colored bundle of spheres in the middle, labeled protons and neutrons. There were probably smaller spheres or dots in a series of concentric circles around that center. This is sometimes referred to as the planetary model by Neils Bohr. As an adult, it's easy to return to that lesson and ridicule it. If nothing else, an atom is obviously not a two-dimensional object.

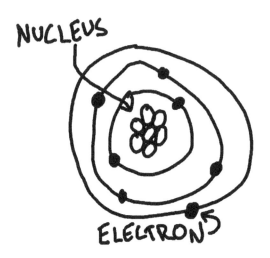

FIGURE 2.1   *A picture of an atom.*

But further, the little balls that make up the protons, neutrons, and electrons in most diagrams are really mostly empty space made up of further subatomic particles. The clustering of neutrons and protons in the center is a bit more vague in real examples. The electrons that orbit the nucleus aren't really orbiting, per se. It's more like they're in all possible spaces and none of the spaces at the same time, with the set of possible spaces being a bulbous wave function.

So why is the first, simplistic model still being taught? There are two reasons. The first paragraph in this chapter about the model is fairly understandable, and probably immediately recognizable to everyone who's attended grade school. The second paragraph is a mess of nonsense and mostly descriptions of what reality isn't. The first paragraph makes more sense than the second, even though they both have roughly the same number of words.

The question then becomes "How much does a precise understanding of an atom affect most peoples' daily lives?" The answer is "almost not at all." But having an effective, basically-as-good-as reality working knowledge of what an atom is made of is a necessary precursor to understanding why we spend money on scientific research, the nature of modern weapons arms races, and many literary references.

There are, therefore, two practical and useful reasons we use this incorrect model of an atom. The first is that it's so much easier to understand that the resources needed to gain a full state-of-the-art understanding far outweigh the costs in time and effort that it took to get there. The second is that the simple model provides a common frame of reference that is accessible to everyone, both in pictures and vocabulary, without requiring complex use of technical jargon and the possible mistakes that come from dealing with it.

In business settings, we have the same set-up that we have in this model of an atom (although we could have used a model of a cell, a picture of the solar system, or any other topic from *The Magic School Bus*): a complex set of interrelating components that require simple and clear communication in order to be most effective. So we address the situation in the same way: by developing models. Some of these models prove ineffective over time,

---

BOX 2.1   Examples of Dead Models

We talked about atoms in this analogy. But atomism is not the first conceptualization of what stuff is made of. Other examples include alchemy, monadism, dualism, and Japanese elementalism.

and others dominate for years. We address several very common and useful models in the appendices.

MAIN STORY: MODELS

Abstraction is the concept of reducing the accuracy of something in order to highlight essential themes. Consider a highway map of the United States. It doesn't include every single small road; it includes only the highways. This is because it's intended to show, at a glance, how to get from one major city to another. A model is a form of abstraction that is intended to demonstrate fundamental principles without getting into levels of detail that would make it difficult to understand the results.

BOX 2.2   Analogies

An analogy is also a model. It presents an unknown, complex concept in terms of a familiar, more simplified idea. Properly, a model is a type of analogy, but the focus is on conceptual models in this chapter. Keep an eye throughout the book on the use of analogies for very simple models.

What is a model used for? A model is an abstraction on a complex concept that strips away some of those complexities in order to emphasize specific components of the concept. For example, in the 2-D atomic model referenced in the analogy, the complexities of movement, Heisenberg's uncertainty, charge levels, and the composite subatomic particles were eliminated to provide enough understanding to allow for further elaboration on concepts like charge, the table of elements, atomic bonding, and understanding the difference between fission and fusion. In the same way, a business model removes some of the subtlety of a situation in order to allow for systematic thinking on a concept. For example, in the seesaw model, process will be placed on the right side of the model, insinuating that nothing on the left side has any process. There are certainly some corner cases where that would be true. But the important part of the model is not that it's a set of rules to adhere to rigidly but that it is an aid for understanding more complex situations. Where the model hinders understanding a concept or where it otherwise causes problems, it should be ignored.

In essence, a model is useful for helping to understand a concept. But adhering to it rigidly will likely cause problems because real-world situations have too many variables to map cleanly onto a model. Models are useful for planning and for double-checking that a proposed plan of action addresses all necessary topics. But a model is useful only as long as everyone is aware that it's an abstraction of the complex issue, not the complex issue itself.

This textbook will revolve around three principal models: the seesaw model, the decision-mode ternary, and the distillation model. These models have been developed specifically for this textbook. Frequently, models are developed and discarded as they evolve among varying levels of usefulness relative to a given task. In this case, effort has been made to develop models that are useful for the specific task of conveying information systems concepts in a nontechnical discussion.

> **BOX 2.3   SDLC**
>
> One more model will also be included: the software development life cycle, or SDLC. However, while it is an important model for the industry, it is not one of the models developed for and integral to this text.

MAIN STORY: THE SEESAW MODEL

The seesaw model is a variation on what we call a "stack" model. In a stack model, each component can interact only with the components on each side of it. This reduces complexity by an order of magnitude, since each component can communicate with only one or two other components, rather than eight to ten other components. "Communicate" in this sense is very loosely used. It just suggests a very broad interactivity or order of events.

The idea of the seesaw model starts with balance. If there are two sides that are broadly divided into the technological side and the people-oriented side, they need to be balanced. Too much technology in an organization and it loses its ability to affect the real world (imagine a video surveillance setup with no one watching). Too little technology and it loses

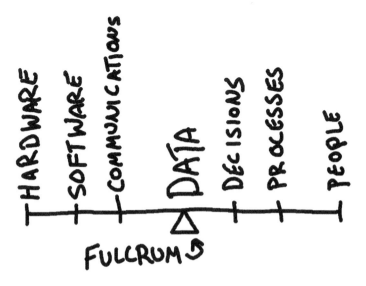

FIGURE 2.2 *The seesaw model.*

opportunities that hardware would have been more effective at doing (imagine an accounting company that prides itself on hand-calculating everything with pencil and paper). Data is the fulcrum point that provides that interface between the two sides. The following list is a simplistic description of each component; more detail will be given in individual chapters.

- Left side: On the left side are the technical components that are necessary in any modern organization.
    - Hardware: The physical components of a technology solution.
    - Software: The nonphysical components of a technology solution. These operate "on" the hardware.
    - Communications: The ability to transfer data or information from one location to another. Communication is facilitated by the software.
- Right side: On the right side are the people-oriented components that are necessary in any organization.
    - People: These are the humans who participate in an organization (they are frequently labeled actors in other contexts, as they don't need to be people). People are the component with the agency and the ability to affect the "real world."
    - Process: Processes give people a series of steps to follow in order to solve problems. They require people to act on them.
    - Decisions: Decisions are the questions that processes try to answer. A process should lead toward the solution for a given decision.
- Data: Data is the fulcrum in that communication sends data from one point to another in order to make decisions.

BOX 2.4   Agency

Agency is an important concept—not from a business perspective but from a philosophy perspective. A good place to start is the Wikipedia entry (https://en.wikipedia.org/wiki/Agency_ (philosophy), making sure to check each of the "see also" links.

SIDE QUEST: SEESAW MODEL MANIPULATION

Models are both fixed and fluid. In order to develop and present a model, its major components should be presented and made static. This way, everyone can refer to the same model with the same concepts. Consider Michael Porter, whose models form a large part of any management expert's repertoire. No matter which schools or practical traditions people come from, they probably still would be able to communicate with each other in terms of Porter's five forces.

However, adhering too tightly to a model is a good way to force concepts or ideas that don't necessarily line up with the real world. Remembering that a model is only an aid, there's no reason it can't be customized to fit the problem. There are three major ways that a model might be adapted to any given situation:

- Scope: The seesaw model is intended to address a broad conceptualization of a generalized organizational information systems function. However, it might be used for an individual department, identifying components in developing a new process, or broadened to an entire industry.
- Substitution: It's possible that, for a particular task, communication doesn't make any sense but something like security protocols does (for example, a sensitive compartmented information facility [SCIF]).
- Combination/separation: Suppose that the model is too complex for a quick diagram on a whiteboard in a meeting about the hardware side. In that case, aggregating the right side of the model into a generic blob might be appropriate. Alternately, if the meeting were specifically about software, breaking the software component into specific pieces might be beneficial.

A beneficial thing to keep in mind is that the seesaw model, at its core, is the balancing of two complex ideas on either side of a central fulcrum. Keeping that in mind allows for application beyond the immediate information systems uses.

Finally, what will be used for this text is, properly, a simplified version of the seesaw model. The broader version balances two ternaries on either side with a distillation model as the fulcrum. This model is overcomplicated and difficult to apply to broader situations, but it's included as a balance to the simplification of a model. Models can be as simple or as complicated as a situation dictates.

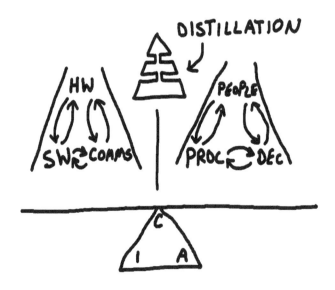

FIGURE 2.3 *The complicated seesaw model.*

MAIN STORY: THE DECISION-MODE TERNARY

There is a classic text in operations management by Robert Anthony (1965) that presents a distinction between the three types of decisions needed to be made in control systems. This is interesting, as it was presented right on the cusp of the newer types of automation that were being afforded by computer control. Subsequently, a fellow named George Morris adapted the concept to information systems and presented it as a triangle with three layers, calling it the Anthony triangle. This is a classic model for distinguishing between different types of decisions. This

FIGURE 2.4 *Decision-mode ternary.*

text will refine the model a little and call it the decision-mode ternary.

If a triangle is a two-dimensional figure with sides and corners, a ternary is the area on the inside. It is, essentially, a way of giving a three-way ratio: The closer to any of the corners a point is, the more what that corner represents is a factor. In the Anthony triangle, each layer of the triangle is a different type of decision making. The decision-mode ternary posits that any given decision-making role contains components of each of the modes. This will be covered more in Chapter 9, but we will present the concepts briefly here:

- Operational: At the operational level, decisions are made that have short-term consequences without direct impact on others.
- Managerial: At the managerial level, decisions are made that have short- or medium-term consequences that likely have direct impact on a small subset of the organization.
- Strategic: At the strategic level, decisions are made that have long-term consequences that have direct impact on a large portion of the organization.

SIDE QUEST: TERNARIES

The decision-mode ternary is not the only application of a ternary. For example, a classic method for choosing colors on a computer is with a ternary color picker. The center is brown, a mix of all the colors, and the points are the primary positive colors red, green, and blue.

The complicated seesaw model uses two ternaries. This is because for most hardware decisions there's going to be some mix of the three areas, and trying to distinguish between the person and the person's decisions/processes is a bit farcical from a business perspective.

The Anthony triangle is one of the fundamental models in the information systems industry. It is what causes Moore's law to be such a disruptive force: It makes operational

> ### BOX 2.5   Positive/Negative Colors
>
> Why did you learn in kindergarten that colors were made up of red, yellow, and blue when in technical contexts the term is RGB for red, green, and blue? It comes down to the distinction between "positive" color sources and "negative" color sources. Effectively, when light is produced by something (like a phone screen), the way colors are mixed is different than when ambient light is reflected off of something (like a painting). Incidentally, this has some effect on sleep cycles.

decision-making roles able to be automated, prescribes the best decision for many of the remaining layers, and shortens the length of a "strategic" decision from 10 to 20 years down to 3 to 5 years. Consider that entire industries can rise to billion-dollar status (Dot-Com, Bitcoin, Ska) and then bust as quickly in less than 3 to 5 years. Compare this with building the first transcontinental railroad—22 years from proposal to completion.

MAIN STORY: DISTILLATION MODEL

The distillation model looks similar to the Anthony triangle, but it is intended to be a broader application. The specific presentation will be used in the capacity of data in this context. Essentially, the distillation model is a series of sets that are connected to each other. Each subsequent set is smaller than the one before it and is produced by the one before it.

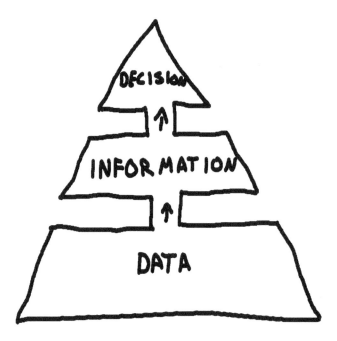

FIGURE 2.5 *Distillation model.*

The intention here is to show that a lot of one thing produces a little of the next. However, in this context, the model will require some definitions that will be reiterated and expanded in Part IV of this text:

- Data: A true fact
    - Technically, it doesn't need to be true or a fact. Any statement that asserts something is valid.
- Information: A useful true fact
- Decision: The selection of a course of action based on information

---

BOX 2.6   Datums

Data derives from Latin and means "many presupposed statements." This is as opposed to *datum*, which means "a presupposed statement." Therefore, when we are discussing "a piece of data," it's a lot like discussing "one of many cattle"—it doesn't make sense when you could say "a cow." In the same way, *datum* is the etymologically proper way to phrase the singular version of *data*. However, like many grammatical forms, society has moved on and largely deprecated *datum*. It is generally acceptable to use the word *data* as a singular conceptualization of an undefined mass of many datums in addition to using the word *data* as the plural word for "a group of facts." Thus, "the data shows that" and "the data show that" are both grammatically acceptable statements.

This leads to the following understanding: Good data leads to good information, and good information leads to good decisions. "Good" in this case means "true." This has been a standard understanding in most of business for a very long time. However, we will need to take it apart and show that there are newer ways of approaching this. In the meantime, the distillation model represents this idea that data produces information and information produces decisions.

See the following example:

I. Data
  1. Collecting a list of the available times of students at a university
  2. Collecting a list of the courses still needed by each student
  3. Collecting a list of professor availability for each course

II. Information
  1. Ruling out times when courses are needed but a professor isn't available
  2. Ruling out times when a professor is available but students aren't
  3. Coming up with a list of times for each class that satisfy as many professors and students as possible
  4. Coming up with a list of classes that take priority for the next semester because there were no appropriate times this semester

III. Decision
    1. Decide which class should be offered at which time based on the list of feasible times

Notice that for each of the components of information the resulting list is shorter than the set of data it was produced from (properly, it could have been expanded to a list of times separated out for each and every class, but that would be a visually boring page), but there are more individual sets of information. Finally, there is only one decision that's being made in this process. This is the idea of this distillation process.

This model is important because, to a certain extent, all information systems, information technology, computer science, and even mathematics have been the process of distilling information from data.

SIDE STORY: DISTILLATION MODEL MANIPULATION

There's no reason this model has to be used only for data/information. In fact, it obviously stems from the process of distilling mash into wort into liquor. The distillation process takes a large amount of water and alcohol and turns it into just the useful part of the alcohol.

For example, turning some raw ingredients into other semiprocessed ingredients, turning those into other processed ingredients, and turning those in turn into finished goods which are then sold is a distillation process. The intent of the model is to reduce a large amount of bulky, undesired, nonfinal product by pulling out a smaller subset that is closer to the desired end result.

There is also no reason it needs to be limited to three stages; simplifying or complicating the model as suited to a particular task would be beneficial.

BONUS LOOT: BUSINESS FUNCTION—HEALTH CARE

One of the most interesting business functions is that of health care. As a population grows larger and larger, it becomes more feasible to predict certain aspects of health care. For example, the 1918 influenza epidemic was shocking to health officials. It spread on a scale nobody had seen nor expected. The Black Plague, similarly, was rife with misinformation about what was happening. The sources were identified as everything from evil spirits to ill humors, to certain kinds of people, to bad meat, to mass hysteria. What was a scary disease turned into a nightmare because it seemed like it could happen to anyone at any time.

However, recent Ebola outbreaks in Africa have garnered much less attention in the news, despite being just as deadly and prone to epidemic. The reason tends to be partly that it's happening "over there." But it's also partly related to the idea that how disease spreads is typically well known in the United States. Everyone is constantly bombarded with messages to wash hands, cover their mouths, and pay attention to sickness. The terror has disappeared because a model of how disease works has been established in our minds.

This is one of the great changes in modern health care: not specific treatments, but global public health initiatives that seek to inform people about how disease works without going into details. Ebola is largely handled by teaching locals in rural locations (who frequently have not had formal schooling) about handwashing, the need to stay away from dead bodies, how to identify symptoms, and so on.

This idea that avoiding sickness is as easy as coughing into one's elbow and washing hands is a model. It's obviously not true, but it is a simplification that makes everyone's lives easier and safer. There are more complex models, such as Centers for Disease Control and Prevention (CDC) or World Health Organization (WHO) projections on how Ebola spreads between regions or countries, with various factors playing into how serious the outbreak should be considered. Even more interesting is the CDC's (2018) recommendations on preparing for zombies.

Understanding that we all are delivered models, actively propagate these models, and are part of the process of updating these models is key to understanding how to implement and use them in an organization.

BONUS LOOT: RESUME BUILDERS—DISTILLATION

The key to making a good model is finding out what's important and only focusing on that. For example, in the seesaw model, the presumption is that the audience doesn't want an in-depth diagnosis on systems analysis and design. They just need a quick rundown regarding their resources and what they are doing. In the distillation model, the idea is to pull from a large grouping of unimportant things and end up with a set of important things.

The same things apply to the development of a resume (or elevator pitch, or sales patter, or interview responses). Sometimes it's important to remember that not everything is important. Consider the person who is reading through your resume. Do they care? For example, while you may be proud of your GPA, does your potential employer care?

Each day, task, and success of your previous jobs are viscerally real to you. You experienced them, in real time. However, when you're trying to express what you did that was worth the money you were paid and prepared you to do those things for a future employer, not all of it needs to be included. There are a couple of key tasks that need to be given attention:

1. Include specifics that are measurable. Did you help someone accomplish some task? Your reader likely doesn't care, because how much your help applied isn't measurable. Did you get credit for a specific amount of income? That's valuable information.

2. Ignore routine tasks. Two-page resumes used to be standard, because when printed they were the front and back of the sheet that was physically handed to a potential employer (consider that, once upon a time, interviews were scheduled before the resume changed hands). However, since resumes are transmitted electronically now, length is less of a concern. Because they're viewed on a screen, hanging white space is not as problematic. What's more important is making sure that every line gets paid attention to, because once your reader begins to gloss over sections, it's easy to continue glossing over sections.

3. Assess and rewrite. Your resume is not a static document. It changes with every success or failure in your current job and/or job search. Pay attention to what

people ask about in interviews and expand that section. Feel free to rotate old jobs off your resume when people stop asking about them. Change what you're including based on the job industry you're applying in.

BONUS LOOT: SOFT SKILLS—ELEVATOR PITCH

The elevator pitch (Wikipedia, 2020) (or elevator speech) is a short description. It can be used to describe an idea (for a product or service or an improvement) or a person (yourself). The idea is to limit the description to a very short time, say the duration of an elevator ride. You do this by using nontechnical language that focuses on the value the idea or person can provide to the listener. "Summary" is a good word. And, having written an elevator pitch, you need to practice it to make it smooth and available on short notice. Of course, real elevator rides have varying durations: 15 seconds up to 2 minutes. This variability leads to the notion that there may be more than one elevator pitch on any given topic, with the level of detail being changed to match the time that is available. For more guidance, go to Barnes & Noble's website and search for how-to books or search for YouTube videos if you prefer that format.

An elevator pitch could be something like, "I work with a nonprofit organization called Bold Idea. We provide education in computer science to students in areas where they may not have access to it. We have a new semester coming up in the fall, and I was hoping to talk with you about how you can help us out."

Remember that this nonprofit (Bold Idea, n.d.) has spent hundreds of hours producing explicit lists of everything related to the organization, developing and designing curriculum, and developing their expertise. Trying to break that down into a 52-word summary that is compelling when delivered in 30 seconds or less is a skill that can be developed and refined. It's also a skill that many organizations find valuable.

BONUS LOOT: CERTIFICATIONS—OPEN BADGES

The modern internet opens up a wide variety of opportunities to decentralize various tasks. One of the current initiatives is the Open Badges initiative from Mozilla. The term that is frequently used is *microcredentialing*. Rather than the current standard of large certification exams that are taken in single sessions (or even across several days for the larger ones), demonstrating mastery of a field should be done in small, regular bursts as the learning occurs.

These badging mechanics are becoming more popular, as they provide a way for learning platforms to demonstrate the completion of their courses. Learning platforms have always provided some form of recognition, but it's typically been a certificate. While some people publicly display every single certificate they receive, the vast majority of people promptly lose them or file them, never to be seen again.

What makes the Open Badges initiative interesting is that it is just a framework; the implementation can be done by anyone. Any learning platform, volunteer organization, or youth activity group can put together a set of badges that are then awarded upon the completion of certain tasks or skill demonstrations. In turn, the display of these badges is available to any platform that wants to do so.

For example, Codeacademy has several courses that can be completed. When they're completed, a student can connect their LinkedIn account to Codeacademy and display the course completion on their LinkedIn account. This means that if a professional is refreshing skills in a new programming language, for example, their progress is immediately demonstrable to potential employers.

REFERENCES

Anthony, R. N. (1965). *Planning and control: A framework for analysis*. Harvard University Press.

Bold Idea. (n.d.). Bold Idea home page. http://www.boldidea.org

Centers for Disease Control and Prevention. (2018). Zombie preparedness. https://www.cdc.gov/cpr/zombie/index.htm

Wikipedia. (2020). Elevator pitch. https://en.wikipedia.org/wiki/Elevator_pitch

CHAPTER 3

Information Security

PRE-READING CHECKLIST

VOCABULARY

> Benign actors

> Malign actors

> Natural disasters

CONCEPTS

> Information security

> Social engineering

> Security specialists

> Security plan

MAIN STORY: GUIDING PRINCIPLES

1. Security is centered on delay, detection, and notification.
2. It is not possible to be secure from every possible attacker. Part of information security is related to recovery.
3. Information security is a practice that is necessary for every member of an organization.

SIDE QUEST: ANALOGY—BANK VAULTS

Bank vaults have a primary purpose: to prevent people from taking what's inside. But there's no way to actually prevent, prohibit, and stop someone from breaking in. Why? What happens if the lock breaks or the key is lost?

Ultimately, someone still has to break in to repair the vault, although we would typically call that person a locksmith.

Instead, bank vaults are rated on three factors. The first factor is how long it would take to break into the vault using the most modern technology. Vault manufacturers use techniques like vibration switches, thick and hard alloyed walls, complex combination sequences, and other proprietary methods to ensure that there is more to breaking into the vault than just taping some TNT onto the side like in a bad Western. However, it's always still possible to carefully navigate each of the preventative measures and ultimately compromise the security of the vault. How long it takes determines the quality of the vault. Older vaults, using older materials and techniques, have lower ratings. Modern vaults from high-quality manufacturers have higher ratings. This rating is typically measured in hours. There's a big difference between a vault that could be broken into in an hour and one that would take a whole weekend to break into (more expensive too!). The reason is that the longer that a safecracker is there, the more chance there is to catch them.

The second factor is harder to measure quantitatively. But it is, effectively, a measure of how obvious it is that the bank vault has been broken into. Imagine the poor bank manager who opens up for business, proceeds through the day, and doesn't find out that the bank vault has been broken into until a customer is brought in to check on their safety deposit box. Any compromise needs to be immediately and obviously visible. Examples might be a giant hole in the casing, scorch marks, or broken visual displays. This measurement tends to be made by qualitative reviews or reputation.

The third factor is also hard to measure quantitatively. It's also, sometimes, hard to define exactly what needs to happen. But the vault should, as soon as possible, notify the responsible party that a break-in has occurred. To draw a further analogy, a home security system that sounds an alarm is secure, but home insurance companies provide a bigger discount if the security system automatically calls the police in the event of an alarm. This method typically takes the form of motion sensors, heat sensors, or oxygen sensors. A vault in a bank that's closed for the night should be cold, motionless, and in extreme cases filled with argon or some other unbreathable gas. Thus, any break in the casing will compromise the static environment, and anyone moving around will generate heat, movement, and breathable gases.

This is a great analogy for information security. It's rarely the case that it is impossible to break into an information system. Every level of security apparatus, from the most community-driven fan site to the highest level of government, has been broken into at one time or another.

BOX 3.1   Heist Movies

Check out *Butch Cassidy and the Sundance Kid* (1969) for an entertaining take on taping TNT onto the side of a safe. Check out *The Italian Job* (2003) for an entertaining take on bank vaults and safecracking. Can you name others?

MAIN STORY: ORGANIZATIONAL SECURITY

This is not an in-depth overview of information security. Information security is a complex, constantly changing technical profession that is a multibillion-dollar industry—one that still struggles to achieve reliability metrics. It is almost a poster child for the adage that a lot of knowledge can be dangerous but a little knowledge is disastrous. Consider medicine: Professional doctors consistently make wrong diagnoses, but overall society judges them to be more helpful than not. However, every person with access to a crank website or an online diagnosis website thinks that they are able to dispense dangerous and unsupportable medical advice.

This is also not a technical overview of information security. Returning to the notion that a single chapter in an undergraduate textbook has the possibility of providing a disastrous level of confidence in the student, security threats update and advance so quickly that by the time this book gets to print, there's a substantive likelihood that any technological response advocated will no longer provide the protection that it promised.

However, in a postinformation age organization, there are basic concepts that every competent manager should be aware of. Information systems can properly place the role of information security in the organization without being expert in that field. There are four overall aspects to operational security that apply to every discipline and every portion of a company:

1. Information security is a necessary part of every employee's job.
2. Information security oversight should be performed only by specialists.
3. Information security should be outsourced whenever feasible.
4. Every department should have an information security response plan.

This chapter is placed near the beginning of the book in an effort to highlight its importance. Using the seesaw model, it might be considered to be the seesaw that all of the other components rest on. The idea is that information security needs to be integral to information systems from the beginning rather than considered as an add-on after the fact.

SIDE QUEST: THREAT SOURCES

There are several sources of threats to examine. First, however, we need to organize the threats themselves. Security threats fall into three basic categories: benign actors, malign actors, and natural disasters. Benign actors are (typically) employees who, through a lack of skill or a legitimate mistake, produce a copy, loss, or change of data in the course of performing their job. Malign actors are internal or external individuals who are actively targeting the organization in an effort to copy, destroy, or change data. Natural disasters are any events outside of the instigation of a person that result in the reproduction, loss, or change of data.

Notice that the definitions of these three categories include the three things that can happen with data. The unauthorized replication of data is when data is copied from its intended location to an unintended location. This typically happens when an employee mistakenly stores the information incorrectly or a malicious user circumvents security measures to actively copy the data to an external site. While it is less common than in the past, it's also possible for natural disasters to cause unauthorized data replications. Natural disasters are a bit of a secondary issue; if a building floods, there's an outside chance that some of the data-carrying hardware is swept to an insecure location.

Data loss is a paramount issue. In this case, the biggest threat tends to be benign actors. Every support technician has a story about knowing someone who worked at a place where the cleaning staff unplugged servers in order to plug in their vacuum cleaners, resulting in data loss. Natural disasters are almost as big of a threat. All data will eventually degrade: magnetic disks lose their magnetism, disk drives wear out, even optical storage has an expiration date as either the foil inside them degrades or the plastic covering gets too scratched to read through. In addition, floods, wars, fires, earthquakes, even the supernova phase of the sun are all potential threats to the longevity of data. Malign actors have historically not been a threat. There are an increasing number of scams that essentially result in lost data because the data is hidden, followed by a blackmail attempt that is neither intended nor possible to follow through on.

Data change is a tricky threat to address. This typically takes the form of a benign actor, in the normal course of their position, accidentally entering wrong data. The person might even introduce an error when attempting to make a correction. Benign actors are by far the biggest source of data change threats. But malign actors can either attempt to change data to their benefit (such as a school child who roughly changes an "F" on their report card to a block "A") or engage in a more common type of "graffiti" by replacing a company's website information with lewd or political messages. The medical industry is certainly concerned about the possibilities. Finally, natural disasters are no longer a huge threat in this area because of modern redundancy and error checking. However, it's still possible for strong electrical fields, like lightning or solar flares, to "flip bits," producing erroneous results that still look correct.

SIDE QUEST: THREAT CATEGORIES

Notice that each of the threats involves data. Typically, crimes against people or hardware are of a more normal variety and only relate to information security with regard to data the person might know or data the hardware might have access to. "Crimes" against software or processes are typically only an attempt to get at the data.

Social engineering is, by far, the most common and successful method of security circumvention. Social engineering is the name given to the process of making the illegitimate desires of a malign actor seem correct. They range from simple sources reflected in popular entertainment, like "always carry a clipboard and nobody will question why you're there," to a more subtle knowledge of human nature, like "always look for the smokers; they tend to leave back doors propped open so they don't have to walk around to the front door to get back in." One of the most common social engineering processes is an attempt to extract either data or a password from a legitimate user. This can be done by posing as a member of tech support, a legitimate contact, or sometimes just by asking.

Software threats are another common and successful method of security circumvention. However, software threats need a way to access a computing environment. But this is readily available by an employee's constant use of the internet; even legitimate sites can be compromised to spread malicious software (malware). A common source of malware is software that purports to scan for malware. A social engineering spin on malware is to put malware onto a portable drive (like a USB thumb drive) and "accidentally" drop it in the lobby of a target organization. The vast majority of people who pick it up almost immediately plug it into their computer to see what's on the drive, which is often enough to install the malware.

Hacking is a broad concept that refers to actively searching for security weaknesses. This is in contrast to a typical software threat, which is more passive. In a hacking attempt, a malign user will tend to scan through all the possible ways to connect to an organization's information system and try to determine one that allows for malformed requests. This would be similar to walking through a locker room with a dummy key and checking to see if any of the locks are broken and will open to any old key. Another method of hacking is called a denial of service attack—the malign user attempts to overload the target system with a series (on the order of millions or more) of nonsense requests in an attempt to break or block their ability to operate.

There are also the more rare (or at least less detected) hardware threats. Most hardware is produced and assembled in a multinational production channel. It is almost impossible to account for all of the potential security problems. It's difficult to detect these areas with accuracy. Hardware threats are a breeding ground for conspiracy theorists and overly cautious security experts. Without specific and expert advice otherwise, it is not necessarily something that can be hedged against.

Finally, there are physical threats. In many organizations, physical security falls under the operation of information security for two reasons. First, most modern security processes (smart ID badges, automated security systems, outsourced security) bear some relation to information technology. Second, physical security is a component of information security. In some situations, it's easier to physically show up at a location and bypass nonexistent physical security than it is to break through a conscientious technological security environment.

There is a side category of security threat. It's not in the same classification scheme as the previous threats, but advanced persistent threats (APTs) are in a classification structure of their own. Whereas most information security is related to one-off or target-of-opportunity attacks, APTs are specifically targeting an organization and will not stop until they are forced to stop or the perpetrators get what they want. In many cases, such a situation would not be problematic, as individuals or small groups typically rely on what amounts to a lucky break. However, larger malign groups (e.g., foreign governments or large corporations) have been documented to attack organizations, and they frequently have the resources to overwhelm any security precautions put in place.

MAIN STORY: INFORMATION SECURITY RESPONSIBILITY

Security threats most often target the average employee. Since most employees aren't trained in threat detection or information security, they are the biggest soft spot of an organization. If a malign user, for example, attempts to target a seasoned and vigilant information security specialist, they risk not only being rebuffed but being caught.

Therefore, every member of an organization needs to be aware of threat sources, threat categories, and how to address each of them. The answer to the last question is consistently going to be "address it in the manner formulated by the information security policy of the organization." But some general methods will be covered here as well.

Benign users are one of the biggest sources of security threat. The possibilities range from accidentally forgetting to save changes to an important document to violating federal law and posting millions of patient records to an external website instead of the hospital's internal website. Stories of employees writing passwords on Post-It notes are standard fare in the security business. There is no solution to this issue aside from properly training employees, checking that each employee is performing correctly, and implementing a well-designed information security policy.

Malign users are generally outside of the scope of what a typical employee is expected to handle. For example, if a retail establishment is held up, most retail employees are trained to cooperate with the assailant. It's more expensive and more disastrous for the company for an individual to try to John McClane a situation. In the same way, a malign user will almost always try to separate the target from the usual control structures. This is because the organization typically has the resources or expertise to counter a malign user, but the bad guy may not be aware of that. So regardless of what seems like a special situation, it is always important to report evidence of malign users to the organization's information security team.

Natural disasters are also typically outside of the scope of a most employees. However, standard safety precautions tend to address most controllable situations. This involves using equipment properly and according to policy. Otherwise, standard safety rules like "don't drive near a tornado" or "evacuate in case of a fire" apply. Broader responses are for the organization to effect. Disaster preparedness and disaster recovery are both huge businesses and very popular topics in information systems literature.

Social engineering responses typically come down to a set of rules. Select strong passwords. Do not hold the door into a secure area open for an unknown person. Never trust someone who comes to you; always attempt to go to them. Never trust anyone who asks for your password. Never trust anyone who asks for your password. This may seem repetitive, but no legitimate employee will ever ask for your password. (Author's note: If you ever suffer negative consequences because you refused to provide your password in a situation where you were legitimately supposed to, please contact me personally and I will be happy to explain the error of their ways to the person who attempted to make password sharing a normal activity.) In general, being wary of unknown contacts and following procedure is the best way to avoid social engineering threats. The best response to a social engineering threat is to let the organization know sooner rather than later.

Software threats are also relatively easy to handle in theory, even if they're harder in practice. Malign users are excellent at providing just enough temptation to make downloading a program or file seem irresistible. Web ads that provide outrageous claims of a product or a news article are frequently misleading and instead lead to a site that distributes malware. Emails especially have a habit of making opening the attached file or clicking on the attached link seem urgent and necessary. However, following the maxim that users should (a) never click on anything that came through email, (b) never connect unknown devices to their computer, and (c) never install programs from a nontrusted source is a good practice.

Hacking, hardware, and APTs are typically not something that can be addressed by the average user. However, there are things that they can do to note them or avoid them. It is easy to antagonize people on the internet by forgetting that the other usernames they are talking with represent real people. Avoiding deliberate antagonism is a good approach. For hardware threats, there are certain locations to which electronic devices should not be taken. The CIA's website provides a list of countries they warn against bringing electronic devices into. Using temporary devices or otherwise avoiding bringing sensitive data in and out of those locations should be a priority. Typically, the rule is that if a computer or device is acting abnormally, it should be reported according to the organization's policy.

Finally, physical threats tend to fall under the same umbrella as social engineering. Don't provide access to malign users. In dangerous situations, comply with any assailant until a security team can handle them. The best way to prevent physical threats is to know the people in an organization. When someone acts oddly or someone is where they're not supposed to be, this provides a measure of advanced warning.

MAIN STORY: SECURITY OVERSIGHT

We used the analogy of a bank vault earlier. However, a castle can be used to draw another analogy that is appropriate to information security in some ways. Historically, if one army was going to battle another army, prevailing wisdom suggested that a 2-to-1 advantage was needed to win. In breaching a castle, however, that ratio leapt up to 10 to 1. Most armies didn't fight with a 10-to-1 advantage, so they would implement siege tactics. The problem with being on the defensive side of a siege is that, in order to win the siege, the defenders need to win against every single strategy of the offensive side. In order for the offensive side to win, they only needed to win once.

The same thing goes for modern organizations. It's a little macabre and depressing to consider that the organization is under siege. But, in a certain sense, it is. Some organizations are under unrelenting and frequent (hundreds of times per second!) probing for security weaknesses by malign users. Standard security apparatuses tend to block those probes. But what about the next day and the day after that? Just like malign users are constantly varying and updating their threats and attacks, security specialists need to adapt and upgrade their responses.

Most employees don't have the time, predilection, or expertise to master this level of security. As a result, an organization should always rely on a security specialist for their security oversight. Defining *specialist* is difficult in an industry where quality employees are very expensive. However, to the extent that the resources are available, it is rarely a poor investment.

SIDE QUEST: SECURITY OUTSOURCING

There are two complementary situations in which security should be outsourced. The first is an organization that is too small to hire a security specialist. There are products and software packages available that provide a modicum of security. These should always be used. However, information security is not a product in and of itself any more than organized criminals provide security to the locations they shake down in movies. Information security should almost always be attached to some process that the organization is already using. For example, when implementing a credit card or payment processing system, questioning the security practices of the vendor is always appropriate.

The other situation is when a company wants to reduce risk. Large organizations are a tempting target for malign users. Who is liable when an organization is compromised and uses its own security team to provide information security? The organization itself. But who is liable when an organization is compromised and outsources their security to a third party? That third party is frequently liable. As a result, hiring a security consulting company is a common decision.

There are two caveats to this guiding principle. The first is that outsourcing information security is not a substitute for developing a comprehensive and sound security policy for the organization. However, the outsourcing company will likely assist with that development. The second is that it's not an automatic decision to outsource information security. Outsourcing necessarily opens up an organization to security risks. In some industries or for some companies, doing so is more problematic (for legal or operational reasons) than the risk associated with being liable for their own security.

MAIN STORY: SECURITY PLAN

Security is like any other process with regard to the need to explicitly state things that might seem obvious otherwise. A good security plan has a stated response to many security threats. This covers the range from benign and malign actors to natural disasters, as well as software through physical attacks.

Going into detail on the scope and breadth of an organization-wide security plan violates the guideline that all security oversight should be handled by a professional. However, there are some aspects of the security plan that need to be addressed by specific departments. For example, if a legal department has stored a number of documents on the organization and someone releases that data to the public, there needs to be a preexisting plan in place that addresses how to handle it.

Therefore, a departmental security plan frequently revolves around threat response. The entire organization's security plan will deal with the rest of the process. But how to recover from a security breach should be part of every department's backup plan. A good departmental response will basically be a branching document that has a series of if-then questions and what to do in response. One bit of advice that appears in every article on disaster recovery is "practice the plan." This not only makes the plan work better, but it can also reveal areas for improvement.

The first issue to consider is whether data was stolen, changed, or destroyed. Data that's destroyed just needs to be recovered. But data that's changed to something embarrassing or offensive likely needs to be found, recovered, and apologized for. Data that is stolen needs to be recovered and apologized for, and it is likely that financial consequences will need to be considered.

The second question is about the sensitivity of the data. A blunt separation would be between important and nonimportant data. Someone changing the cafeteria's menu to something amusing is changing non-important data. That should obviously be handled differently than someone changing the front page of the company to something offensive. The biggest distinction will likely be who is notified and the timeline to correct it. For example, if customer data is involved, there is a strong legal position that the customers need to be informed immediately.

Finally, there's an important question of who the malefactor is. If it's nature or a benign actor or a small opportunist, there is an urgency to address the situation. But that urgency is not as substantive as when it's a large organization or an advanced persistent threat. Again, the biggest distinction is who will be notified: internal dispute resolution structures, police, or FBI.

Typically, the center point of a departmental security protocol will be the backup schedule. Backups should always be taken of all data. This is the primary defense, because many problems are not fixable. The "solution" is to erase all of the affected data and restore it from the appropriate backup. Ideally, backup data would be taken every few minutes of the entire organization and stored indefinitely. But that would be prohibitively expensive for all but the smallest organizations. A more reasonable solution focuses on a three-stage backup: operational backups taken hourly or daily, scheduled long-term backups that are stored in a more secure manner such as a tape backup, and off-site storage.

For nontechnical managers, this could seem like a lot of nuisance. However, it's effectively like purchasing health insurance and having to go in for an annual physical. Ideally, 99% of the time, nothing is found. But the physical is intended for that 1% of the time when something is wrong. Similarly, backups are, in an ideal world, never needed. But in the real world, they're the most common solution for restoring data. The process is typically an automated process for the hourly or daily backups, and a more manual process for the weekly backups. That more manual process has, historically, involved physically swapping the backup between the off-site and the local routine location. But with the advent of cloud hosting, it may take a more automated approach.

The second largest portion of a departmental security procedure is to define contacts for various types of security incidents. For example, the procedure might indicate that if there is a security breach involving customer data found in an insecure location, the employee is to immediately inform the departmental supervisor who will contact legal and marketing to develop a response plan for informing customers who may have been affected. Another example might be a situation in which a user receives a specific, credible information security threat; they may be instructed to inform their supervisor and the information security team immediately. The security team will then be tasked with determining the immediacy of the threat and what information should be shared with law enforcement.

MAIN STORY: INFORMATION SECURITY AND THE SEESAW MODEL

Remember that the seesaw model is ideal for creating example problems so that a manager can then use the model to formulate a comprehensive approach to the problem. This would be an excellent example of how to develop a new policy. When developing the policy, specifically addressing each component of the seesaw model is a good approach.

For hardware security, the primary threat avoidance measure is access. Someone typically needs physical access to hardware in order to present a credible security threat. The most secure data centers tend to be in abandoned (no people) salt (low humidity) mines (no weather threat) where the facility is sealed and filled with a noncombustible gas (no fire threat), locked with heavy armored materials, and guarded by armed guards who, themselves, have no access (no human threats). The primary response tends to be similar to any other break-in: Ensure there are no lingering threats and repair the damage.

For software security, the primary threat avoidance measure is education. If users are educated to know what sorts of activities are appropriate for their position, they are less likely to engage in risky online behavior. Similarly, if they are warned of specific types of threats, they are more likely to identify and respond appropriately to those threats. Failing that, many organizations institute limitations on the use of the internet. The primary response tends to be immediate IT support who will take necessary measures to repair or replace damage and check to see whether the software threat spread to any other systems.

Data security primarily rests on the other security measures. Since data has no active or moving components, there isn't any way to secure it once the software or the processes are compromised. The primary concern, however, is legal and moral. There are no universal industry codes of ethics for companies with regard to sensitive data. However, there is a growing body of legal precedent suggesting that data is, itself, not protected beyond that of broad "speech" classifications. The organizations that handle it tend to have a legal obligation to protect it and must demonstrate a bona fide effort to do so.

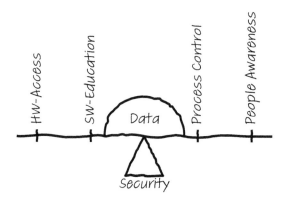

FIGURE 3.1 *Seesaw model for information security.*

For process security, the primary threat avoidance measure should emphasize adherence to established processes. If the process is developed ideally, it should produce the intended results with no unintended results. An ideal process should have enough checks and evaluation points to be sure that possible security threats are blocked before becoming problematic. Ideal process design points should be designed with security in mind, but more about that in a moment. Typical response patterns tend to be focused on identifying and repairing the security vulnerability in the process. A common joke is that every weird line in a syllabus is there because someone did something correspondingly weird in class. Similarly, processes that have a large number of specific caveats tend to be the result of revision in response to previous events.

Finally, for people security the primary threat avoidance measure typically relies on education. When employees know their roles and who they should be interfacing with, they are less likely to present a target. Employees should be trained to double-check who they're communicating with. They should also be reminded that if a situation sounds too good to be true, it bears an instant resemblance to most scams. The primary response for process security breaches should tend toward education. However, in the real world it frequently devolves into one of punishment and scapegoating. Education results in wiser employees; punishment and scapegoating result in the development of an untrusting and possibly hostile environment.

MAIN STORY: SECURITY PRIORITY

In every design process, security should be a priority. It might be helpful to return to the bank vault analogy. For a vault to be effective, it should be designed into the structure of the building with conscientious effort to follow best practices for such installations. However, many home safes are just installed into the studded sheetrock between rooms. Thieves may not be able to break into the safe immediately, but they could easily cut the safe out and steal the whole thing to break into at their leisure. Similarly, for security measures to be effective, the entire design process should keep them in mind rather than adding them in after the fact.

Typically, however, what happens in a lot of process design is that organizations try to do as much as possible while using as few resources as possible. As a result, when a process or a piece of software is designed, there is a choice between making it flashier and more outwardly impressive or spending time on infrastructure and security measures. For a project that is hanging by a budgetary thread, it's very tempting to forgo security until the project has proven itself.

This process management approach leads to poor performance. It's routine, during the development process, to propose a new feature and immediately say, "Is it secure? How can it be made secure?" But after the process or product has developed, trying to return and then evaluate every aspect of the product in hindsight means that small, obscure situations likely will be overlooked. And it's these small, obscure situations that have historically been the target of hackers and malign actors.

Security is a priority. It's a necessary part of information systems, and it's also the part of information systems that most directly affects the routine management of every other department.

BONUS LOOT: BUSINESS FUNCTIONS—OPERATIONS

Operations and information systems have a back-and-forth relationship, historically. Operations runs more efficiently with information systems support. Systems analysis and design falls squarely in information systems, but it is most effective at improving operations tasks. However, at a certain point the question becomes "If information systems is so good at doing it, why don't they just take it over?"

The results of an information systems takeover tend to go poorly. Operations tend to better relate to the actual function of the organization. In many ways, operations drive all organizations. Information systems are support functions and can't direct the path of an organization. So the information systems takeover creates an immediate dichotomy that eventually results in operations regaining control.

A good boundary between operations and information systems tends to be that information systems cover analytics, security, and outsourcing, whereas operations cover mission-oriented processes. This means that information systems handle the analytical capabilities of an organization, the information and physical security aspects of an organization, and contracts and negotiations.

This last area seems a little odd. But because information systems are already frequently vested in outsourcing relationships like software vendor contracts, hardware maintenance contracts, secure disposal contracts, and the like, it is not unusual for them to end up responsible for more routine outsourcing relationships like cleaning or consulting. This is not always the case. But it does make some sense when combined with the security aspect, as it means that information systems are responsible for addressing all of the concerns related to any outsourced functions.

BONUS LOOT: RESUME BUILDERS—IT CERTIFICATIONS

IT certifications are either vendor-specific or vendor-neutral certifications that provide a baseline of competency. This is a broad definition, as different certifications measure that competency differently. But, for example, Microsoft proposes that their certifications enable professionals who obtain them to perform certain job functions at a certain level (for example, an MCSE is qualified to develop and run a new enterprise-wide information system using Microsoft products). On the other hand, CompTIA's certifications tend to imply that a person has a certain amount of knowledge (for example, their A+ certification suggests a level of knowledge comparable to someone with 6 months of experience in an IT function).

Some certifications can be huge undertakings requiring demonstration of years of industry experience and multiple, rigorous testing sessions. But there are a number of certifications that require only a single test. For example, Microsoft Office Specialist (MOS) certifications are intended to be an objective demonstration of a certain level of expertise in specific versions of specific Microsoft products. Many of the CompTIA certifications are related to low-level skill sets. Even some non-IT certifications like the Six Sigma Yellow Belt or Six Sigma Green Belt have relatively short turnaround times.

These nonintensive certifications are great resume boosters. The certifications won't mean much on their own outside of the industry, and they are not intended to replace a college education; however, when combined with an education and as a subtle indicator that a candidate is technologically capable, they are a good way to help shore up any potential weak points in a resume.

We discussed skill decay a bit in Chapter 1. The idea was that all skills in information systems tend to decay when the technology they are founded on becomes obsolete. However, there are two excellent situations where that is not necessarily problematic. The first is for a product that is long-lived in the industry. For example, Microsoft Word MOS certifications become obsolete after a while, such as when new products come out. But a similar certification will become available, and it's an implied statement about a person's commitment to self-training and currency to demonstrate a pattern of updated certifications. The second is, as implied, when a certification is obtained as an incredibly short-term attempt to bolster a person's chances at getting a job.

Attaining a certification is not always a minor process, but it is a process worth considering.

BONUS LOOT: SOFT SKILLS—PERSONAL/ONLINE SECURITY

As I write this, another credit card company is disclosing that their security has been compromised. Here is some of what they have to say to their customers (I've redacted the company name):

> **What happened:**
>
> On <date>, we determined that an outside individual gained unauthorized access and obtained certain types of personal information about <credit bank> credit card customers and individuals who had applied for our credit card products.
>
> **What we've done:**
>
> <Credit bank> immediately fixed the issue and promptly began working with federal law enforcement. The person responsible was arrested. Based on our analysis to date, we believe it is unlikely that the information was used for fraud or disseminated by this individual. However, we will continue to investigate.

From there, the credit bank outlined steps for customers to follow if they receive phishing attempts related to the data breach. The steps include do not reply to the email, do not click on links within the email, forward the email to their fraud department, delete the email, and continue to monitor. Also inside the document is a link to a new document that describes ways to prevent identity theft. That is a subject with plenty of detail. The U.S. government (2020) has a website devoted to public information on personal security.

We've included several cases in Chapter 22. A few of them come from an associate director in an IT Services Department at a small Midwestern private college. The AD had a fair number of students working for him; they were dispatched to faculty and staff offices on a number of repair missions. The AD asked the student workers to keep a record of the number of offices where the computer password was found taped under the keyboard. These numbers were alarmingly large. Best practices for password security is a lengthy topic; rest assured that it does not involve writing passwords on paper for posting. These best practices don't change in intent, but they do slowly evolve over time (for example, a recommendation of a minimum of 6 characters moved to 8 characters around 2000 and is currently moving to 10 characters). It's important to find a reputable site to return to every so often for a refresh (Netwrix, n.d.).

BONUS LOOT: CERTIFICATIONS—SECURITY CERTIFICATIONS

Security certifications are a little more advanced than run-of-the-mill certifications. One problem from a holistic standpoint is that there is only one metric for success in information security: the ongoing process of not having a security breach. Alternately, there are only negative metrics (having a security breach), with the few positive metrics largely being an absence of negativity.

However, there are three layers of security certification that are useful to any professional:

1. Routine professional development. Almost every single organization requires that their employees go through routine training on information security. This is particularly true in any industry that is dependent on HIPAA (Health Insurance Portability and Accountability Act) or FERPA (Family Educational Rights Protection Act). If you are part of an organization that does not routinely require information security training, it's likely worth proposing.

2. Security+. CompTIA has what they consider a "baseline" security certification. It is a technically oriented certification that represents what someone who has mastered entry-level information security issues should know. It is worth studying for and passing, as it says what it is right in the name and would be a good value for a smaller organization.

3. CISSP (Certified Information Systems Security Professional). This certification is effectively the gold standard of security certifications. It is the baseline to be considered for a skilled information security professional in a number of different industries (particularly anything involving the federal government of the United States). It requires several years of documented industry work experience and exams over several broad areas.

Realistically, information security is a specialized field, and this list is more useful in evaluating potential candidates. Every organization should have at least one person who is knowledgeable about information security, and larger organizations should outlay for higher level and more specialized certifications. This list of three is targeted at the nonprofessionals, as they are a realistic goal to work toward regardless of current industry and experience.

REFERENCES

De Line, D. & Gray, F. G. (2003). *The Italian job.* De Line Pictures.

Foreman, J, & Hill, G. R. (1969). *Butch Cassidy and the Sundance kid.* Campanile Productions.

Netwrix. (n.d.). Password policy best practices. https://www.netwrix.com/password_best_practice.html

U.S. Government. (2020). Identity theft. https://www.usa.gov/identity-theft

PART II

The Seesaw Model

P art II consists of 9 chapters, each one detailing an aspect of the seesaw model.

WHERE WE'VE BEEN

In Part I, we established the background and context for this book. It's a book about managing in an information systems field, but it's written for the nontechnical manager. Information systems is like the seesaw model. Of course this model is the preferred framework for decomposing information systems into smaller, more tractable portions for more detailed study.

LOOK AHEAD

The left side of the seesaw model consists of hardware (Chapter 4), software (Chapter 5), and communications (Chapter 6). These items are pretty clearly goods and services (stuff you can buy). The purchases are often planned for in projects, and their purchases and installations are supported, respectively, by feasibility analyses and the tools that help schedule. The purchases will show up on "the books" as assets or expenses (i.e., the cost of doing business). What to acquire, when, and how to finance it are key concerns that are addressed in Part II.

A firm employs people (Chapter 7). People create processes (Chapter 8) that result in decisions (Chapter 9). One would hope that high-quality employees create processes that result in high-quality decisions, but it's quite a complicated dance, and a lot can go wrong. Nobel Lauriat Herbert A. Simon had a lot to say about decisions and decision making. His thoughts on the subject are worth a look, starting with Box 9.3 (Chapter 9).

Hardware

SIDE QUEST: ANALOGY—FIRE

Grilling is potentially the oldest form of cooking. There are even examples of animals in the wild starting forest fires. Zoologists would suggest it's because they're trying to herd prey animals out from under their cover. True grill aficionados know that it's because heat and smoke make food taste better. In fact, grilling over a campfire can provide a useful analogy for hardware and software—two requirements for a computer to work.

A good frontier chef knows that the best way to handle any food preparation process is to separate all of the components and stages of the cooking process into different areas or locations. For example, there might be an area for raw ingredients, an area for cooked dishes, an area for active cooking, and someplace for holding food that needs to stay warm. To visualize further, imagine a large campfire that's burned down into hot coals that are just right. The chef might set aside the left side of the fire as a place to store raw meat and the right side as the place where people come in to get their cooked food.

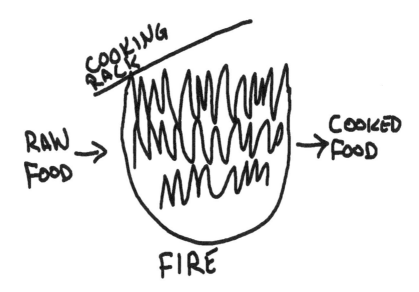

FIGURE 4.1 *Four-component fire.*

There might be a main spit where whole animals are roasted slowly over the coals, and then racks over the edges of the fire (where the coals aren't as hot) to stage the meat while it rests. Our analogy introduces several great, concurrent concepts that we can use to better understand complex ideas.

The first concept is the divide-and-conquer method (used throughout history as "divide and rule," but also a well-known method for algorithm design, now widely adopted through most business processes). No chef is going to be happy with cooked food and partially cooked food and raw food intermingling. No health inspector would be happy with that either. Not only that, but making sure everything is accounted for and properly situated is easier when things have been broken down into smaller groups.

The second useful concept revealed by our analogy is scope. We could break each of the areas we described earlier into smaller and smaller areas. Take the spot for cooked dishes. People may be coming by for their food, but the chef might want more than just a pickup station. Suppose there was a person there who takes the cooked food as it comes in, dresses and plates it using a *mise en place* method, and then gives it to the people waiting for their food. The same picture we had for the cookfire as a whole now could be applied to this smaller aspect of the cookfire analogy. The best models are the ones that apply on multiple or recursive levels. You, the model user, end up with a multifunctional model and plenty of opportunity to practice using it.

The third important concept revealed by this analogy is, we hope, revealed by all of our analogies. That is, why would we restrict the use of our campfire analogy? Could a five-star restaurant in an urban area use this same model? What about a winery that takes raw grapes, stores them while they mature, and then ships them out? What about a TV dinner factory that takes in raw ingredients, stores them, prepares the meals, and ships out (questionably) tasty victuals? Remember that a model is, at its core, an analogy. Since an analogy is always imprecise, this means that the model could apply, just as imprecisely, to a number of situations. The model itself is just a tool that leads to an aid in understanding.

MAIN STORY: DRIVING PRINCIPLES

1. It's not necessary to know all the minute details of hardware; a broad strokes understanding is enough.
2. Hiring an expert to make hardware decisions is appropriate, but you should know enough to understand the recommendations.
3. Hardware decisions can be made by price point as much as by the technological factors.

MAIN STORY: THE FOUR-COMPONENT MODEL

There is a basic model of computers that has been around as long as modern computing. A computer has four basic components: input, output, processing, and storage. Without any one of these, a computer isn't a computer; it's something qualitatively different. We'll address each of these in turn, but it's important to reiterate that this is just a model. It will fail in some cases. It is an aid to understanding hardware (and thus computing), not the definition of how hardware works.

You may have already noticed that the input, output, processing, and storage would fit easily over the cookfire analogy we just described. There are a dozen different targets for analysis that we could consider (processes of life, manufacturing, car engines, etc.), and they can all be easily conceptualized using this model. In turn, each of these functions can be described by the model or the whole computer might just be one component of a larger system.

Input is like the raw ingredient. A programmer might type on a keyboard to produce instruction sets. An actor might tap dance in front of a camera. An Olympic swimmer might wear a set of sensors all over his body while training. All of these count as input, which is anything that enters the system from outside. Without input, a system is essentially a random-number generator with no way to know what the output relates to.

FIGURE 4.2 *Four-component model.*

Output is like the cooked food. Anything that moves from the system to outside the system is the output. You look at a monitor while using a computer. An engineer might use a 3-D printer to prototype the design for a new and better mousetrap. A myopic inventor might design a smell printer for the internet. Without output, a system is essentially deep storage, the contents of which are never intended to be used.

Processing is like the main cooking spit. Any system ought to be changing the input in some preplanned way or there would be no reason for it to exist. Processing happens when an action game hero beats a monster and the loot is calculated. It happens after a customer makes an order and the system checks to see if the product is still in stock to determine whether that product should still be offered for sale. It happens when a scanned document gets compared to the English language to determine what it says. Without processing, a system is just passing things through, possibly just holding it for later use.

Finally, storage is like the warming area. Not everything can be processed at the exact same time (in a modern system); instead, some of it is stored while another part is processed and then vice versa. Storage is like when a music playlist is currently playing only one song out of however many are in it. It's like when a website might have hundreds of pages but a user is reading only one at a time. It's like when a calculator is solving an equation and needs to store the answer in parentheses. We call a system without storage a finite state machine (FSM, because there are only a fixed number of states that the machine can exist in), which is very useful in computer science but is vastly less effective than a fully equipped computer.

This four-component model has broader applications than just for defining a computer. It would also be an appropriate framework for establishing and defining new processes. It will be used in the chapter on processes. It could also be used as defining the software side, but it becomes a bit strained.

SIDE QUEST: SCOPE

One important concept in any systems thinking is that of scope. A micromanager is not doing anything different from what a well-balanced manager does. The micromanager is directing subordinates and describing desired outcomes. However, the micromanager runs into a

---

BOX 4.1   Scope

The idea of scope should relate to anything -scope, like a microscope or a telescope or rifle scope. The idea is that scopes are defined by their degree of magnification. Someone shooting long-distance target practice at a gun range is going to need to consider magnification carefully. Using a 2x (doubling the size of the image) scope on a 1-mile shot likely defeats the purpose of using a scope at all. On the other hand, someone using a high-powered 1,000x scope to shoot at a 10-yard target is likely going to be unable to recognize what they're seeing through the scope. They will only see blurs as they try to aim. Just like selecting the right optical magnification (from the Latin scopus, meaning "target," implying distance) is vital visually, it's also metaphorically important concept.

problem in choosing an appropriate scope. The subordinates were hired to take ownership of the tasks that fall closer to the operational vertex of the Anthony triangle. The manager is intended to operate closer to the managerial layer.

When discussing hardware, it becomes more difficult to define exactly what a computer is as technology improves. For example, a printer is obviously an output device because it produces something in the real world from the computer. But on its own, a printer has an input from the computer, it has to process the electrical signals into the pattern its print heads expect, it typically stores recent and future printing tasks in a storage buffer, and it outputs paper to a tray and error messages back to the computer.

The printer is a computer in its own right on one scope, but on another scope it's just one component of the larger machine. We could go further and demonstrate how any given computer is just the input/output of a broader computer network or how the processor that drives the display of the printer is itself comparable to a computer.

This is not a problem. The description and function of any given object changes based on scope. Just like an individual's vote at the state level is largely irrelevant for national presidential elections based on the electoral college and just as the role of a midlevel manager is as a subordinate in one context and as the boss in another context, any component in a complex system can be described in greater or less detail.

Going hand in hand with scope is the concept of abstraction that was discussed earlier. Abstraction is the process of ignoring fine details in order to emphasize certain aspects of a problem or system. Abstraction lets the printer be considered an atomic component of a computer system, even though it's got component pieces.

This may seem simple, but the adroit use of scope definition and appropriate abstraction is a widely useful skill for many business functions. It allows for the precise definition of many processes without getting distracted by unrelated aspects. Consider, for example, the video game industry. When big games get behind schedule, the development process enters "crunch time," where all of the employees are expected to work ludicrously long hours in order to meet an arbitrary release date. However, a well-designed process for development would have both prevented the causes of the game getting behind schedule as well as realized that the design processes needed to occur in an appropriate manner and that adding more work hours would not necessarily speed up the process.

BOX 4.2   The Mythical Man-Month

Fred Brooks published *The Mythical Man-Month: Essays on Software Engineering* in 1975 with updated editions in 1982 and 1995. The book is the story of Brooks's experiences in managing software engineering projects at IBM. The premise is that adding personnel to a late software engineering project does nothing to repair the lateness. In fact, it makes the project later. This is referred to as Brooks's law. Brooks had some more (good) things to say about prototyping methodologies (Wikipedia, 2020).

MAIN STORY: CONSULTATION

One area that information systems frequently ends up supervising is consulting. This reveals a basic dichotomy in the realm of information systems. Tech expertise is expensive for a small company to develop in-house. Assume that a single technical expert can support somewhere between 50–100 employees. If a small business only has half a dozen computers, they'd be wasting 90% of a full-time expert's time. So small companies typically select one of two suboptimal solutions:

- Hire a non-IT employee who spends a small number of hours each week supporting computers. This allows the employee to spend more time supporting the computers as the number of computers increases. However, the problem becomes one of expertise. An employee who is the only "techie" at an organization for 4 hours a week, in addition to their other duties, can't possibly attain the same level of expertise that a full-time employee could. This means that they'll miss out on basic things a full-time expert would catch. This also violates the idea that security issues should be built into an organization from the very beginning, as the part-time tech almost certainly won't have the expertise to do so.
- Hire an outsourcing company to handle all technical details until the company grows to the point where it can hire its own full-time tech. The problem with this solution is the old adage that "there's nothing more permanent than a temporary solution that works." Just like using an old brick as a doorstop instead of installing a better latching mechanism, once a consulting company has taken over the technical side of an organization, it's frequently hard to take on the extra time and cost to bring the information departments in-house.

These two options ignore some less common possibilities like hiring a consultant who guarantees to come on full time when the company is big enough or hiring a consulting company that is designed to hand over control at a certain point. Those are not common solutions, and finding someone who follows through is even rarer.

The result is that a large number of companies, small and large alike, have their entire technology department designed and supported by an external consulting company. This is problematic for the same reason that having any third-party company responsible for a key component of business is a problem. What happens if the consulting company goes out of business? Can the consulting company be said to have the same commitments and ideals that the client has? At what point is the growth of the client limited by the size of the consulting company?

But there are a number of possible benefits. Much of the risk in technology is taken on by the consulting company. For example, one reason franchising fast-food restaurants is so popular is because the franchisor provides a turnkey set of hardware for the location that has already been tested and effectively guaranteed to work. There's no development time, there are fewer bugs, and there is less cost associated with the mass-produced solutions.

Similarly, what happens if there's a data breach? If the company is handling its information security and technology concerns in-house, there's a significant chance that personal feelings, pride, or other issues will come into play. But the third-party organization should handle the breach dispassionately and with specific expertise.

So, in general, if there is no technical expertise at all in an organization, hiring reputable technical consultants to handle the entirety of the hardware or technology side of the company is perfectly reasonable, given that the person responsible for interfacing with the consultant is at least superficially conversant in tech issues. There is likely still a greater benefit to keeping all of the technical side in-house, but the margin of that benefit becomes slimmer over time.

MAIN STORY: PRICE POINTS

Hardware and software are purchased differently. Software is typically purchased in volume licenses for a set rate. As far as that goes, our purchases don't exactly result in our owning software. We typically purchase the right to use the software in limited ways. Software purchasing decisions are typically made based on preexisting needs (e.g., the database administrator knows only one type of database, all of the documents are saved in a specific format, partner organizations prefer to have some of the integrations that come from using a specific utility). When that isn't the case, a more in-depth decision needs to be made by someone with training in application selection.

Hardware, on the other hand, presents an interesting conundrum. We've already seen that everything eventually becomes free. So why should an organization buy new computers now if they'll be about half the price in 18 months? Of course, the question would reappear in 18 months and again in 36 months, and so on. But eventually new computers will need to be obtained just because of standard wear and tear on the old ones. So how can decisions be made?

One helpful approach is to consider price points. From the purchaser's point of view, the question is, "How much stuff can I get for as little cost as possible?" and from the seller's perspective, "How much can I charge for this much stuff?" Welcome to classical economics! But the reality tends to be more complex, and those questions typically are resolved in factories. In a factory for technical components, there typically isn't a continuous supply/demand curve for all possible outputs. Instead, for every change in the hardware, the entire production line needs to be redesigned. This leads to a tendency to prefer as few product lines as possible for a certain hardware function. But how does the manufacturer know which products will be the most successful?

Like most industries, the answer tends to come from analyzing past consumer performance. But when we have exponential growth laws in effect, trying to ask consumers the important questions about products is so difficult that it's ultimately futile. However, management of a hardware production process can examine prices. This is where price points come in. For example, a basic assumption is made that if hard drives sold successfully at $120 in the past, then they will do so in the future. The production question then becomes,

"How much functionality can I provide at this particular price point?" In turn, the consumer should be asking, "How much can I get for this set price point?"

What makes this useful for the nontechnical manager is that the cost of hardware very frequently stays more or less static in the short run. There is some change over time, but it's much more gradual than the exponential growth rates of performance might otherwise suggest.

BONUS LOOT: BUSINESS FUNCTION—CUSTOMER SUPPORT

Most people have used a customer support number at some point. Because of the nature of telephone communication, it's often difficult to visualize what's happening on the other side of the line. But there's typically a very routine operation. Call centers are expensive, and as a result, operators are typically rated on a large number of different factors to determine success.

The process of handling a call is typically very streamlined. Most call centers utilize a multi-tier structure with new calls going into the first-tier support center. This section is for new or inexperienced employees. They typically have a large binder or an interactive program that tells them how to handle any given problem in a large set of if-then questions. If the operator can't solve the problem (or can't solve it within a certain time period), they're typically instructed to pass it up to tier 2. Tier 2 can typically pass it up to tier 3 and, depending on the organization, this is frequently where it stops. At tier 3 (or wherever the top tier is), something new has occurred, which requires active problem solving over the course of days or more.

Managing a call center is a standard skill. Whether it's a tech support line, a billing support line, or anything similar, the processes tend to be the same. As a result, understanding the technology and the processes behind them are important; however, being able to motivate people and help employees solve productivity problems is also paramount.

Further, technology is slowly absorbing the bottom layers. For example, calling into a customer center with a basic question, such as "How much do I owe?" is typically handled by an interactive voice menu. Those automated solutions are exponentially cheaper than a live person, so most call centers prefer to route everyone through this new "tier 0" layer first. But as voice processing and semantic contextualization by the machine learning programs becomes more effective, they can take increasingly complex calls.

This doesn't mean that the call center is disappearing, but it does mean that the skills necessary for managing them are changing. Rather than focusing on the ability to keep new employees on track and able to read through a binder, it's becoming more important to know how to bring new employees up to problem-solving status quickly. Training on specific applications is becoming more intense, and the metrics tend to veer away from how short a call is and how few complaints there are toward how the problem gets solved and what the positive response rate from the customers looks like.

BONUS LOOT: RESUME BUILDERS—TECHNICAL SUPPORT

"Handy" skills is a hard skill set to place. For many careers, it falls more under "hobby" than an applicable skill set. However, it's probably worth noting at some point in discussions with employers or professional partners when those skills exist. What are they? Suppose that a printer breaks in an office. There exist offices where they immediately contact a printer repair person, and the office can't print anything until it's fixed. But having at least one person in the office who might say, "Let's turn it off and then back on again and see if that fixes it," is frequently a boon.

This technical support side fits in with a lot of the other resume-builder skills. Learning a little bit of programming helps with the mind-set of systematically tracing down bugs and identifying where they are. When a machine beeps three times and then doesn't work, knowing that someone should do an internet search for the serial number and "three beeps" is a good skill. Employers want to hire those people, and others like to work with those problem solvers.

However, unless the job is specifically looking for those low-level "office grease" type skills, it's probably not good to put on a resume. However, an anecdote, for example, "The office phone system went down and I was able to fix it by unplugging each phone one by one until I found one that wasn't working, so we only had 15 minutes of downtime instead of waiting until the technician could come the next day," is probably good to keep in mind for when it fits the answer to interview questions or other inquiries. On the flip side, if you can quantify this skill in terms of how many dollars were saved, it could be a valid line to put into a resume.

BONUS LOOT: SOFT SKILLS—NEGOTIATION

Your authors have degrees in technical and/or quantitative subjects. A topic like negotiation, wherein two or more groups come to a joint agreement, is naturally suspect. Yet it is impossible to read anything about national politics and not encounter the concept, if not actual examples. In business schools and similar contexts, negotiation is often centered around prices that are accepted for goods and services. Of course, individuals might negotiate salaries and benefits.

Some of the best texts on negotiation come from books written for sales. Og Mandino's (1968) *The Greatest Salesman in the World*, Dale Carnegie's (1936) *How to Win Friends and Influence People*, and Stephen Covey's (1989) *7 Habits of Highly Effective People* are all classic texts to read in this regard. But these recommendations come with some caveats. They're books written in their time and may have turns of phrase or presumptions that don't sit well with a modern audience. They're also written by people who are just writing. From an academic perspective, it's important to realize that these are starting points, not end points. Their claims should be verified by readers, and further reading is always a good idea.

Finally, another good area to do some research in is game theory. Game theory is more than just chess or video games or board games (although it has applications there). It is the science and theory of deciding on optimum courses of action. For example, the ultimate goal of game theory is to identify what both parties want and set up an agreement where everyone gets that. In essence, a good negotiator can take a situation that is a zero-sum game and set it up as a non-zero-sum game where the output contains more utility to every stakeholder than the inputs.

BONUS LOOT: CERTIFICATIONS—A+

CompTIA's A+ certification represents the equivalent of 6 months' experience in a generalized IT role. Typically, this means a hardware role, being the person who actually turns the screwdriver to remove and replace components or strings cable from one side of a building to another.

Without mitigating the value of the A+ certification, it is not intended necessarily for college graduates. It is more of a way for nonindustry people to demonstrate that they've taken just enough tech training to learn what to do or for a younger employee to demonstrate their expertise after 6 or 12 months on the job.

A good rule of thumb for what an A+ certification represents is if everything is going right and there are no problems, a person could open up a desktop computer, identify all of the things inside, and generally know what they do. This has two outcomes for the average business school graduate. Even the least technical person has learned how to study and should be able to study for and pass the A+ certification exam. This may not have any direct effect, but it at least opens up the opportunity to interface with more technically oriented companies (for example, a hardware assembly company that wants to hire HR staff but can't do so if the candidates don't know how to assemble hardware).

The other side is that being able to demonstrate at least that A+ level of knowledge is a good minimum qualification for hiring technical employees. A common solution for very small businesses is to hire the owner's mother's neighbor's nephew who likes to play video games. However, encouraging that person to get an entry-level certification before being hired is a good way of mitigating the risk of that decision.

REFERENCES

Brooks, F. (1995). *The mythical man-month*. Addison-Wesley.

Carnegie, D. (1936). *How to win friends and influence people*. Simon and Schuster.

Covey, S. (1989). *7 habits of highly effective people*. Free Press.

Mandino, O. (1968). *The greatest saleman in the world*. Bantam Books.

Wikipedia. (2020). The mythical man-month. https://en.wikipedia.org/wiki/The_Mythical_Man-Month

CHAPTER 5

Software

VOCABULARY

> Software

> License

> EULA

> Operating system

> Application

CONCEPTS

> License types

> As a service

> Price variability

MAIN STORY: DRIVING PRINCIPLES

1. Software licenses are complicated, so be sure to have a specialist address any concerns.
2. Subscription models are not historically the best deal, but they may become more beneficial over time.
3. Organizations do best when they select a specific platform; however, individuals are most successful when they have a wide variety of platforms they're familiar with.

SIDE QUEST: ANALOGY—LIQUOR SALES

Ellis County (n.d.), Texas, is a damp county (which means that beer and wine can be sold, but not liquor). Texas, in general, is becoming less conservative in its vice restrictions as time goes on. It has recently relaxed some of its definitions regarding what constitutes a prohibited weapon, it opened up certain vectors for alcohol sale, and it has had state-level debates on the feasibility of opening gambling ventures inside the state.

Further, Ellis County does not have a relatively low alcohol consumption rate. So who are the primary motivators of maintaining the current status of alcohol sales? The straightforward answer has been the same for decades: puritanical influences who frown on the consumption of alcohol.

The problem is that conclusion doesn't hold water, as it were. Religious sources typically have better things to do and often partake of alcohol themselves. There isn't a lot of money that can be raised in denying people access to something that they can drive to the next county to purchase.

But that's exactly the issue: People have to drive to the next county to purchase liquor. Assuming that the purchase and consumption of alcohol is not substantively different from one county to the next, it means that liquor stores don't have to compete with extra stores in Ellis County. Instead, they can operate immediately across the county line and get their regular business as well as the broader business from Ellis County. So, in fact, it's the liquor stores themselves that have a tendency to promote the maintenance of restrictions on alcohol sales in certain counties.

In a similar vein, Texas has a ban on selling liquor on Sundays. But the idea of a modern politician defending the practice by saying "You can't drink; you're supposed to be in church" is a bit retro focused. Instead, once again, it's the liquor stores that prefer to limit their hours of operation. The assumption is that people don't stop drinking their standard amount of alcohol on Sundays; they just get in the habit of buying double on Saturdays. This means that the liquor store only has, at most, a minor decrease in weekly sales but can reduce its staffing and operations costs by one seventh.

Software sales are similarly deceptive in their approach. Alcohol is a luxury item, but software is a fundamental need by almost every modern organization. And rather than being a service-oriented industry, there have been several practices that have become standard that are contrary to the interests of the clients.

MAIN STORY: SOFTWARE LICENSING

Software is not the same as hardware. When an organization purchases a piece of hardware, there is a physical object that ownership transfers on. The organization can put an ownership sticker and bar code on it, and it has a location and a place and is part of the organization's IT audit.

Software, however, doesn't have a physical representation. When software is purchased, what change in ownership happens? Electrons don't physically leave one location and arrive at the other location. Instead, a copy of the software is made and the data transfers ineffably to the purchaser's computer (whether "digitally" over the internet or via physical medium like a CD or USB drive). So what has been purchased?

The typical answer has become that "purchasing" software is the process of obtaining a license to use the software for some length of time. Retroactively, software that didn't specify that period of time effectively licensed it forever. But every modern piece of software contains some variation of a EULA (end user license agreement). These used to be called shrink-wrap agreements because the phrasing tended to start with "By opening this software, you agree to ..." The assumption was that the user had to remove the shrink-wrap to install the software. In the same way, every piece of modern software requires the user to consent to some form of licensing agreement before it will function. This is one of the few places where absolutes like "every" and "all" are appropriate, because even modern software that doesn't have an explicit EULA is covered by a wide, overlapping, confusing array of generally applicable licensing terms.

There is a split opinion on the legality of EULA as a limiter to operation. One side says that they're firm and valid contracts, enforceable by either party. The other side says that they're a legal gray area and that there are a number of unanswered questions. For example, suppose a child uses a mobile device, installs an app, agrees to the EULA, and purchases too many pieces of software. If a child is unable to sign a contract, how can the EULA be enforced since it was agreed to under fraudulent circumstances? If it's under fraudulent circumstances, why aren't the companies held liable for it? There will have to be a number of court decisions that firm up exactly what the contract of using a piece of software looks like, but the existence of the EULA will almost certainly have to stay.

The gist is that any organization that uses software should almost certainly have some expert on the use of software. Depending on the size of the organization, it should be part of the technical expert's responsibility (whether that's in-house or a consultant), part of the service provided by a general legal counsel, or fall under the role of a specialist in software licensing. Software licensing is confusing, and it is generally accepted that a valid defense is whether something is a standard practice in the industry. But, overall, it's important to have some sort of explicit plan.

BOX 5.1 Valid Defense

One of the interesting ways that laws are written is "valid defense." Frequently a law will express when someone can be arrested or when a lawsuit is reasonable. But it will also outline "valid defenses." For example, many municipalities will note that it is a valid defense if a person is speeding because of a genuine emergency, and the municipality will then outline what those emergencies are. The person will still get a speeding ticket, but they will have the opportunity to present that valid defense in court.

SIDE QUEST: LICENSE TYPES

Software licenses can be, imprecisely, considered a spectrum with two representative extremities:

- Open source software. On one end is the ideology that software is by nature free. Since there is no actual good exchanging hands and the original author is not at a loss in time or goods for each additional sale, the actual distribution of the software should be free. Note that there exist for-profit companies who hold to this philosophy, the idea being that they make their money off service calls and their expertise in installing and maintaining the software while providing the software itself for free.
- Proprietary software. The other end of the spectrum is the idea that not only does the ability to use a piece of software have to be acquired in exchange for money, but that the "rights" can't actually be transferred to the end user. Instead, the original copyright holder is graciously allowing the user to operate the software for a fixed amount of time, assuming that they agree to behave in a way the copyright holder approves of.

There are myriad variations between these two different categories. Going into detail on each and every minute variation is time consuming and potentially dangerous as it would give the impression that software licensing is cookie-cutter. Rather, every organization's use of every individual piece of software is a separate legal contract that needs to be tracked and reviewed.

BOX 5.2   Individual Licenses

Properly, individuals should also consider each and every individual piece of software as a separate legal contract. Every piece of software has a separate and unrelated EULA that should be read and understood before the software is used. This is the same vein of advice that demands that every driver read the manual for their car, coffee maker, and screwdriver. Companies know that it won't happen. (For example, some companies hide prize money in their EULA (Scwartz, 2019).) But currently the bulk of legal precedent is on the side of the companies. The presumption is that the user has read and agreed to the EULA.

Instead, here are a few significant variations:

- Open source
  - Public domain. First, it's important to note that no piece of software is ever in the public domain. Ever. In fact, there is no legal mechanism for relegating any piece of copyrightable work to the public domain aside from the expiration of copyright protection after the better part of a century. For example, if a person announces that they relegate their software to the public domain, there is absolutely nothing stopping them from later changing their license to a more restrictive one.

❑ Free licenses. There are a variety of licenses that are essentially intended to provide software to users for free. The bulk of programming tools operate under this license. There are differences, but examples include the various Creative Commons licenses, MIT license, variations on GNU, Apache Public license, and Mozilla Public license.

❑ Restricted licenses. These licenses provide a variation on "free" licensing in that they require something from the user other than money. This may be a limitation on use, duration of installation, publication of product, or other concerns.

■ Proprietary

❑ Seat licenses. Most software is sold in some variation of "so many people using it at the same time." This may mean that the number of licenses an organization purchases is based on the number of computers it has, the number of employees it has, the number of expected users it has, or some other metric agreed on by both parties. For utility software, like an operating system or productivity suite, there tends to be a one-sided declaration by the selling organization.

❑ Subscription licenses. Acronyms that end with "aaS" (such as software as a service (SaaS), platform as a service (PaaS), and infrastructure as a service (IaaS)) are a new, increasingly common example of subscription licenses. Essentially, rather than purchasing the indefinite use of a piece of software, a subscription license requires the consistent renewal of that license on typically either a monthly or yearly basis. Software companies prefer to move to the as-a-service model because not only is the software on a subscription but the client can access it only through a web interface, which provides almost absolute control to the software company.

One issue to consider is that selection of a platform is typically something that happens only once. For example, selecting Microsoft Word as a platform is functionally a permanent decision. There are costs associated with switching to a new platform. Using technical tomfoolery, companies tend to sabotage the ability to migrate to different platforms (for example, at one point Microsoft Word did not adhere to its own published standard for saved files; therefore, moving to WordPerfect would make the file look wrong, because WordPerfect showed it right, but the "right" way was different than the way it appeared in Word).

The as-a-service model increases the difficulty in migrating. Since the software is accessible only through an online portal, it may be difficult or impossible to move all of the data to a different platform. Consider, for example, how hard or even impossible it would be to move all of the purchased licenses off of Apple's e-book platform to Amazon's (or vice versa). There's no benefit to the company to allow it, thus the technology often refuses to assist.

MAIN STORY: SOFTWARE TYPES

Keep in mind that software is a little different from hardware for a number of different reasons. The first one is cost: Both hardware and software require large sums of money to develop, but the actual production of software is only as expensive as the electricity it takes to send it over the internet (effectively zero). Secondly, most people don't worry about the hardware that they're using. For example, whether a computer uses an Intel or an AMD processor is irrelevant to the tasks of most people. But there is a visual component to software that is fundamental to the user interface/experience. As a result, users tend to identify with software decisions more than hardware decisions.

We could consider applying the four-component model to software, but it becomes a little tedious. Any given application software works well in the four-component model. But it becomes a little more effective to combine input/output and use the three-tier model, which we'll introduce in the next chapter. For now, let's review the different types of software that are most important.

There are two (or three) main divisions in the software world: operating systems and applications (and other). Operating systems (OSs) are the central authority on a computer. The operating system is what tells a computer when to listen for input and when to produce output. The OS checks for whether a program is malfunctioning, handles security for the average user, simplifies accessing other machines, and so on. OSs were originally designed as a method of allowing multiple users to access a computer at the same time, and that use has eventually morphed into allowing the use of multiple programs at once and removing many of the technical hurdles for computer use.

Applications are the programs that do a specific task. When a user sits down to a computer and turns it on, the OS starts automatically, but the user selects which applications will address their needs. Common examples of applications include but are not limited to word processors, email clients, internet browsers, database management systems, spreadsheets, and programming suites.

For the business world, it is often useful to consider a third category of software that we are calling "other." Technically, our third category could fall under "applications," but there's a subtle distinction. Whereas applications do something that benefits the organization, not all software does. A computer game doesn't have any particular benefit to the organization. Common other software might include music streaming apps, personal social media programs, and so on. It's important to keep in mind that not all applications are productivity suite applications.

SIDE QUEST: SOFTWARE PRICE POINTS

Software does not work on the same price point model that hardware does. This returns to the concept of what it costs to produce. If an office building purchases a door, there are a fixed number of variable costs associated with the materials for that door. There's so much wood, so many fittings, a latch, a lock, and so on. Those materials had to be grown or mined, and they are inextricably tied with that specific door. When the construction company sells the door, the construction company loses those goods and the office building gains those goods. This is all elementary, but it's so elementary that it's necessary to explicitly state since those basic concepts do not apply to software.

If a company makes a piece of software and a client purchases it, what fixed costs are associated with that software? The electricity to transmit it out of the company is an (typically negligible) operational cost that the client does not gain. The standard practice is that the client pays for internet access to download the software. The software itself is a copy of the original, but the original remains with the software company. So all of those variable material costs disappear.

If the additional per-unit cost of each piece of software sold is effectively $0.00, what's the justification for the cost? Obviously, it's the fixed costs: power, lights, office space, programmer time, administrative costs, and so on. Therefore, a simplistic model for a software pricing model is to either project or tally the total cost for its development, project how many sales can be expected, and then divide one over the other. Anything past that target number is profit.

BOX 5.3   Software Sales Formula

Total cost per unit = $0 variable cost + [total development expenses / projected total sales]

This lack of a variable cost is the crux of the issue. Using basic supply/demand curves, suppose that a company sells their product for $100 and needs to make $100,000 to recoup their development costs. If they expected 1,000 sales, the numbers all line up. (Where's the profit? Such a situation likely involves an independent developer, and that $100,000 represents their back salary over the last 12 to 24 months, so profit is nice, but it is of minimal comparative importance.) Suppose that sales are brisk and the 1,000 unit goal is met in 3 months before tapering off severely. Increasing the supply by decreasing the price to 50% should dramatically increase the demand. Without getting into more detail, the question becomes "Why would a client purchase the product immediately instead of waiting until it goes on 'sale' for 50% off?" Hence, price point doesn't apply so much for software sales: The price can vary substantively with little cause.

A good example of this is Steam—a video game sales site. All the products are distributed digitally and, several times a year, games are put on sale for 50 to 90% off. But it's the exact same game. Compare this with Black Friday sales (first Friday after American Thanksgiving). Most electronics manufacturers produce a separate serial numbered line of their product solely for sale during Black Friday. The reason the product costs half as much is because the components put into it reflect the comparatively lower quality and longevity of the product.

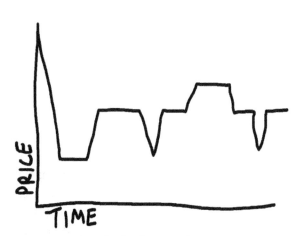

FIGURE 5.1 *Graph of software sales.*

MAIN STORY: ... AS A SERVICE

Historically, software was always purchased as a fixed unit. Simplistically, if a company had 10 computers, it bought 10 copies of each piece of software it needed. For small companies, this is still feasible. However, when companies begin to have thousands or tens of thousands of computers, with a comparative number of employee and nonemployee stakeholders, they need a better solution.

This need for a better solution intersects with software companies' preference to maintain a constant stream of software sales (following the basic accounting principle of matching costs to expenses). What keeps an individual from purchasing a copy of Microsoft Word 2000 (published in the year 2000) and using it for 20 years, possibly transferring the license from computer to computer? If that person doesn't need more than basic functionality, it's doable. But software companies do not like that "loss" of revenue. They'd rather see the individual purchase and use Microsoft Word 2003, 2007, 2010, 2013, 2016, and so on.

Therefore, many software companies are moving to a service model of software sales. Software is not sold; instead, users sign up for an account with a monthly fee. Frequently, this also means that the software can be used only through an internet client. The benefit is that the user always gets the latest version of the software. The downside is that there is no product past the end of the account's subscription.

The benefit for an organization is that they no longer have to project costs based on number of machines. They can set up automated processes to automatically sign employees up for accounts with the appropriate subscriptions. This makes managing software an easy project from this point.

One final note is that software as a service is not the only line. There are a large number of variations on the same theme. But one easy set of divisions to remember is shown here:

- Software as a service: An application that performs given tasks (e.g., subscribing to a television content provider like Netflix or Hulu)
- Platform as a service: A suite of applications (possibly an entire operating system) that are unified and consistent (e.g., Google Docs or Microsoft Office 365)
- Infrastructure as a service: Not only the applications, but the hardware and resources to run and operate tasks on them (e.g., Amazon Web Services or Microsoft Azure).

SIDE QUEST: THE VIRUS EFFECT

The virus effect is a descriptive analogy regarding the ubiquity of certain programs (with hardware and technology, this is often described as the *network* effect). Seventy percent of American adults use Facebook (Gramlich, 2019). So if a consumer decides that they're going to sign up to a new social media service, what is the most likely one that they'll select? Certainly, one of the biggest factors is going to be the social media platform the people who they know use. And with a market penetration of 70%, Facebook is likely going to be that platform. The virus effect presumes that the utility of a product increases as more people use it. There are a large number of historical examples: VHS won out against Betamax because more people used it, despite Betamax's potential technological superiority, as well as the 8-track versus cassette; Blu-ray versus Microsoft's HD DVD; and micro-USB versus Thunderbolt.

This is important to recognize for two reasons. The first is that when selecting an option it's important to consider the most popular option. Popularity is a strong support for making a decision in the technological world. For example, very few companies or governmental organizations would say, "We don't accept Microsoft Word .doc format; we accept only WordPerfect .wpd format." Popularity shouldn't be the only consideration, but for many selections it's indefensible to select the nonubiquitous solution.

The other reason for this importance is to realize that the most utile solution changes over time. It's difficult to see a time when Google will not be the search engine of choice. So it's likely a good platform of choice for advertisement or other commitments. But 20 years ago the same could have been said about Yahoo!, AltaVista, or even Gopher. Disruptive technological changes need to be responded to, and some caution should be taken in committing too much of a business model to an external company. For example, Google has a strong history of introducing new services and then cancelling them after a few years, leaving companies that relied on that service with few options (Hartmans, 2020).

This has an important individual correlation. While a company may have the resources to pivot relatively quickly when a service it relied on disappears, individuals do not always have the resources to do so. As an individual in any field, it's important to develop skill in a broad range of platforms. A very minor reason is so that if one platform fails, the individual can switch to another. But a much stronger reason is that it demonstrates that the individual has a proven track record of adaptability and can switch to new platforms with ease. (One final note: There are those who would argue against this, preferring to develop expertise in only one longevity-proven technology.)

BONUS LOOT: BUSINESS FUNCTION—ACCOUNTING

The field of accounting is very concerned with the rapid improvement of technology. Because entry-level positions in accounting are typically performed at the bookkeeper level, it is difficult to entrust that position to inexperienced employees. Inexperienced employees will make more mistakes and are less capable of identifying the mistakes that they've made. Accounting information systems, on the other hand, tend to perform basic bookkeeper tasks with accuracy, speed, and an increasing ability to identify problem areas.

The result is that the World War II vision (immortalized in the Pixar short *Paperman*) of a roomful of accountants typing away at manual 10-key calculators has been replaced by a few accountants in a room with a computer operating virtually nearby. And industry forecasts indicate that the trend will continue such that most functions of an organization can be performed by a single human who maintains oversight of the processes.

That's not to say that the role of accountant is going away. There are always going to be functions that operate at a higher conceptual level than a computer can understand. A computer may be able to calculate numbers, but it may not be able to understand when there's an error in those numbers (for example, 1 pen sold for $100, when it should have been 100 pens for $1). Even if a computer is programmed to identify those errors, a human will always need to be around to identify how to handle those errors the first time.

Further, there's a need for humans to engage in accounting research, in tax law analysis, and in explaining what certain concepts or strategies mean in real terms to clients. The human side of accounting will always exist, and that human side will need to know the mechanics of accounting. Even if the computer does most of those mechanics better for routine operations, the human is necessary to put the information into context.

BONUS LOOT: RESUME BUILDERS—OPEN SOURCE CONTRIBUTION

One constant demand by resume reviewers is the inclusion of technical skills. If you know how to use Excel and you're in a field where it's a benefit but can't be assumed, you need to incorporate it into your resume in some way. There are two reasons to do this: The first reason is that hiring managers probably legitimately need to know that you know how to use Excel. But the second reason is that most large organizations process applications through a machine learning algorithm that checks the applications for certain keywords, and you can't know ahead of time whether Excel is one of those keywords.

There's not much that can be done on the second area, except to make it a practice of knowing what keywords are frequently included in your industry or job function. But for the former, it becomes a little difficult to demonstrate competency in some fields where the number of applications in regular usage might top a hundred. There's not an effective way to demonstrate skill in any given application on demand in a static and unchanging environment like a resume.

That's where it's important to build a portfolio. Rather than have a list that says, "Here are five programs that I've used," produce a set of deliverables using those programs that effectively demonstrate competence. Most hiring managers would be more impressed with that than just having to trust you that you've done it correctly.

However, that only helps in a final in-person interview stage. Few hiring managers are going to track down a dozen links on each of the several dozen applications that they're reviewing for a single job. Everything needs to be right on the resume. That's where it's good to find some online projects that you can contribute to. Open source programs are always looking for help adding features to their programs. Testing new features is also an area that many applications consistently require help with. And being able to include in a resume that not only have you used a utility before but that you have been selected as a development tester for new features on a similar product should quickly demonstrate excellence in technical topics.

Finally, open source projects aren't the only possibility for contribution, but they are one of the easiest places to describe what you've contributed. Other places may look for basic data entry, transcription, review, or editing of online work. The benefit is that you can find an area of interest to you, contribute to it, and have it reflected professionally.

BONUS LOOT: SOFT SKILLS—FIRST IMPRESSIONS

By Fawn Walker

As an ambitious postal employee with good skills and an honest, conscientious approach to my work, I was promoted in 1993 to customer service supervisor. I was an expert who would go to a poorly performing station, bring it back into compliance with the rules, and improve performance. I worked at several stations and became an acting manager and postmaster, cleaning up processes at each location I was assigned to.

I later had an opportunity to transfer to operations support in 2006. I learned computer skills on my own at work and at home. I later became the acting manager of delivery and customer service for operations support. In this position, I made the manager of operations programs support (MOPS), my boss, look good, and he frequently recognized me with both praise and awards.

The postal service structure has 67 districts, with district managers distributed across seven areas administered by area vice presidents. However, despite hard work, great results, and recognition, my chance of advancing any further came to a halt when the district manager of the large district I worked in called me to her office. Apparently, a person in the area finance department had developed a report similar to one that I created in district operations. I kept up with my area operations counterparts, but not area finance, so I did not know about this report. She wanted me to tell her why my report was different than their report. She would not allow me to look at the two reports to determine what the difference was. She wanted to know right then and there, and since I couldn't answer without guessing, she became very angry. I refused to give a guess as an answer and, as expected, it only took a couple of minutes back in my office to determine that the two reports were tracking different metrics. This particular manager formed strong opinions of people and never changed them, no matter what happened in the future. She had taken a dislike to someone who worked for me, and I heard her say he would never get promoted in her district. However, once she liked a person, she was intensely loyal to them, even if they were incompetent. I made a poor impression on her but continued to make a great impression on every other person I worked with.

While she was district manager and, later, area vice president, I never received an actual promotion to anything, even though my performance was so good that, at the time she retired, I was an acting manager in a different district seven levels above my actual pay grade. As the manager in charge of delivery and customer service, our district was number 1 in the nation for performance. After she retired, I was quickly promoted from 2012 to 2017 to customer service manager, area operations analyst, area complement coordinator, headquarters field staffing analyst senior, and principal headquarters data analyst, which is my current position.

Be prepared for anything; monitor what your manager is monitoring. If their concern is financial performance, you should be following the finance department, even if you don't work in finance. Even though I went so many years without a promotion, I still kept my performance up and improved my skills. So when the roadblock was removed, I was promoted nearly immediately.

We fully believe Ms. Walker's overview of her situation. However, let's pretend for a moment that she had done something to justify the initial first impression. Her conclusions still seem reasonable: People make long-term conclusions based on instantaneous judgments. Further, it's important to continue performing at a high level even in situations where someone has made an incorrect judgment based on a first impression. What's interesting about this anecdote is that it could also apply to technology and platforms: People frequently make snap decisions about the utility and effectiveness of physical products in the same way that they make these decisions about platforms.

BONUS LOOT: CERTIFICATIONS—FURTHER MICROSOFT

Microsoft (n.d.) is an interesting target for certifications because it is such a ubiquitous platform in most modern business environments. Further, almost every product they have has some form of certification related to it. These certifications come in two types: exams and tracks. The tracks cover specific roles that Microsoft has identified as core to their platform offering. The tracks are also offered at several levels. Both the tracks and the levels change slightly over time. Getting an expert-level certification (e.g., a Microsoft Certified Systems Developer) is often the result of several years of experience, study, and testing. They are, according to their certification, well versed in almost every major aspect of Microsoft development products.

Most people are probably not interested in these certifications. However, when hiring for a technical position, it's probably worth being sure that the applicant is using the appropriate nomenclature from Microsoft and that the level they have is what they're representing. Microsoft certification is expected for certain roles, and it's possible to be familiar with what those roles cover without knowing all of the details of the knowledge covered.

However, these tracks are typically made up of several exams each. These exams alone are not frequently viewed as sufficient (although they can indicate that someone is on the path toward a full certification). For the nontechnical manager, identifying a specific technology and a specific exam to is a little bit of a tip that the person has some technical ability. For example, passing the Microsoft 365 Fundamentals exam (more technically oriented than an MOS) and being able to explain the underlying concepts of the cloud architecture will likely have applications in a wide variety of business roles.

REFERENCES

Ellis County. (n.d.). County ordinance. https://co.ellis.tx.us/DocumentCenter/View/10008/Alcohol---Ellis-County

Gramlich, J. (2019, May 16). 10 facts about Americans and Facebook. Pew Research Center. https://www.pewresearch.org/fact-tank/2019/05/16/facts-about-americans-and-facebook/

Hartmans, A. (2020, August 5). Google's inbox by Gmail service is about to shut down for good. Here are 19 other Google products that bombed, died, or disappeared. *Business Insider*. https://www.businessinsider.com/discontinued-google-products-2016-8

Microsoft. (n.d.). Microsoft certifications. https://www.microsoft.com/en-us/learning/certification-overview.aspx

Scwartz, M. (2019, March 8). When not reading the fine print can cost your soul. NPR. https://www.npr.org/2019/03/08/701417140/when-not-reading-the-fine-print-can-cost-your-soul

CHAPTER 6

Communications

PRE-READING CHECKLIST

VOCABULARY

> Scalability

> Fungibility

> Communication

> Internet

> Networks

> WiFi

> LAN and WAN

> Medium, media

> Fiber optic cable

CONCEPTS

> Differing perspectives on communication

> LAN vs. WAN

> Information overload

> The cloud

MAIN STORY: DRIVING PRINCIPLES

1. Communication is the process of transferring data for the purposes of distilling information.
2. Communication from a technical perspective is completely different from communication from a human perspective.
3. Information overload is a problem that grows over time.

SIDE QUEST: ANALOGY—NUCLEAR POWER PLANTS

The bike shed problem is a famous analogy related to communication (Northcote Parkinson, 1958). Imagine a municipal oversight committee that is in charge of reviewing business plans for a small city. These are not experts; they are just citizens who are appointed to make sure that nothing fraudulent or counter to the interests of the citizens is occurring. Then suppose that they are given the plans to a nuclear power plant that will be built on the outskirts of town and told to find all of the issues they have with the power plant.

With sage faces, they all pore through the dozens of pages of technical blueprints pretending they understand what they're seeing. Each person has two unthinkable options: They can either (a) declare that there's nothing wrong and write up a two-sentence report saying that everything's fine with the huge project or (b) declare that they don't know what they're talking about and that it was a stupid idea to assign this task to them. In either case they are going to look incompetent.

After hemming and hawing, one person finally sees something that cuts across both of those issues. In the back of the facility, there's a bike rack for employees to store their bicycles. The person may not know much about nuclear physics, but they have lots of opinions on the relative merit of reducing carbon emissions by biking to work. "This is too small! There needs to be more incentive to bike to work!" Another person disagrees and does so vociferously. And that leads to another comment, and so on.

After 3 months of committee meetings, they have assembled an exhaustive and thoroughly researched 250-page report, 249 pages of which discuss the relative merits of different options for the bike rack at the edge of the parking lot and 1 page that says, "Everything else is fine."

The moral is that people will center a discussion on the areas they are comfortable with, and they will ignore the areas that are outside of their comfort zone. A broader principle is that communications are frequently not about what they seem to be about. In short, communication is hard.

MAIN STORY: WHAT IS COMMUNICATION?

Communication is the process of transferring data from one point to another point. There is a large number of variations on this definition, though. The key to remember is that highly specific definitions don't more accurately define communications; they reveal the predilections of the definer.

A discussion about communication in information systems is difficult. A large part of the discussion centers around the technical aspects of communication. A regional branch in one state has a certain amount of bandwidth that it can transfer to another branch, and that requires a certain category of data cables or other situations. But those details need to be relegated to a technical expert.

Instead, recall the seesaw model, that hardware exists for software to run on, software exists to facilitate communications, and communications exist to transfer data from one place to another. There's still a large amount of communication occurring outside on the nontechnical side. It is important to be aware of and manage that communication.

> **BOX 6.1   Station Wagon of Tapes**
>
> There's a famous saying, "Never underestimate the bandwidth of a station wagon filled with backup tapes!" At one point in the early days of networking, some academics got fed up with the slow speed of their network connection and realized it would be faster to just load all of their backups into a station wagon, drive them to the destination, and copy them manually. Sometimes the most technical solution is not the ideal solution.

One of the easiest ways to do this is to try to unify two different perspectives on communication: the technical and the human perspective. In the technical perspective, data is broken into small, uniformly sized pieces and transmitted from one network location to another. From the human perspective, communication is a free-form flow of surface thoughts broadcast to one or many people. The key to unifying these is to remember that the definition of communication reveals the bias of the definer.

In this case, the bias we want to focus on is that of the organization (or the system, as in information systems). In this case, the uniform packetization of data that occurs in the technical definition can be merged with the free form of the human definition. This means that communication is the measured and defined transmission of data from one actor to one or many actors. The word *actor* is used to emphasize that it may be an automatic process, a data store, an external target, or a human. The word *defined* provides a way to delineate the form of a specific transfer of data without limiting the range of possibilities. But the most important word is *measured*. It doesn't matter what is communicated from the organization's perspective so much as that someone is aware of it and that it is part of the broader plan for the organization.

SIDE QUEST: NETWORKS

Networks are an interesting corollary to communications. They're firmly on the technical side, but they provide the first truly novel capacity for computers. Prior to networking, computers did what humans did, but faster. But with the introduction of networking, that ability to do what humans did elevated itself to a new level. For example, a person can have a meeting with someone in New York or with someone in Tokyo. But add a modern network as a tool and that same person can have the meeting in New York and Tokyo at the same time.

The term *network* has two general applications in information systems. On the one hand, we can use the word *network* to describe situations where multiple computer systems are transmitting data to each other. On the other hand, we might also use it to refer to any group of devices communicating with each other. This is a bit of a specious distinction, since computers are devices. But when we make that distinction, we're normally considering levels of complexity. For example, when we have a computer that is interacting with another computer, the system of rules for negotiating and affecting the transmissions is quite complicated. But when we consider a computer interacting with its associated Bluetooth keyboard, there is only a minimal amount of data being transmitted.

This distinction is important because, for the most part, networks in the broader realm of information systems deal with the first definition. Networks of devices working together (i.e., the second definition) are typically relegated to the realms of information technology. There is a broader principle here: When we deal with systems, we don't need to worry about some of the little fiddly bits. We want to consider the flow of information, and exactly what the technical device is doing is a little bit irrelevant.

The primary intent of the word *network* in this chapter is multifaceted interaction between several computers. Networks are typically described, classified, and categorized by a number of different functions. In the technical space, the definitions of functions are typically focused on specific protocols and version numbers. We will delve into the distinctions among networks only to the point that we have a qualitative difference (that is, a difference in kind, not just a difference in capacity), because this distinguishes how we can use networks to enhance our computing systems.

The first distinction is between a wired versus a wireless system. The term that describes the connections is *medium* (the same term that is used when referring to digital media). Medium refers to the physical format that data is transmitted on. This book is either on the media of the printed page or on the media of a digital e-book. Wired networks are typically on the media of copper cabling or fiber optic (or fibre optic or optical fiber) cable. Copper uses electrical impulses to transmit data; it is reaching the peak of its transmitting capacity due to basic physics, and it is subject to electrical interference. Fiber optic cables use photonic impulses (light waves) to transmit data across glass or plastic strands; it is more difficult and expensive to install, but it is lighter, faster, and a little more secure than copper.

Wireless systems transmit data across a broad medium as opposed to the narrow medium used by the wired systems. Almost any electromagnetic energy can be used, but the frequently encountered wireless media are typically radio waves and lasers. There are others that are common in select industries; for instance, satellite transmissions are generally microwaves. Radio waves typically go under the term *WiFi*, which stands for "wireless fidelity." Radio waves are convenient because they go through physical barriers and they attenuate (that is, the signal strength degrades) in a roughly circular pattern. Lasers are convenient because they don't go through physical barriers and attenuate related to their physical environments. Laser networks are not in the public market yet. But they are the next evolution and will address a large number of the security issues presented by radio networks passing through, for example, the external walls of a building. Almost uniformly, wireless networks are less secure than wired networks. Wireless networks are also much slower than wired networks, but that is only currently true; it is not guaranteed to always be true.

The second distinction between network types is between LAN and WAN networks. A LAN is a local area network that exists within the confines of an organization. A WAN is a wide area network that expands beyond the organization in some fashion. One way of making the distinction is deciding who owns the medium. It's a LAN if the organization owns all of the wires or all of the area where the wireless signals travel. It's a WAN if the wires or wireless signal are leased from a third party. The biggest distinctions between these two types lie in security: LAN security depends on physical security on site, whereas WAN security depends more on how secure the information is in transit.

The third distinction between network types lies in the communication characteristics of the channel. There are simplex, half-duplex, and duplex communications methods. Simplex communications can pass in only one direction, like a television or radio broadcast. Half-duplex communications can pass in two directions but only one at a time, like personal letters or a citizen's band radio (CB). Duplex communications pass in both directions at the same time, like a telephone call. Every modern network is designed around requiring a full duplex communication scheme. However, the intent needs to be considered (for example, point-of-sale systems tend to pass information to higher organizational levels, whereas phone systems want that ability for real-time back-and-forth communication).

SIDE QUEST: THE INTERNET

A network is many computers interacting together, and scope is when we consider different layers of abstraction. At a high level of abstraction (i.e., if we abstract away those details of the individual computers) we can consider the network as a single construct. What happens if multiple networks interact? This is called an internetwork. The most famous internetwork is the internet. There exist others, such as internet II (an unsuccessful attempt to replace the internet), SIPRNet and NIPRNet (secret internet protocol router network and nonclassified internet protocol router network, networks that connect to each other for the U.S. Defense industry), and various large corporate networks.

Communication over the internet typically follows several protocols. Without going into detail, we'll break them down into content broadcasting, communication, social media, and autonomous communications protocols. Content broadcasting is the production and dissemination of visual material, replacing newsletters or catalogs of previous years. The most common examples are web pages or other storefronts.

The internet is a foundational component of international communications, acting as a nongovernmental infrastructure for message and content relay. This is important, because it is not a thing that has happened before. Historically, almost all international communication was government or government-sanctioned in nature. But we are quickly moving to a point at which most of the communications are private in purpose, and this introduces new areas for interaction. Alternately, we could consider the newness of the internet in its ability to allow everyone to have free and instantaneous worldwide communications with an audience of unlimited size. Prior to that, our only comparable technology was shouting.

It is important to conceive of the internet as a black box. There is too much complexity to map it out in detail, but modern businesses need access to the new technologies inherent in or made possible by the internet. So rather than assume any level of control over the internet, organizations should control their networks and monitor the internet itself in more detail.

MAIN STORY: INFORMATION OVERLOAD

One problem that increases in complexity over time is information overload. This is a bit of a self-defeating term, as information is not the problem. Information is useful facts. But information overload is the overwhelming production and communication of data such that the data becomes useless with its quantity.

Moore's law was discussed earlier as the primary driver of information systems. But there are other laws that correlate to other metrics. For example, Nielsen's (2019) law tells us that the rate that data can be transmitted grows by 50% every year. Data storage is harder to pin down to a practical metric, but a variation on Kryder's law (Internet Archive, 2006) shows us that the price of storage halves every year. So the problem is that the amount of data that can be stored is increasing at an exponentially faster rate than the amount that can be transferred or processed.

Imagine the worst, most confusing graph possible. That graph was probably bad and confusing because not enough time and thought was put into its production. But the goal of the graph was the same as that of the good graph: to distill a lot of data into a few useful facts and then present that information. But if the amount of data being produced is exceeding the amount that computers can process and analyze, there are problems.

This is the true cause of information overload. This is important because one of the most effective strategies for reducing complexity and confusion in an organization is to reduce the number of available choices because that reduces the amount of data that needs to be communicated. This sounds restrictive, and it is not intended to be a universal solution. However, clear and direct instructions allow operational employees to know what they are expected to do. Limiting the scope of managerial problems allows a managerial employee to make better decisions with the data at hand.

This is an issue that is at the forefront of the current push for data analytics, business intelligence, and visualization. Success in this area now will likely imply first-mover advantage over time. Remember that communication is never about just numbers; it's about telling a story.

BOX 6.2 Moore, Kryder, and Nielsen

Who are these people? Essentially, they're more or less random tech industry workers who made an observation that was either coincidentally accurate or controversial enough that people referred to it by the person's name. Why, then, is Kryder's law referred to as harder to pin down? Two slow processors don't make a processor that's twice as fast without substantial overhead, and 10 processors are definitely not 10 times faster because of that overhead. But 10 storage drives have 10 times as much storage capacity as 1 drive that's 100 times the size. So for the vast majority of situations, storage density is not as important as the cost of storage. But (a) Kryder's law originally referred to storage density and (b) the form of storage starts bringing a lot of variation to the argument from experts.

SIDE QUEST: THE CLOUD

Recently, a newer attribute of the internet has presented itself. Technology has reached a saturation level that allows for the seamless integration of multiple resources. Remembering that as time goes on processing and transmitting costs will hit zero, it has now become effectively free to pass resource requests to a third party. The cloud is a fungible and scalable reallocation of distributed resources. Talking about the cloud is ubiquitous and inevitable; everyone tends to have an idea of what it means. Unfortunately, definitions are not standardized. Most definitions tend to focus on the two important considerations: fungible and scalable.

First, when we discuss the cloud, we're discussing the ability to distribute resources beyond first-party interactions. An example might be an internet service provider (say, ISPa) with a fixed amount of space available in a network operations center to rent to customers. When that amount fills up, does it make sense for ISPa to put a sign on a web page saying "no vacancy"? Or would it make a certain amount of sense to assume that ISPa's business is going well and find another organization (say, ISPb) whose business either isn't going as well or who bought too much space in their network operations center and now needs to quickly rent it out. So ISPa can rent it from ISPb at a lower rate than ISPa sells to customers. But what happens if, later, ISPb no longer has the space? Do they tell ISPa to find someone else or do they try to find a way to continue that income? Likely, they'll find ISPc and negotiate yet another layer. And when ISPc needs more space, they'll find someone else. But suppose that somewhere down the line, at ISPg, when they need space, they happen to find that ISPa is having a sale and decide to purchase excess capacity from them? The point is that the arrangement(s) is not simple and linear; the cloud is a quick cover term for a system of deals occurring on the back end that change relatively frequently and are likely too complicated to map out.

When we talk about fungibility, we're talking about the ability of the resources on the cloud to be split up to any desired level. Currency is the classic example: Gold can be transferred in tons, pounds, or fractions of an ounce. Likewise, an organization that rents processor space might have physical devices that operate in the billions of operations per second. But most of their clients might want to rent only on the thousands of operations per second. Or perhaps they have one client who wants to rent on the tens of billions of operations per second but who wants what he's renting to appear to be only a single processor. Another term that is used for this concept of fungibility is *virtualization*. Virtualization is the process of creating an illusion of resources that combine many or part of physical resources in a manner that is seamless to the user.

Scalability is the other primary attribute of the cloud. Scalability is the ability of a requirement to handle small or large changes in amount. For example, an extensible ladder might be able to scale from 8 feet to 16 feet. But if someone needs to get on top of a 30-foot platform, they'll need a different solution. The cloud is considered to be infinitely scalable: If a client needs more resources, they are available from somewhere. An example of this might be a small, independent video game designer who releases a new video game expecting around a hundred people to purchase it in the first month. That video game designer would historically have had to weigh paying for excess and unused capacity with the risk of overloading the servers. But if they used a modern service provider, part of their contract likely includes automatically increasing the amount of resources allocated based on need. If the game suddenly gets featured on a large video game review site and, instead of 100 downloads, 100,000 people download the game, the servers should be able to respond accordingly.

In the 1800s, cocaine was hailed as a wonder cure-all and prescribed to almost everyone for the smallest to the largest medical problems. It found its way into the ingredient list for carbonated soft drinks! It was considered by many to be the next wave of modern medical science, but we stopped using because of the very detrimental side effects. Similarly, in the 1950s, computers came into nongovernmental use and their utility was at the early stages of exploration; people were starting to hail it as a foundational component for the future. It's hard to see in hindsight, but there was a very real possibility that computers would have hit some unforeseen hurdle that made them not an ideal solution. In the late 2010s, however, it would be ridiculous to suggest that computers are not a fundamental part of the modern environment. Similarly, in the mid-1990s, the internet was probably going to be beneficial, but there were a lot of technical and societal hurdles involved in its eventual ubiquity. In the same way, the cloud has had a number of very large problems, but it is now foundational to the way the modern internet works and very unlikely to disappear.

Those large problems are still around. The biggest issue with the cloud is security. When an organization signs an agreement for cloud storage, there is typically a large section detailing the fact that the actual physical location of the data is not guaranteed. So, for example, data that originates in the United States and is stored with another U.S. company might actually be housed in an eastern European data center. There are obviously large security problems there.

The cloud is a fantastic system for storing and handling online activities for anything where security is not a concern. It's likely a good thing for any application where security requirements aren't substantive. But it is a bad idea for any area where security is an issue, for example military, governmental, or medical industries. And part of that insecurity goes back to the analogy at the beginning of the chapter.

BONUS LOOT: BUSINESS FUNCTION—PUBLIC RELATIONS

Public relations is possibly the single most changed field in business over the last 20 years. The advent of social media has changed how companies can communicate with the public as well as how the public expects to be communicated with. This, however, leads to some sharply divided opinions on the right ways to handle social media.

One side suggests that it's impossible for social media to ever be of benefit to a company. Companies can make mistakes on social media but never benefit from it. For example, when has someone ever switched toilet paper brands because their toilet paper manufacturer was particularly responsive on Twitter? On the other hand, it seems reasonable to assume that a toilet paper manufacturer could lose customers by making an offensive statement (intentionally or unintentionally) in their attempt to be witty on social media.

The other side says that social media is the new method of communication. All companies are now deeply connected companies, and there are opportunities to build social capital in the environment. For example, video game companies spend a large amount of time specifically designing how they relate to their customers online in an effort to build loyal followers who will purchase future video games just because the game is related to that company.

A more balanced perspective might suggest that there are two types of companies in this regard. There are some companies for whom a social media presence is of little value, like a metallurgy processor. But small companies who rely on word of mouth or otherwise need aspects of their company sensationalized by the nature of their industry (movie production studios, musicians, museums) need to embrace the new hypersocial reality. *Hypersocial* is the term used for companies that make social media a priority, and it is worth further reading in its own right.

BONUS LOOT: RESUME BUILDERS—LEADERSHIP

Leadership examples take many forms. And these forms are more varied and ubiquitous than ever. For example, unofficial round-robin financing groups in parts of Kenya are very different from the bureaucratic and documented structure of an American nonprofit group.

However, these leadership groups are a good way to document the soft skills that employers are looking for. The person who goes out of their way to volunteer at and take a leadership role in a local meet-up for professionals relating to an industry is going to have a good leg up on others at their same level. Good examples are makers clubs, professional organizations, nonprofits, church groups, or other structures that can be defined and followed up on.

But not everyone cares about these leadership roles. For example, a resume might list "work experience" and "volunteer experience," and many resume reviewers will ignore the volunteer experience section. But that doesn't change the fact that the actual skills learned are still fundamental and valuable. Someone who has several years in a leadership role will have developed skills and leadership abilities that they didn't have before, and that should come across outside the scope of the resume.

Finally, remember that many places have formal structures. Nonprofits have boards of directors. Committees and local chapters of professional organizations have presidents, vice presidents, secretaries, and treasurers. Having specific titles that are well known will go a long way toward increasing the validity of these leadership roles on a resume.

BONUS LOOT: SOFT SKILLS—ONLINE FIRST IMPRESSIONS

First impressions are important. While it's feasible to say that not everyone operates on the instantaneous judgment of first impressions, it's certainly a common fallacy of human psychology (Glikson et al., 2017). However, what is not always evident is how we are perceived through online first impressions. This is because it is simultaneously a limited subset of nonverbal cues as well as the substitution of a different set of a nonverbal cues.

When communicating online, the human brain is given just enough stimulation to try to respond in the same manner as in a face-to-face meeting. However, the information lines are severely restricted. For example, in an email, there are no body postures, facial cues, voice tone indicators, or other cues that humans are used to relying on. Instead, the flow is restricted solely to word choice, grammar, and punctuation. This makes it vitally important to ensure that those things are well developed. It is important to develop a work voice and work tone for digital communications that are in a limited medium like text, regardless of whether it's on a website or over email.

Along those lines, the extra set of cues comes into play. Historically, when a person showed up to a job interview, they were there on their own recognizance. They just showed up and expressed themselves. There were probably some reference checks, but otherwise, it was a low-bandwidth process. In the modern, information-rich era, it's possible to Google a person and find their previous employers, rating sites that might discuss them, social media sites, news articles, and numerous other information sources with minimal effort.

As a result, it's important to keep those things in mind. The personal and professional world are very easy to blur together (Tarpey, 2018). A personal social media site is currently fair game for evaluators to use. On the other hand, many professionals find a lack of social media presence suspicious, so there's a balancing act between the need to have and maintain a social media presence and the need to keep that presence professional.

BONUS LOOT: CERTIFICATIONS—TRAINING WEBSITES

Websites are becoming much more social in their use of training options. For example, when discussing microcredentialing, Codeacademy was mentioned. There are a number of sites like this, such as LinkedIn Learning, DataCamp, and Khan Academy. There are even colleges that offer free courses, for example Stanford's (n.d.) free online course database is one of the earliest and most extensive. These sites are a good source of not just learning something but also providing documentation of that learning.

These online websites vary in both utility and respectability. It is valid to ask, "What sites do you use to learn new topics?" Because there are so many sites available, it's reasonable to match the site used with a target industry or company. For example, some people love Khan Academy's YouTube videos and learning site, but others hate it. Wikipedia is an excellent site to learn material (and make edits to, which in turn can be documented and referenced as a career booster), but many academics or self-conceived "purists" do not find it to be a valid source.

In short, when looking to learn a new skill, try to find a free or low-cost site (ideally) that, in addition to providing training on the subject, provides documentation of that training. Even if it's a printed certificate, it's something that can be used to objectively describe what was learned. If it's on a platform that others are also familiar with, it provides a common frame of reference so that both parties can understand the scope of the specific skill set gained.

REFERENCES

Glikson, E., Cheshin, A., & van Kleef, G. (2017). The dark side of a smiley: Effects of smiling emoticons on virtual first impressions. *Social Psychological and Personality Science*, *9*(5), 614–625. https://journals.sagepub.com/doi/abs/10.1177/1948550617720269

Internet Archive. (2006, April 10). Kryder's law. https://web.archive.org/web/20060410141312/http://www.mattscomputertrends.com/Kryder%27s.html

Nielsen, J. (2019, September 27). Nielsen's law of internet bandwidth. Nielsen Norman Group. https://www.nngroup.com/articles/law-of-bandwidth/

Northcote Parkinson, C. (1958). *Parkinson's law, or the pursuit of progress*. Penguin.

Stanford University. (n.d.). Search catalog. https://online.stanford.edu/courses

Tarpey, M. (2018, August 9). Not getting job offers? Your social media could be the reason. *CareerBuilder*. https://www.careerbuilder.com/advice/not-getting-job-offers-your-social-media-could-be-the-reason

People

VOCABULARY

> Roles

> Operational/managerial/strategic

> Semantics

> ERP

> Dissonance

CONCEPTS

> Type of decision making

> Soft skills

> How people are part of IS

> Decision-making ternary

MAIN STORY: DRIVING PRINCIPLES

1. Systems can document roles, which are simple constructs comparable with any other component of the system. But they are just an abstraction of the actual person performing that role.
2. People need a certain amount of structure in their role definition, but that structure should be appropriate to the complexity of their decision-making role.
3. People are one of the biggest security risks in an organization.

SIDE QUEST: ANALOGY—CHARACTERS VERSUS NPCS

In any novel or story, there are characters that fulfill certain functions. The difference between literature and pulp novels is in the development of those characters. In a dime-novel space opera from the 1930s, a damsel in distress is a one-dimensional character who only exists to buttress the perception of the main character as the hero. On the other side, good literature typically tries to show the flaws of protagonists and justify the rationale of the villains. One example of this might be in the evolution of video games.

There is an increasing perception of video games as an art form, largely because of the increase in characterization that occurs in many story-driven games. Consider the standard platform. Forty years ago it was enough for the plumber to have to save the princess. But over time, it became necessary to intrigue the player by introducing a short backstory in the intro, justifying why the villain kidnapped the princess and why the plumber has to save her. In the most recent iterations of similar game types, there is even typically some metric of motivation in a postgame scenario showing the independence of the princess and what her goals are. It doesn't address everything, but for a game whose target is typically children under 10 years old, there are orders of magnitude in the improvement of the characterization.

In video games, these characters who aren't controlled by player are called NPCs, or nonplayer characters. These characters are the ones who offer quests to the character, explain backstory, or exposit plot points in a second-person narrative. Their reactions to the player are relatively simplistic, however. Typically, a character triggers a certain piece of in-game code, and that makes the NPC react a certain way. The range of these NPC reactions are limited by the complexity of the code. This level of complexity becomes more interesting over time as programmers are able to develop more complicated branching trees for the NPCs to respond with. But it's also frustrating when compared with the more full realization of the depth of characterization in a well-written novel or video format.

Systems have this same level of complexity. Some roles in an organization are very simple with an easy-to-describe set of appropriate reactions to stimuli. Other roles in an organization become increasingly more complex over time, with the ability to document what is occurring becoming more difficult. Ultimately, however, it's important to remember that documenting just the organizational perspective of a given role does not categorize the person. The person and the role are different, and the system can document only the role.

MAIN STORY: ROLES

A person who works in an organization doesn't do so in a vacuum. In this area, information systems departments work alongside human resources in definitions and structure. Human resource departments tend to be the ultimate definers of what a given role can be required to do. Information systems departments, on the other hand, take a more documentation-oriented role. This distinction between definition and documentation is the overlap between human resources and information systems departments.

For example, for a given department, after documenting the roles of everyone in the department and the ways in which information is passed between them, information systems and various modeling languages allow a manager to identify places where unneeded inefficiencies are occurring ("unneeded inefficiencies" is not a redundant statement in this particular case). Suppose that a department has 10 people working in it, and after redesigning the process, 10% savings occur. What happens with that extra person whose role is now unimportant? Again, this is where working alongside human resources is important for any systems approach to the people component.

This is one area where the term *information systems* tends to be too abstract. It is important for managers to remember that there are real people and their representation within any systems diagram or modeling is only a representation of their activities in the company. An extreme example might be that a (bad) information systems person can analyze an employee's time and note that they answer an average of 10 emails per hour. Therefore, in a 40-hour week, they can answer 400 emails. If a particular department only gets 200 emails, they should be able to have their role split between answering email and other roles.

From a non–information systems perspective, there are the soft skills aspects to consider. For example, if the person can answer 10 emails in an hour, can they keep that pace up for 20 hours a week? What about breaks, time for following up with finding the answer to difficult emails, interacting with departmental requirements, and so on? There are also other soft skills to consider: If a person develops an expertise at the customer service component of answering emails, does that expertise necessarily roll over to other areas?

This is where the phrase "unneeded inefficiencies" comes into play. There are both legally mandated and managerially appropriate reasons to not use all employees to their absolute technical limits, as it may cause more problems than it solves. It's like running a car engine at its highest speed setting: That may work well for short bursts, but it can't be maintained indefinitely without damaging the engine. In a similar way, the people component of the seesaw model is the most important component to ensure full collaboration with other departments.

SIDE QUEST: SEMANTICS

What is the point of all of this technology? The answer is, surprisingly, not much. Ultimately, there always needs to be a human component. In the 1980s, the phrase "garbage in, garbage out" was coined to help people understand how computers worked. The idea was that the computer and the technology didn't really do anything on their own without a human instructing the computer. Four decades later, computers are more capable of independent action, but ultimately semantic meaning still resides with a human.

Semantics is the concept of "meaning." When a person is asked to think of a cup, they might imagine a glass, a mug, a plastic cup, a red Solo Cup, someone cupping their hands together, or a unit of measurement. Regardless of what they are visualizing, if they explained it, other fluent English speakers would immediately understand how their visualization fit the term *cup*. A computer is not capable of making that association independently. For a computer, the word *cup* is just three letters. This may not always be the case, but it will be for the foreseeable future.

While the left side of the seesaw model can perform fast and complicated processing on the data in order to come up with information that has meaning, the computer can't infer that meaning. It doesn't "get it." A human is still required to, for example, understand that the number 90.17 is the price in dollars of a new, pink kids' bicycle without the extra basket and including tax. The computer can retain that association, but there is no semantic understanding of the concept; for example, if someone wanted to know the price of a new, pink kids' bicycle with the extra basket and including tax, the computer would be lost without additional instruction.

The principle to take away here is that humans are just as much a part of the information systems environment as the hardware or software. Granted, humans are all individuals, and each has separate and unique value. But from the perspective of an organization, a human's utility lies in the actions that they perform on behalf of the organization. The fact that a computer calculates the quarterly finances but a CPA still needs to sign off on them doesn't change the end result: The entire organization's financial data has been rendered into the quarterly statement information.

It's important to keep in mind that people are complicated and more difficult to account for than the hardware, but they're no less a part of the process of developing and operating an information system.

MAIN STORY: DECISION-MODE TERNARY

The first chapter discussed the models that act as presumptions. One of those is the decision-mode ternary, which is based on Anthony's triangle. This needs more detail, as it affects the roles of people in any given system. There are three levels of decision making: operational, managerial, and strategic. Anthony's triangle ranks the decision-making modes with operational roles at the bottom and strategic roles at the top. This is done not to imply the importance of the roles but to align with types of decisions.

Operational decision making is the most immediate decision-making role. At its most extreme, operational decision making is the decision to follow an appropriately scripted set of instructions. For example, McDonald's has spent decades and millions of dollars refining their instructions for creating the perfect crispy fry. This is a monumental achievement, potentially on par with any engineering task in this history of humanity. Consider that, across the world, regardless of culture or distance from McDonald's headquarters, a french fry tastes pretty similar. McDonald's research and development spends a large amount of time defining french fry size, freezer temperature, cooking time, salt content, portion size, holding time, and any other metric they can think of to maximize consistency. When an employee is assigned the role of cooking french fries, there's very little analysis that needs to be put into the decision.

Managerial decision making is more complicated than operational decision making. A comparable task would be a chef in a fine dining restaurant who wants to add french fries (or pommes frites) to the menu. The chef is not necessarily a manager, but the decision will affect the line cook who is responsible for executing the recipe, and the chef has wide

> **BOX 7.1 McDonald's and Transnationalism**
>
> McDonald's is one of the classic examples of international management. One model of international management considers that a company can be local, move to national when it opens in multiple states or provinces, international when it begins to interact in any capacity with a second country, and transnational when it no longer has a primary cultural focus. McDonald's has very clearly gone through each of these stages and, from a process and systems perspective, is worth reviewing. International management is much more of a specialized field in information systems than in other fields. McDonald's is also one of the companies discussed in *In Search of Excellence* (Waterman & Peters, 1982).

freedom in decision making. The chef can choose what kind of potatoes to use, how to source them, what method of cooking to use, how they will look, and so on. But, ultimately, it is still a decision about french fries.

Finally, strategic decision making is a bit more complicated still. This level of decision making opens things up even further. At this level, a restaurant owner or an executive chef might decide that french fries are not healthy, and so the chef may open the search to alternatives like kelp chips or zucchini spears. The solution might even be to shut down the restaurant or open a new restaurant, completely ignoring the french fry decision. The idea is that there are broader decisions to be made based on evaluating market trends that may take years to come to fruition.

The way that these restaurant employees fit into information systems is that they still fall under the seesaw model in the people component. But how they're represented should be handled very differently. In the documentation process, each and every step of an operational level role should be documented. However, moving on to the managerial level, it's more reasonable to emphasize what decisions need to be made and what the end result should be, but how to get there can frequently be glossed over.

However, the strategic level is a completely different story. It's very difficult to describe what makes a successful strategic manager. The best generalization of a successful strategic manager is that they wander around and talk to people and then things happen. (Realistically, if the exact requirements to succeed as a CEO were easy to define, they'd be defined and then everyone would be a CEO.) This means that it's difficult to document the role of a strategic decision maker, and it tends to be much more vague.

SIDE QUEST: OPERATIONALIZATION

At one point in defining what data actually was, the maxim was given that one of the prime goals of every quantitative field has been the distillation of information from data. In the same vein, it might be said that the goal of every step of industrialization has been to move more decision making into the operational decision-making level. Consider the operational example just given. Prior to the development of fast-food restaurants, every restaurant had a chef that made their own decisions on how to cook french fries. But the advances in systems and process definition have allowed that french fry cooking process to move from the managerial level to the operational level.

One important effect of information systems is the routine conversion of strategic tasks to managerial and managerial tasks to operational.

BOX 7.2   Industrial Revolution

By one estimate (Word Economic Forum, n.d.), global society is on the brink of the fourth industrial revolution. After the agricultural revolution, the first industrial revolution included automation and standardization concepts. The second industrial revolution introduced longer-ranged transportation and communication. The third industrial revolution drastically reduced labor costs and increased computability. The fourth industrial revolution is difficult to conceptualize until it happens, but it will likely center around data and forecasting and the independence of automation tools. Notice the bias in the phrasing of this description of the industrial revolution as emphasizing information systems ideals when compared with that of Schwab's (the original author).

MAIN STORY: SECURITY VULNERABILITY

In the chapter on information security, there were three sources of security threat listed: benign users, malicious users, and natural disasters. Notice that users are there twice. Even more shocking, an employee can be a security vulnerability just while doing their job. For example, there are anecdotal stories about servers crashing every night at about the same time, and no matter how much analysis was done, nobody could find the source. Finally, a tech decided to sit in the server room and watch to see what the hardware did, when they noticed the cleaning crew come in, unplug the server, and plug in their cleaning equipment.

There are two important solutions to routine security threats caused by benign users. The first is to ensure that all processes are fully documented. For example, if a user receives an email telling them not to contact IT because of a vague or specific threat, they will frequently not contact IT. However, if they are told explicitly that even in those cases the sender of the email is likely bluffing and they should still contact IT, the user is more likely to contact IT. Similarly, if there's a process for turning in unidentified data sources notifying about possible insecure practices, and explicit rules about securing access locations, it is more likely to be done than if each user is left to determine these responses for themselves.

The second solution is training. Computer usage and security process are learned skills. Some users may already have those skills, but it is unlikely that every user has them. Further, security is a degradable skill that needs to be updated routinely. As a result, it is important for education processes to be implemented routinely, requiring refreshers of all users as to potential security threat vectors (for example, if an employee finds a USB drive sitting in the middle of a public place, they should definitely not go plug it into their work computer) as well as their appropriate responses (if an unknown individual follows an employee into a secure area, how should the user respond in the organization's specific framework?).

SIDE QUEST: FURTHER TRAINING

People are potentially the most difficult part of any organization. This is amusing, since an organization is only an organization because of the people being part of it. However, it turns out that from a technological and process perspective, the people component is difficult to update. There is only one demonstrably effective approach to effectively implementing updates: training.

Prior to any technological update or process update, it's important to begin engaging in training sessions. Even 6 months before a change occurs, training should begin detailing what will be different and what will be new. Most people can handle change as long as the change has become routine and dull. One effect of frequent and early trainings is that the user becomes so confident they can handle the change that they begin to look forward to the change.

This solution applies to the following:

- Software updates: A new operating system or a major update to an office productivity application
- Hardware updates: New computers or new interfaces for the computers
- Other technology updates: New log-in screens, new time-card devices, and so on
- Process changes: New approaches to accomplishing familiar tasks

BONUS LOOT: BUSINESS FUNCTION—HUMAN RESOURCES

Human resources departments operate in an immediately dissonant matter. The name itself tells us that it's about humans but also about resources. However, no (normal) person has ever considered themselves a "resource" to the same extent that a forest is full of lumber resources or a camel has excess resources of calories stored in its hump.

A human resources department needs to interact with its constituents in a manner that both recognizes their individuality and proffers them a sense of agency and self-worth. But at the same time, a business runs on capital; people cost money and require training. Human resources need to satisfy both of these necessary functions without letting either interfere with the other.

This is where the idea of process comes in. Further, information systems departments help design the processes that interface with human resources departments by fundamentally offering a new set of tools. Learning management systems are a tool most college students are familiar with, but they have a reflection on the industry side to represent high-quality training with minimal overhead. Personnel management systems are also a common tool, frequently part of an ERP. The ERP allows human resources to track the hiring process; consider performance; ensure all of the pay, benefits, and so on are accruing appropriately; and ultimately allows for permanent records of larger and larger organizations.

Ultimately, that's what information systems provides to human resources: an extension of what used to be a set of singular interfaces. The owner of a small retail establishment, for example, might hire a small handful of personnel or even use their own family. However, now that the idea of an organization is potentially so much larger by orders of magnitude, it's possible for human resources to interface with each employee in their own frame of reference while still reporting the calculations obtained from the information system to the strategic level to demonstrate how the human resources aspect is providing a positive return.

BONUS LOOT: RESUME BUILDERS—PROFESSIONAL ORGANIZATIONS

A professional organization is an excellent way to build a resume. Not only does membership in an organization immediately draw others who are part of that organization, but longevity always conveys a certain sense of maturity as a professional.

Further, professional organizations provide an excellent networking opportunity. Some networking opportunities are a bit on the shady side. Showing up to a charity event, talking oneself up, and then taking a job that one isn't qualified for is an approach that works, but it eventually backfires as often as not. In a professional organization, however, colleagues are able to see each other for who they are over long periods of time. Being successful in contributing to the organization can have a direct implication of ability to successfully contribute to any organization. Finally, attaining any level of formal position in the organization is an excellent way of demonstrating, in a low-stakes environment, the ability to handle certain functions.

As a result, participating in one professional organization (at least one, but not so many that it seems like you are spread too thin) is a good idea. Here are some of the professional organizations related to information systems:

ACM (Association for Computing Machinery): To keep abreast of the latest in technological standards.

ISO (International Organization for Standardization): Not just technology but a wide variety of protocols and standards.

SIM (Society for Information Management): A more academic-oriented professional organization that engages in a lot of research and member education initiatives.

Toastmasters: Ostensibly this organization is about public speaking, and that's a valuable skill for most managers, especially in information systems (some business functions tend to attract more introverts than extroverts).

ASQ (American Society for Quality): Continual quality improvement is one of the current trends, and information systems is rife with it and enriched by it.

BONUS LOOT: SOFT SKILLS—MEETINGS

Running and attending meetings are skills that are hard to master. It's easy to find a number of sources about how to improve meetings, but it's important to pay attention to the source. For example, the *Harvard Business Review* is probably a good source (Axtell, 2018), but Jack's *Heavy Metal* weblog might not be. The skill of attending a meeting has a lot of different moving factors that are a bit outside the scope of this textbook. It is better to emulate other people who are successful in an industry (Do they take notes? Do they skip certain kinds of meetings? Do they talk often? First? Never?).

But employers are frequently looking for the ability to run a meeting that maintains the attendees' interest. One complaint that few managers want to field (and frequently can't do anything about) is, "So and so made us go to a meeting and it was so boring!"

There are a few keys that can be utilized to make meetings better, but there's a preliminary question that takes in the technology side of information systems first: Does the meeting need to happen at all? Can it be a recorded video? Can it be done online through a screen broadcasting application? Can it be handled in an asynchronous matter like email? Can it be broken up into a training module in a content management system so attendees can go through it at their own pace?

One novel approach to avoiding meetings is to utilize a community-editing tool like a wiki. The Wikimedia foundation runs Wikipedia. They also produce a product called Mediawiki, which is the actual program that drives Wikipedia. Mediawiki is open source and can be installed on an internal web server. As a result, frequent daily touch points can be relegated to a team-editable page where team members perform many of the functions of a daily meeting without many of the drawbacks.

That being the case, there's still frequently a need for physical, in-person meetings. Keeping them short, relevant, and moving is important. The leader needs to seem (regardless of actuality) expert in the subject matter and exhibit a dynamic presence that implies forward momentum.

BONUS LOOT: CERTIFICATIONS—SPEECH AND PUBLIC SPEAKING

There are two issues that are of concern to many people. The urban legend is that speaking in public is the absolute biggest fear of the largest number of Americans. But being able to speak and interact with others is fundamental to the modern business environment, so it's important to make sure those things are satisfied. There are a few layers of skill, each of which has concrete steps to advance:

- Uncommunicative: As a technical executive stated, "When I walk into the room, all of my data people stick their heads down and won't look at or talk to me." Many professionals are surprisingly uncertain how to communicate with each other in a professional manner. For many of them, counseling is an effective method of resolving their underlying concern.

- Language acquisition: Many people suffer from diction or accent issues. This is not a recommendation that people in America speak English, so much as that people should speak the language of their organization and speak it well. Learning a new language as an adult is hard, but for second languages, attending a constant language learning class is a good idea.
- Diction: Many native language speakers suffer from diction or tone problems. Utilizing a speech coach to develop a broader diction, remove certain speech habits (such as frequent "ums," speech impediments that cause the speaker embarrassment, or acquiring or discarding specific accents) is something that can allow a professional greater opportunity.
- Public reading: All of the previous issues can lead to public speaking. There are a number of organizations that promulgate more and better public speaking. But the best approach is just to engage in more public speaking. The first step can be public reading: Libraries need people who will read to children, public functions need announcement readers, worship centers need scripture readers, and so on. Reading when the purpose is reading is a good half-step toward public speaking.
- Public speaking: This is where the certification aspect comes in. Every single public speaking engagement is, in effect, its own certification. How does one get selected for public speaking? Just volunteer. That is frequently a good start. But failing that, booking a library or a conference room for a speech on some topic with self-directed advertising is enough to start getting a reputation as a good and available public speaker.

Having a track record and a history of speaking engagements is an excellent way to demonstrate competence to both managers and colleagues.

REFERENCES

Axtell, P. (2018, June 4). 5 common complaints about meetings and what to do about them. *Harvard Business Review*. https://hbr.org/2018/06/5-common-complaints-about-meetings-and-what-to-do-about-them

Waterman, R., & Peters, T. (1982). *In search of excellence*. HarperBusiness.

World Economic Forum. (n.d.). *The fourth industrial revolution*, by Klaus Schwab [Book review]. https://www.weforum.org/about/the-fourth-industrial-revolution-by-klaus-schwab

CHAPTER 8

Process

PRE-READING CHECKLIST

VOCABULARY

> Pseudo code

> ISO 9000

CONCEPTS

> Four-component model

> Six Sigma

MAIN STORY: DRIVING PRINCIPLES

1. Information systems develop over time.
2. Information systems must be constantly refined.
3. For an individual to learn a new program or process takes time and practice, just like any other skill.

SIDE QUEST: ANALOGY—CARPENTRY

Carpentry is an ancient trade. Humans have been making things out of wood for almost all of recorded history. Carpentry occurs in most cultures because wood is available in most geographies. Not only that, but because wood is a relatively durable material, the products of carpentry frequently last throughout decades or centuries. The oldest wooden structure in the world, Hōryū-ji Temple in Japan, is over 1,400 years old!

With all these artifacts, the research done on them, written records of the craftsmen at the time, and the wealth of tools available, it should be easy to

> **BOX 8.1   Carbon Dating**
>
> You can tell how old wood or other organic materials are by using radiocarbon dating, or carbon dating. Inorganic materials, like building stone, are a lot more difficult to date.

pick up some lumber, buy some tools, and craft anything. And yet, for anyone who's tried, there's a fundamental discontinuity between conceptually understanding the steps it takes to create something and the practical knowledge to do it right and do it in a reasonable amount of time.

In the same way, information systems run into a practical knowledge problem. Any organization can go out and buy a full suit of computers, servers, and software. They can purchase a methodology for using the hardware, and they can hire experts to run it; however, there's always a period of development in order to align the purchases with the organization's goals and practices. This learning curve is something that can't be bought; it must be developed.

Similarly, an individual can purchase a piece of hardware or a computer program. And an individual can watch training sessions. But no matter how much they're guided through the process, it doesn't prevent the moment when that individual will have to sit down and start a project from scratch. Watching another person do a task or following really detailed instructions to complete a task is categorically different from performing that task independently. The individual's ability to succeed comes down to the same process of skill development as it does for the organization.

This chapter is about that development. Succinctly, the difference between information systems and information technology is the extra bits that need to be developed and refined over time. At its core, information systems are processes of continual refinement and improvement. It's this development that allows information systems concepts to apply to other fields and support organizations at any level.

MAIN STORY: FOUR-COMPONENT MODEL

Imagine the DMV, but without any rules. Anyone showing up has access to the entire DMV database. Anyone can edit their status to show that they can drive motorcycles, fly helicopters, or don't need medically necessary corrective lenses. Anyone can access anyone else's data, changing it as they want. Not only is it anarchy, but if something were to go wrong, how would an investigator be able to make any sense of what happened?

This is where the idea of a process comes in. A process is a simple concept. It's literally when we say that input becomes output. However, it's also convenient to think of it in terms of the four-component model from the chapter on hardware. The point of all of this detail is that because a process needs to be explicitly described in order to be effective it is possible to see how the input became the output.

When we talk about a process in the information systems sense, we're normally talking about a mélange of ideas. With a computer, it was easy to simplify the input and output. Input was anything that goes into the computer from the user, and output was anything that comes out of the computer to the user. However, with processes, there needs to be more consideration in terms of what it is that's going into and out of the system. But here's the catch: It doesn't substantively matter what it is that's acting as the input or the output so long as it's documented.

Effectively, a process is a free-form description of a computer. Rather than using electricity and code, a process is defined with words, definitions, and explicit descriptions of what should occur. In this chapter, all that matters is this broad definition. There'll be an example of one specific method of this delineation in Part V of the text.

Breaking a process down in terms of the four-component model gives us something like this:

- Input: What needs to exist before the process can begin, what informs the process about the outside world, or what gets passed into the process. An example would be that in order to apply for a job, an applicant should already have a resume written; that would act as one input for the job application process.
- Output: The deliverable of the process, what changes should occur as a result of the process having successfully completed, or what gets sent somewhere else at the end of the process. An example would be a maintenance crew completing repairs on the HVAC system after hours or on the weekends and then logging the completion of their task and activating the security system on their way out.
- Processing: The series of steps that occurs between receiving the input and delivering the output. In essence, the process should be the act of converting the input to the output. For example, in a very high-level sense, a car factory takes raw iron as input and produces cars as output. Each step of the process is detailed somewhere in the description of their factory line and is composed of a series of subprocesses (which, in turn, might have further subprocesses).
- Storage: There may or may not be a storage component to a process. Storage is, effectively, useful only when it persists between projects. It's what allows for subsequent iterations of the process to take advantage of lessons learned in earlier iterations. An example might be employee reviews that are kept in file: Every year, part of the employee review process should be checking to see if unresolved opportunities from the previous year were taken advantage of and determining whether the employee has improved over the previous year.

In considering the concept of a process, it's important to remember where it falls on the seesaw model. People provide an interface with the rest of the world, but ultimately they need to make decisions and take action steps. Processes are the sequence of events that lead to that output, whether the decision or the action steps. Documented processes are important because they ensure that whoever engages in it comes to the same best-practice conclusion and is able to justify the results using the extant process.

Another way to look at the seesaw model is as a continuum: Moving further to the left side moves toward concrete, purchased changes. Moving further to the right side moves toward gradual, procedural changes that are part of the development of an organization's operation. This continuum can be viewed through a number of filters (the left side is harder for the average employee at an organization to be trained in, while the right side tends to be easier; the left side is easier to outsource to experts, while the right is harder; the left side is more static and the right side is more dynamic), but considering the incremental development of the right side is part of what leads toward identifying and taking advantage of an organization's core competencies.

SIDE QUEST: PSEUDO CODE

Programming is a very rigorous set of specific code phrases ordered in a specific way that is recognizable by a computer. But does it start that way? Typically not. Most software engineering begins with a concept called pseudo code, which is intended to mimic the specificity and organization of programming without worrying about whether a period or a semicolon is in the wrong place. The idea is that there are all the advantages of step-by-step instruction programming, but it is still easy for humans to read and improve on.

Pseudo code is one method for putting together processes: It explicitly describes what should happen, but it is also human readable so that the person enacting the process knows where they are supposed to be and what they are supposed to be doing.

BOX 8.2   Pseudo Code Example

Here's an example of simple pseudo code:

Taking an order online

Prerequisite: Website is operational and client submits an order.

Objects: Order (data), OrderProcessor (employee)

Step 1: OrderProcessor accesses and displays Order.

Step 2: OrderProcessor reviews order for errors. If item is out of stock or understocked, use OutOfStockNotification process. If special instructions are unclear or infeasible, use OrderClarificationRequest process.

Step 3: OrderProcessor executes PaymentProcessing process using Order total details. If the payment is declined or other problems occur, send Order to CustomerServiceAgent. If payment is approved, send Receipt to user.

Step 4: OrderProcessor prints Order details and sends to FulfillmentCenter.

Notice that this is a general process. Details can be overridden by specific departments, but otherwise it can apply to anything from ordering pizza to ordering furniture, to ordering industrial levels of office supplies. In addition, notice that there is not a lot of "why" these steps are occurring. The processes are largely focused on the "what," but there might be room for notes or comments detailing more incidental information.

Pseudo code is typically not going to be the end product of an organization's process design. There are a number of methodologies available to delineate the format and phrasing of process description. Further, they will tend to change over time as acronyms, industry jargon, and other complexities creep in. That's unavoidable, but good process description will have all of the terms defined at some level (for example, a glossary that defines RTM as "return to manufacturer"). Database designers call this the data dictionary.

MAIN STORY: IMPORTANCE OF PROCESS

One issue that frequently occurs is the conflation of information systems with information technology (or, rather IS with IT). Properly, they are different fields. Information systems is focused on the relations of different actors and departments within organizations and the flow of information and data between them, regardless of whether it is technology based. Information technology is focused on the technological solutions to routine problems. This distinction is further complicated by the fact that technology provides solutions for almost every problem within information systems and many of the nontechnological systems mimic technological approaches (for example, pseudo code).

Thus, the distinction is a little academic. Practically, an organization will tend to have information systems (or computer information systems or management information systems; IS, CIS, BCIS, and MIS are effectively synonymous) or an Information Technology Department that covers both areas. However, since this is an academic text, that distinction needs to be explored a little further. At the broadest approach, information systems is a strategic field, emphasizing long-term solutions and high-level approaches to organizational design. Information technology tends toward being a more operational field, with immediate solutions like purchasing and installing a new computer or implementing a new network cabling.

What makes information systems a strategic function then? Looking at the seesaw model, everything on the left side can broadly be considered IT, with data traditionally being lumped into that (although the section on data will suggest that it is moving away from IT categorically). In the chapter on software, three major areas of the as-a-service model were explored: Software as a service incorporates the software component, platform as a service incorporates the software and hardware components, and infrastructure as a service incorporates all three. This leads to the conclusion that the IT portion of the seesaw model can be purchased or outsourced. Data can also be purchased or outsourced, and it is accumulated by all organizations.

On the right side of the seesaw model people are typically not components that can be controlled, and much of their function is defined by human resources. While information systems treat them as components within a broader system and as, effectively, more complex hardware systems, that should be immediately recognized as a level of abstraction and not applied too rigorously in the real world.

If data, people, and the entire left side of the seesaw model are removed, what remains? Process and decisions. These two components of the seesaw model are what separate information systems from information technology. They are important enough that they have sections devoted more fully to them (process is examined in Part V of this text, and Part IV discusses the intersection of data and decisions).

SIDE QUEST: UML

UML stands for "unified modeling language." It is a method of documenting the processes (and everything else) of an organization. The result of using UML is a visual diagram that describes what certain portions of a system should look like. It was originally developed for use by software engineers to describe increasingly complex systems, but it was adopted for more broad use by a number of different applications. UML is a standard, but it is not the only available method for this documentation. However, it is readily identifiable by most people in information systems and industrial engineering, and it is likely the most popular model. Large portions of UML are also international standards maintained by the International Organization for Standardization (ISO).

Detailing the use and creation of UML documents is a separate but tangential field to information systems. Serious information systems specialists should have some experience in UML, and complex systems should be defined by either UML or a similar competing standard. At least some exposure to UML is beneficial for all managers, as it provides a clean, uniform, accepted method of documenting systems concepts. It is then useful for drawing messy and customized explanations for complex topics in a manner that is sometimes more helpful than words alone.

There are a large number of different UML diagrams that can be broadly broken down into two categories. One category describes static system perspectives, and the other describes more dynamic system components, even though they are both describing the same system. One way of looking at it is the same as the distinction between accounting having a balance sheet and a statement of cash flows. They're both describing the same thing in different perspectives to address different constructs.

UML is intended to be a detailed and multifaceted approach to systems documentation. It is, at its core, an object-oriented modeling language. This means that it is intended to describe all of the objects in a system (objects, in this case, being people, computers, data stores, or similar) and then how those objects can relate to each other. It is large and cumbersome, which lends toward its unsuitability for nonspecialists. In general, comprehensive documentation of an organization should be done by an expert in UML. However, smaller portions or more temporary documentation are well within the skill sets of nontechnical managers.

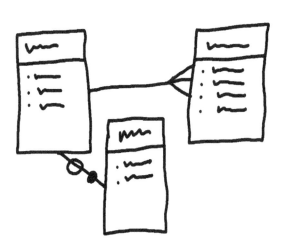

FIGURE 8.1 *UML example.*

SIDE QUEST: BPMN

BPMN stands for "business process management notation," another method of systems documentation. However, while UML is an object-oriented modeling language, BPMN is a process-oriented modeling language. This distinction is important, because while UML has a wide variety of diagrams that seek to most accurately describe every facet of a system, BPMN is largely focused only on the processes themselves. BPMN is also an ISO standard.

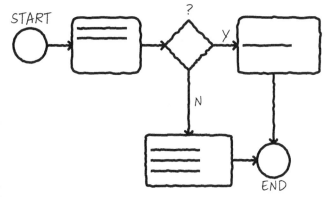

FIGURE 8.2 *BMPN example.*

Strictly speaking, BPMN and UML are completely different standards. However, practically they cover much of the same territory. They aren't intended to be mixed, but there is some value in being aware of and familiar with both of them. The primary benefit to BPMN is that it is action oriented. Since it's largely focused on creating flowcharts that document processes, it excels at that one area. So while UML is beneficial for a wide variety of tasks, BPMN may be more beneficial for simply describing an incremental series of steps (such as in the pseudo code example).

SIDE QUEST: ISO 9000 CERTIFICATION

If BPMN is more beneficial to the process of describing a process (properly, the metaprocess of describing a process), why was UML mentioned first? The short answer is ISO 9000 certification. ISO 9000 is a category of different certifications for business process documentation. It has two intents: The first is to demonstrate that an organization is committed to process documentation and the quality improvement cycle. The second is to facilitate the integration of processes between separate companies.

The biggest benefactors of ISO 9000 tend to be the bulkier industries such as transportation, construction, and manufacturing. Consider, for example, a company that makes folding tables. Folding tables are in huge demand from government agencies, church or community center picnics, and even as computer desks of certain information systems textbook authors. These folding tables are designed with a specific type of bolt, and it would be possible to calculate how many of those bolts the company goes through in a given day.

However, those bolts need to be stored before they're used. And that storage space has an opportunity cost of more manufacturing space. Historically, a company might have ordered a month's worth of bolts and stored them in a giant bin at one end of their floor. With advances in transportation and ordering, they can probably shorten their ordering capacity to just what they need for a day. Of course, that has the converse problem of both increased shipping costs and a hard limit for what they can produce in a given day. A better solution might be to have their manufacturing and storage processes documented to such a degree that their source can automatically ship bolts. The folding table manufacturer can order a batch of bolts at an amount that optimizes both storage space and shipping costs and then set up a process that allows the bolt manufacturing company to automatically ship a new batch of bolts once a certain minimum buffer is crossed.

This integration of processes is at the core of the benefit of ISO 9000 certification. And ISO 9000 certification requires a much more detailed process documentation than BPMN. ISO 9000 certification is an extreme case (and with enough of an operational cost to implement that it is only worthwhile in specific, not general, cases) of process documentation. But if the benefits are worthwhile there, then a less-detailed version of UML documentation might benefit other companies.

BONUS LOOT: BUSINESS FUNCTION—INDUSTRIAL ENGINEERING

Industrial engineering, to a certain extent, is the engineering of process. For example, Disney lauds itself on its use of industrial engineering to streamline the flow of attending their resorts and other attractions (Atencio, 2009). There is a sort of push-and-pull relationship between industrial engineering and systems analysis and design. They tend to come at the same problems and address the same problems from different perspectives. Industrial engineering tends to be more engineering and nonbusiness focused, looking at it as a problem to be solved. Analysis and design tend to come at problems from a more business perspective, looking at them in terms of business processes.

This is a bit of a specious distinction, since from the outside it would be relatively hard to make a distinction between them. However, it would be reasonable to look at industrial engineering as focused on the practical and applied aspects, while analysis and design looks at problems from the perspective of what they mean for an organization. If an organization wants to improve their office workers' efficiency, they may want to consider a systems person. If they want their factory set-up to be more efficient, they'll want to look at industrial engineers.

But, again, either field could likely moonlight as the other field. And the reality is that for experienced professionals, expertise is going to be developed more by the trajectory of their career.

BONUS LOOT: RESUME BUILDERS—PROCESS DESCRIPTION

Resume design is always a balancing act. Whether a particular resume should be one page, two pages, or longer is worth determining. A specific person's resume should even change length based on the application. However, one possible approach is to define a sort of "mother resume" from which all of the other resumes spawn.

Remember that much of a person's career experience is useful for decades. But consider whether the day-to-day operation of a job from 20 years ago will be clear in a way that can be used in a resume. What about 5 years and two job changes ago? Steps should be taken to make sure that the important, salient points are included.

In this mother resume not only are the routine bullet points about job duties and successes listed, but even small details can be included in case they happen to be relevant to the verbiage in a specific job posting. These small details could include portions of time spent on minor activities, specific people engaged with, processes improved, efficiencies gained, and so on.

Further, while a production resume would likely not benefit from process definitions or UML documentation, this mother resume might benefit from including some of those elements. Describing the various roles a job entailed, along with their responsibilities and the deliverables made to other roles in the organization, might help spark some memories later down the line.

BONUS LOOT: SOFT SKILLS—WORK ETHIC

Employers are constantly asking questions to try to identify work ethic. There have been numerous anecdotal stories about things like hiring managers asking potential employees out to lunch but then concocting a story about why the manager can't drive as an excuse to scope out the applicant's car. A messy car meant a messy work ethic, while a clean car obviously meant a good potential employee. Many of the strategies were ludicrous, but there is a strong desire for hiring managers to find someone who will go the extra mile to solve problems.

That's what they're looking for: "Never pass a problem without solving it." Rather than passing the issue on to others, there's a drive to take ownership of problems and find a solution. This is frequently tied to returning phone calls to customers when it's not necessary, ensuring processes are working more efficiently than is necessary, and otherwise trying to go above and beyond the requirements of a position.

There's a darker side of this soft skill, where organizational culture begins to expect workers to work unhealthy hours (e.g., the infamous video game development crunch time (Schreier, 2006), when employees report being expected to work 100-hour weeks for weeks on end). But the idea of a strong work ethic is to preclude situations like that by addressing the problems that lead to such situations proactively, at the front end. It's not about working more hours; it's about ensuring that everything is working well.

BONUS LOOT: CERTIFICATIONS—SIX SIGMA

In statistics, sigma is the symbol for standard deviation. It's used in the form of "a certain number of standard deviations above or below the mean." Recalling that one standard deviation above the mean is the 86th percentile, two standard deviations is the 95th percentile, and three is over the 99th percentile, six standard deviations above the mean is the 99.9997th percentile. The phrase translates roughly to "one in a million."

The Six Sigma process is, effectively, intended to remove errors in manufacturing or other pursuits down to one in a million. Six Sigma certification is intended to demonstrate a certain level of mastery in project management according to the Six Sigma process. The certification typically has five levels: white belt, yellow belt, green belt, black belt, and then a training level. These certifications tend to be highly sought after, but they require a certain amount of project management experience as part of the certification process.

One of the bigger problems with Six Sigma certification is that there is no centralized certification authority. Instead, the Six Sigma process as it was originally envisioned has been modified and updated through the years, and a number of different organizations offer their own in-house variations on Six Sigma certification. Historically, this has meant that only employees of those organizations were able to get Six Sigma certifications. Pairing the certification with employment at one of the larger organizations that has a certification program is typically very beneficial in demonstrating professional excellence.

However, there are also a number of industry groups offering Six Sigma certification that is widely accepted as the same or higher level of quality as the original corporate-based trainings. One such organization in a number of cities is ASQ, the American Society for Quality.

REFERENCES

Atencio, G. (2009, May 3). *Industrial engineering the magic at Disney* [Video file]. https://www.youtube.com/watch?v=krCjsxDhNyM&_ga=2.24234554.104523068.1566874545-2141536589.1566874545

Schreier, J. (2016, September 26). The horrible world of video game crunch. *Kotaku*. https://kotaku.com/crunch-time-why-game-developers-work-such-insane-hours-1704744577

Decisions

VOCABULARY

> Structured

> Semistructured

> Unstructured

CONCEPTS

> Organization as an organism

> Integration of models

> Structured/ unstructured model

> Wil Wheaton rule

MAIN STORY: DRIVING PRINCIPLES

1. Decisions are made by people using predefined processes.
2. Unstructured problems are the most difficult but most interesting of business problems.
3. Decisions can and should lead back into processes that cause people to affect change outside of the organization.

SIDE QUEST: ANALOGY—PETS

Pet ownership in the United States is big business. Depending on whose statistics you believe, it could be that more households have pets than not. Lots of money changes hands in order to acquire, sustain, medicate, insure, amuse, and lay to rest our friends. There are a lot of different types of animals that can play the role of beloved pet. As you would expect, the top two are dogs and cats. These two make up about three quarters of the U.S. pet landscape (Ollila, 2016). Most people would agree that owning a dog is not the same as owning a cat. Can we compare and contrast ownership of these creatures? Comparisons are pretty easy: You'll need to buy food, provide clean water, and some regular medical care (annual shots, teeth cleaning, etc.) will be required. The gross structure is pretty consistent: two eyes, two ears, four legs. Contrasts are quite a bit more difficult due to the variability with the species. According to the Hill Science folks (they make pet food), some key differences are the way each exercises, how each plays, their biorhythms (e.g., cats are usually nocturnal), their group structure (or pack mentality), what they need to eat, and how they sound (Insurance Information Institute, n.d.).

The study of decisions and decision making requires similar compare-and-contrast analyses. For the commonalities among decisions, the framework offered by Simon is good. In 1978, the Nobel Prize in Economics was awarded to Herbert A. Simon for "his pioneering research into the decision-making process within economic organizations" (Wikipedia, 2020). Simon pointed out that we do make the best decisions that we can but we are limited by our humanity, in particular limits on our cognitive abilities and our lack of complete information. He defined the three stages of rational decision making: intelligence gathering, design, and choice (Lewis, 2001).

For contrasting decisions, we offer models for this chapter that decompose decisions into differing categories based on the organizational roles (described as levels) and the nature of the problem that requires a decision. Like cats and dogs, decisions made at different levels will tend to have different qualities across categories and similarities within.

MAIN STORY: WHO MAKES DECISIONS?

As we've already seen, everyone in an organization makes decisions about the organization on a daily basis. If nothing else, every single employee has to make the decision to come into work and do their job. Attitude is normally more innate than environmental, and that decision needs to come from the employee.

Why is decision making being discussed in information systems? Historically, decision making has been made in the strategic management or organizational behavior function. But as more employees are being empowered, through technological solutions, to make more decisions, the concept of decision making is being more firmly rooted in information systems.

To one extent, that means that the fundamental purpose of information systems in the modern era is that information systems exist to allow every employee to make the best decisions possible.

Indeed, in the past access to computers was typically reserved for only specific roles within the organization, typically those roles found higher in the organizational hierarchy. But as time has passed, it's become more common for a larger portion of an organization's employees to have access to a computer. In the past, those with access to computers were frequently restricted to specific software; however, as time has gone on, it's become more common for everyone to have access to general purpose programs. In the same way, this transition to higher levels of computer availability is opening the way for more employees to have access to high-level decision support structures. This, in turn, is allowing strategic decision makers to make better decisions because they have access to better decisions from their subordinates. The process is a wonderful circle in which good decisions lead to further good decisions.

MAIN STORY: WHAT'S THE POINT OF INFORMATION SYSTEMS?

It has been said in other contexts that "data is the fulcrum." According to the distillation model, good data leads to good information, and good information leads to good decision making. But what good is a decision?

The word *organization* derives from the same root word as *organism*. And, in fact, there are many similarities that are used in understanding how organizations operate. One approach is to consider that organisms operate in a stimuli-and-response manner. That is, as the organism is stimulated by the outside world, it considers that stimulus and then—based on instinct or calculation—it responds to the environment around it.

Breaking down that description of an organism very quickly evinces similarities to the four-component model that's been used to describe several parts of the organization. As a result, it could be said that an organization is stimulated by the outside world; it processes that stimulus based on its stored knowledge and processes in order to produce a response.

The key point here is so basic that it doesn't seem worth saying. However, with all of the emphasis on design, systems, process, and documentation, it's important to remember that an organization has to interface with the outside world. A manufacturing company that has the most advanced production line and the most efficient business processes is useless without actually selling the cars it makes.

At the ultimate level of abstraction, the goal of information systems is to ensure that when the organization is stimulated by outside factors, it makes the objectively correct response. Obviously, that is impossible at a practical level, as a complete guarantee is outside the practical set of possibilities, and frequently there is no objectively correct response. But that perfection is always the aspirational goal.

BOX 9.1   Mathematical Correctness

One thing that draws most theoretical mathematicians and computer scientists is the concept of proofs. In science or common phrasing, the word *proof* just means "something that's enough to convince." In a legal sense, there is a concept of "burden of proof," which means that the prosecution has to demonstrate "beyond reasonable doubt" that a person committed a crime (as opposed to a civil case, in which the winner is the one with a "preponderance of evidence").

However, in mathematic fields, *proof* means an absolute, 100% guarantee that something is true. The entirety of math would have to be wrong before a given proof is wrong. Math is an abstract field. However, providing a mathematical proof that some function, process, or other aspect of business works as intended is the ultimate goal of many technically oriented professionals.

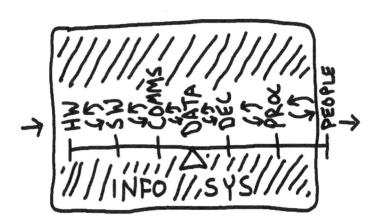

FIGURE 9.1   *Outside world perspective of seesaw model.*

The point, however, is that an organization interacts with the real world. If the left side of the seesaw model leads to the creation and manipulation of data, and the right side deals with people and process; the culmination is in the decision component. This component is where something changes. But that change has to be a result of some direct or indirect stimulus and in turn has to propagate back out to some action steps that occur. People use processes to make decisions, but those decisions also lead to new processes. This cycle allows interaction with the outside world.

SIDE QUEST: IMPACT

Later, the metrics related to a process will be defined as efficiency and effectiveness. However, nonprofits add an extra metric that's worth considering. This is not a standard business consideration, but it makes sense in some situations. Nonprofits typically measure efficiency, effectiveness, and impact. What was the end result of doing something? Was it just more of the same, or did the key stakeholders have the outcome that they were looking for?

Remember that nonprofits exist to do something. Businesses traditionally exist solely to increase stakeholder wealth (although from a social responsibility perspective this is no longer strictly true), so it makes sense that the quantitative metrics of efficiency and effectiveness are the primary metrics. But to the extent that there is something more than just money involved, impact should be considered.

This is more than simple things like "everyone obeyed the law, and therefore nobody went to jail." It's more along the lines of "the value of people's lives and their dignity are immeasurable by traditional means; therefore, those indefinable situations were improved by this course of action." Nonprofit management has traditionally tried to adopt for-profit business techniques. However, as a separate industry, it's worth some evaluation to see where they differ and how their unique viewpoints can be adopted.

MAIN STORY: STRUCTURE OF PROBLEMS

There's a complementary model we can use to the operational, managerial, strategic decision-making model. Whereas that first model focuses on the role within an organization, this second model focuses on the nature of the problem that needs a decision. The underlying reality is still a continuum rather than a set of categories (thus, the model for this text is the decision-mode ternary as a successor to the Anthony triangle). Using the model still requires a level of abstraction to a set of categories. Effectively, we can divide problems into either structured or unstructured problems.

Structured problems have only one outcome. The extreme example of this is following directions. If the directions for a particular process define each step, with no room for interpretation, then implementing the process is a very structured problem. There is only one answer to the problem, and that is "follow the instructions." The nature of the problem is very immediate, and there is a fixed and explicit series of steps to get to the solution.

BOX 9.2 Heuristics

A set of steps or process to get to a solution is called a heuristic. You might have a personal heuristic for solving a Sudoku puzzle. There is no guarantee of an optimal outcome in a finite amount of time.

Unstructured problems are the opposite. There is no clear answer to the problem. It's not even always possible to determine whether the problem has an answer. Upon arriving at a solution, there may not be a way to determine the correctness of the solution. Extreme examples of unstructured problems are philosophical questions such as, "What is justice?" There is no commonly held agreement on the definition of justice, let alone ways to determine practical examples of it. For any solution, there are likely supporters and detractors with no way to objectively measure which is which. The classic business example is, "Where do I locate our new manufacturing facility?"

It's likely apparent that this second structured/unstructured model relates well with the operational, managerial, strategic model of decision making. They are not the same model, but it's typical that the more unstructured problems are found on the strategic end, with more structured problems at the operational end. An easy visualization of this progression is to consider employee evaluations. At the operational end, evaluations are typically measured in numbers such as success rate, jobs completed, or work produced. At the managerial level, evaluations are typically measured as an aggregation of the operational performance of the team members being supervised. Figuring out how to motivate and lead that team is a mix of fixed, structured processes and unstructured creative thinking. At the strategic end, the evaluation may be difficult for a leader who institutes a process that won't see measurable results for 5 or 10 years. For example, how would one measure a chief innovation officer's performance? The number of new ideas doesn't necessarily equate to good or profitable ideas. But is having a single good or profitable idea over the course of 12 months and dozens of bad ideas a good or poor indicator of performance?

There is one more category of problem that is very important and has its origins in computer science. Semistructured problems are unstructured problems that are moved toward the structured end of the spectrum in some manner. This is typically done by adding constraints to the problem in some way. Semistructured problems tend to mimic unstructured problems; however, the outcome tends to be a "good" solution, even if it's not demonstrably the best solution. For example, the question "Where is the best place to open a new branch?" is very unstructured. The metric of "best" is ill-defined, and the number of possible solutions across the globe is almost infinite. However, introducing constraints such as "in a city of a certain size, with a certain percentage of engineers in the population, located on a major highway with a minimum amount of traffic, and the price for construction and land must be below a certain amount" yields a heuristic that allows the production of a set of results. Choosing between them is still an unstructured task, but selecting between a hundred possible options is still vastly simpler than the original, infinite number of options.

BOX 9.3   Satisficing

Nobel Lauriat Herbert A. Simon coined the term *satisficing* to indicate a suboptimal yet satisfactory solution to a problem. Very often, natural problems are not amenable to mathematical optimization.

The distinction between structured, semistructured, and unstructured problems is important in the realm of information systems because of the skill sets of the parts of a system. Computers are excellent at solving structured problems but are incapable of generally even recognizing unstructured problems. Conversely, people can be good at unstructured problems, but repeatedly solving the same type of structured problem leads to boredom, followed by mistakes. This model correlates with the decision-mode ternary:

- Positions that lean closer to the operational mode tend to solve more structured problems.
- Positions that lean closer to the strategic mode tend to solve more unstructured problems.
- Positions that lean closer to the managerial mode tend to solve more semistructured problems.

As an aside, this process is routinely portrayed as computers taking people's jobs. And, to a certain extent, that's true. But more broadly, the intent is to free people up to take higher

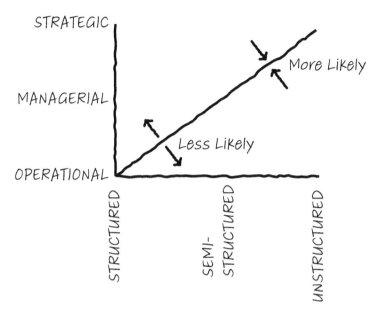

FIGURE 9.2 *Decision mode ternary versus structured problem.*

levels of responsibility and move up to higher levels of decision-making complexity where the human brain is more successful than computers.

SIDE QUEST: MODEL APPLICATION

One last consideration regarding both the decision-mode ternary and the structured/unstructured decision-making model is that they apply in several different sets of circumstances. We discussed this earlier when we discussed scope.

We've seen already that both of these models apply to individuals. A bookkeeper has one level of routine responsibility with simple decisions. An accountant has a higher level of responsibility that entails some decisions that require judgment calls. But the comptroller or CFO of an organization needs to make unstructured decisions targeting long-term productivity.

However, these models also apply at the team or department level. Some teams routinely operate on the operational level, such as a maintenance team. The team requires multiple people to accomplish a task, but the majority of the work is routine and is solved using a fixed set of repair steps. Others operate at a strategic level, such as a final appeal committee for an industry association's ethics board. By the time an issue gets to a final level of appeal, it's likely that it doesn't follow the usual patterns that can be handled at lower levels.

Finally, in some ways, these models can be applied to an entire organization. For example, retail organizations typically operate according to much more operational parameters, with outcomes measured in rates related to sales. On the other hand, think tanks often operate at a strategic level, considering policy decisions. Even the strategic-level employees in the retail organization will be focused on metrics derived from structured problems, and the operational employees in a think tank need to be focused on strategic problems.

Also, note that while there is a strong correlation between the two models, it's not a fixed correlation. For example, a media design team typically works with operational decision making: They're given a set of tasks to complete and a strict set of directives to adhere to. But most of their problems are unstructured in that there's no way to know whether a stylized icon of a lion is going to be a more successful motif than the cute pictures of kittens. And, practically, there's not always an objective way of measuring which would have been better.

BONUS LOOT: BUSINESS FUNCTION—CUSTOMER SUPPORT

Customer support is a great example of the complexity behind the different levels of decision making. Typically, in a call center a customer calls into an automated system. Fifty years ago, every problem had to be handled by a human. Even calling long distance typically required multiple operators transferring calls between switchboards. Now, however, routine, structured decisions like checking a balance, reporting an outage, or requesting routine information can be interpreted and handled in an automated fashion by a computer.

Sometimes, however, customers have more specific problems. Tech support, for example, handles problems that don't have an easy solution. However, the unstructured problem "this computer doesn't work" is frequently simplified to the semistructured problem "have the following solutions been attempted?" As a result, the first line of contact for a tech support is typically a nontechnical call center employee walking the customer through the basic steps of turning the device on and off again, updating drivers, and checking the pattern of the blinking lights on various devices. These steps likely solve the vast majority of the problems customers face and are easy for anyone to offer guidance for.

However, at times, even this first level of customer support is exhausted with a small minority of problems. In a sales call center, for example, when a customer requires special treatment, has requests for the order that are outside of the fields in the standard form, or just wants to complain about the company, the supervisor gets involved. Supervisors typically have fairly broad authority to solve problems because it's impossible to predict what issues people are going to call with. The supervisor needs to be able to address problems that don't have simple and straightforward solutions.

BONUS LOOT: RESUME BUILDERS—PERSONAL BRAND

It's important to remember that for any position there are likely dozens or hundreds of applicants, qualified and not. In any group of a hundred applicants, it's very easy for qualified applicants to be overlooked. Being an unknown person applying for a job is a daunting proposition.

One modern solution is the formation of a personal brand. The first step of forming a personal brand is to follow the Wil Wheaton rule: Don't be a jerk. On the internet, it's easy to let the facelessness and anonymity tempt one into posting things that are condemning in the wrong light. This is why many organizations do quick internet searches on any serious applicants, looking for pictures or descriptions of excessive drinking (one of the biggest hurdles for new college graduates), rude behavior, or association with unsavory ideologies. Avoiding posting things in the permanence of the internet is one of the easiest ways to keep from being unfairly prejudged by a potential employer.

The second step of forming a personal brand is to identify a target platform and identity. Just like a celebrity, this identity isn't necessarily the real person; it's an exaggeration of the real person to highlight the core principles that person wants to express. The easiest platform to form this identity is LinkedIn, but doing so on reddit, Twitter, or in industry groups is also a valid solution. The identity is the modern interpretation of the self-descriptive resume line. Rather than having a few words at the beginning of the resume saying "I am a hard-working, self-motivated learner seeking a positive work environment," it's possible to establish a track record of statements actually demonstrating that ideal. That identity doesn't need to be perfect, but it should be fairly consistent.

Finally, one of the most effective steps in forming a personal brand is to communicate with people. It's scary to talk to unknowns. But helping others leads to becoming known in a professional community. Answering questions, asking intelligent questions, and presenting well-researched and insightful comments are all great ways of demonstrating the sort of attributes that most employers are looking for.

BONUS LOOT: SOFT SKILLS—GETTING EMPLOYEE BUY-IN

Making decisions is easy. A flip of the coin will do it. But making the right decision is what differentiates the successful professionals from the less successful. But where do those right decisions come from? Frequently, it's not an issue of just making a decision that is supported by the data, but it's in ensuring that everyone is committed to the implementation of that decision.

The most classic example of this is in politics. The 18th Amendment to the U.S. Constitution effectively banned alcohol. But just 14 years later the amendment was repealed. A small group of people wanted to ban alcohol, but it turned out that a much larger group of people opposed the idea. The temperance movement felt it had facts on its side, but because it didn't check for buy-in from the rest of the country or seek to develop a consensus, it was overturned.

Similarly, in a business setting, just declaring that a decision is the correct way and things are going to change will frequently have people digging their heels in. Even simple changes like updating a computer operating system will cause people to declare that the old way was so much better (for example, Windows XP still has a measurable percentage of users (W3Schools.com, n.d.), despite Microsoft declaring that it would no longer receive any support of any kind in April 2014). The better solution than the correct solution tends to be to work with people to identify how new solutions will affect them, demonstrate or train them on the new solution repeatedly ahead of time, and check in with them frequently immediately after the new implementation.

Buy-in addresses a fundamental human need to feel in control of the environment. When changes are dictated, that need is thwarted. Instead, when employees feel a part of that process, the need is fulfilled.

BONUS LOOT: CERTIFICATIONS—SAS

SAS (Statistical Analysis System) is a tool for enterprise-wide data collection and analysis. It is a broad utility that allows analysts to reach into almost any part of an organization and pull data in an effort to make connections between disparate divisions.

One of the reasons why SAS is so popular is its longevity. It's been relatively ubiquitous for about 20 years. But that longevity also means that it's identified how its users want to interact with it and, as a result, has developed a visual interface for its primary software portals. In programming terms, a visual language is one where typing out code is significantly reduced or eliminated in favor of drag and drop. The idea is that what most development-oriented end users want to do is relatively routine. By providing visual representations of tasks with simple ways to connect those tasks, it's possible to provide a relatively comprehensive situation. To misappropriate P. T. Barnum, they have a solution that addresses most of the people most of the time.

This leaves open an interesting situation where professionals can study for and be certified in SAS with a minimum of code-oriented experience. Instead, they can learn to use the visual programming interface, which may be similar to their previous experience in Excel, Access, or other Office utilities.

REFERENCES

Insurance Information Institute. (n.d.). Facts + statistics: Pet statistics. https://www.iii.org/fact-statistic/facts-statistics-pet-statistics

Lewis, P. (2001, February 10). Herbert A. Simon, Nobel winner for economics, dies at 84. *New York Times*. http://www.umsl.edu/~sauterv/DSS/10SIMON.html

Ollila E. (2016, November 16). Differences between dogs and cats: Learn what makes each one special. *Hill*. https://www.hillspet.com/pet-care/resources/differences-between-cats-and-dogs

W3Schools.com. (n.d.). OS platform statistics. https://www.w3schools.com/browsers/browsers_os.asp

Wikipedia. (2020). Herbert A. Simon. https://en.wikipedia.org/wiki/Herbert_A._Simon

CHAPTER 10

Data

PRE-READING CHECKLIST

VOCABULARY

> Data
> Integers

> Strings
> ETS/ETL

> CRM
> Tableau

CONCEPTS

> Distillation model
> Sources of data

> Data types
> SIPRNet

> Levels of security
> Clearance

MAIN STORY: DRIVING PRINCIPLES

1. Data is a commodity that accrues to every organization as it proceeds.
2. Data is acquired and distributed in an almost fungible manner.
3. Data should be retained, effectively, forever; conversely, once data is created, it's difficult to ensure that it won't be retained forever.

SIDE QUEST: ANALOGY—WEALTH

One of the core models is the distillation model. The idea is that something large or of middling value can be concentrated into a small amount of something useful. The mental image should be of an old time still from a clan of moonshiners in the Kentucky Bluegrass region. They made huge vats of mash in an effort to draw the sugars and carbohydrates out of vegetable matter and then, after it cured for a while, boiled off all the alcohol that had formed and discarded the water. What they were left with is a very high proof alcohol suitable for stripping the polish off of either a car or a digestive tract.

There are a thousand different comparisons that could be used. Huge quantities of tree go into making every single sheet of paper. The number of apples in a glass of apple juice is always surprising. The amount of vegetation in a wheat field compared to the amount of wheat that's actually harvested is a large ratio.

However, one of the most apropos analogies to use is wealth. Wealth is like data because it is something that every single person produces in the process of living. And just like data, it will belong to someone else if specific precautions aren't taken and a plan followed. But what's even more important is that wealth, when used correctly, should lead to knowledge and excellence. And that knowledge and excellence should lead to decisions that improve the lot of others.

Similarly, the data that every company begins to acquire should be used wisely in order to make not just information but valuable conclusions that reinforce the company's core competencies. And then those reinforcements in the company's core competencies should be used to increase the ability of the company to enact its socially responsible decisions that lead back to improving the lot of others around it.

MAIN STORY: WHAT IS DATA?

The short answer is that data is any true fact.

BOX 10.1   Datum and Latin

Typically, you might see *data* defined as "any true fact." But the reality is that we can't verify the truth of data. On the one hand we know that some facts are going to be untrue due to transcription errors, degradation, or miscalculation. But because we can't verify the truth, we presume that the facts are true in the context of most processes. This is why the definition is that data is "any true fact"—not because it's limiting the scope of data so much as it is presuming that any presented fact is true for the sake of continuing a process.

Most people can visualize the most basic forms of data. For example, when a researcher engages in a survey, the responses to that survey are data. This is exactly the same as a physicist who takes readings from an electron telescope or a doctor who requires their patient to keep a daily log of how much they sleep and exercise. But if that was all the kinds of data that were there, it would be easy to set up information systems. Effectively similar processes could be used in each of those scenarios to handle the data.

But what about the paper that the researcher writes? Are the words and the order they're written in data? What about the survey itself? Is that data? If the physicist acquires data from another source, say, a chemist, and wants to merge observations, how do the incomparable types of data get merged? Is the expertise of the physicist in knowing how to use, maintain, and take output from the electron telescope a form of data? Is the place where the doctor finds a recommendation to have their patient keep daily logs a source of data? What about if the patient notes extra comments like "slept 6 hours, but it was really fitful"? Is "it was really fitful" data? Obviously, the answer to all of these questions is yes, but the problem then becomes identifying and coding the data such that it has some sort of value.

The easiest way to categorize the data types is to consider the source:

- Operational quantitative sources: These are the data sources that easily map into numeric formats (e.g., prices, quantities, distances, times). These are all operational sources that companies constantly create. They should be captured and retained for future use. This would include data like what a customer bought but also how fast the cashier rang them up.

- Operational qualitative sources: There are more data sources than just the numeric data. For example, customer feedback is typically done in a free text format. Location data is numeric, but it's also sometimes easier to note qualitatively (the such and such campus rather than x- and y-coordinates).

- Purchased data: This is data that can be purchased from other sources. For example, while one convenience store in a city might be able to use its data to help it make good decisions, all of the convenience stores in the city could share their data and each be able to make even more effective decisions (this is an offshoot from the central tendency theorem in business statistics).

- Process and employee expertise: All of the processes that have been discussed are, themselves, data. Further, the expertise of every employee in the organization in performing the tasks assigned to their roles is also data. This type of data is one of the hardest to encode, but it allows for some of the most effective tools to be developed.

- Metadata: There is an important aspect to data called metadata. This is "data about the data." So, for example, it's not always a complete record of a transaction to note that Mr. Smythe purchased 24 tangerines at 39 cents each. But the metadata would include things like payment type, what the transaction number is, and even the timestamp.

SIDE QUEST: DATA TYPES

There are several different data types. For the most part, they should affect the end user. Good design typically means that something should "just work." However, understanding some of these distinctions may help in working with developers to determine if there's a problem. This is not a technical list of data types, but a broad grouping of them:

- Integers: Numbers that are counting numbers are called integers. These are always whole numbers. They're also any data in the form of only numbers, such as a phone number or a Social Security number, but not a license plate number.

- Decimals: Sometimes called floating points, these numbers have more complicated math on the back end to allow for the complexity of a decimal point. (For example, consider that adding the numbers 0.2 and 0.4 results in a number of format X.X, but multiplying them results in a number of format X.XX.)
- Strings: These are strings of letters smooshed together, such as in an address, a name, or a long paragraph. Numbers are allowable, so this would be where a license plate number is categorized.
- Blob: There's a wide variety of different data types (Access, at one point, called them "blobs") that aren't really human readable, such as specialized executable files, encrypted or compressed files, or other data types. This category gets really messy from a design end.

Generally, the idea is that on the back end there are some operations that can only be done on certain data types. For example, if a field wants to check if a user is over 13 years of age and has an age field, having the user enter the word "fifteen" may be accurate, but the computer likely doesn't know how to subtract 13 from 15. Instead, forms and data collection apparatus will likely be filtered to only accept data of the appropriate format.

MAIN STORY: DATA ETS/ETL

Data is used by most companies to inform decision making. If data is useful to the company, more data is more useful to them. A simple example would be that if a company knows what it's doing and makes decisions based on that, their decisions could be even better if they knew what their competitors were doing as well.

Like every other resource that someone finds useful, data has developed a secondary market. The primary market would be one company offering to sell its data to another, but that can only go so far. A historical example would be the steel industry in the early part of the 19th century. Rather than having large consumers trying to separately negotiate with smaller producers, a large exchange was established that allowed consumers and producers to buy and sell in a larger, secondary market.

As a result, data is available from a wide variety of sources. The problem is that the formatting of the data is frequently very different. A simple example would be that almost every transaction probably has a timestamp (noting the date and the time of the transaction). But is it set to Greenwich mean time? Is it set to local time? What if the local time is in different time zones? What if one database calls it time, another calls it date, and another separates it into two categories, time and date?

This is where the extract-transform-store (ETS) process comes in (sometimes called extract-transform-load (ETL) depending on the context). ETS is, properly, a function of a data warehouse (which will be covered in chapter). The ETS function is intended to provide a structured way of considering data from disparate sources and then putting them together into a single database.

The first step is extract, which means pulling out the desired data from the target data source. This has lots of different uses. For example, many contexts place restrictions on personally identifiable information (PII), so anything that individually identifies a person doesn't need to be extracted. Alternately, it's possible that some data is unnecessary, for example, if a sale occurs but it was an accident and immediately reversed, that data might not need to be retained. In particular, this extract phase is heavily dependent on the particular use that the data is going to be put to. In a main data store for a company, probably almost everything will be extracted. But if it's for the specific purpose of market research or operations analysis, there may be a much smaller subset.

The second step is transform. In this phase, rules are put into place to automatically convert the data into a different format. For example, in the case of different time zones, data may automatically be converted to the same time zone. The person in charge of the transform process will likely determine when different column names are really describing the same data and ensure that they are converted to the same name. In addition, this would be where the data is structured to fit into the specific structure or peculiarity of the target database.

Finally, in the store phase, the data is specifically saved to the organization's database. This final phase is sometimes called the load phase. The distinction is largely whether the data is going to be put into a write-once-type data warehouse and saved forever or placed into a production database that will be used for real-time or operational purposes.

This ETS process is a very standard approach to data acquisition. It's used whenever data is purchased from a broker, acquired from other outside sources, or even from disparate internal sources (for example, the hourly accounting for a lawyer on retainer is likely going to be very different from the hourly accounting of a salaried front-desk employee).

There are also other types of data that tend to be input into systems called decision support systems (DSSs). These DSSs will be covered in a separate chapter.

MAIN STORY: DATA SECURITY

Remembering that information security should be "baked in" to every aspect of information systems (and likely the company as a whole), what is the most likely target of a malicious user? While cash would be nice, that's not typically within the realm of most malicious users. One thing that makes cash a unit of currency, however, is its fungibility. When something is fungible, it can be split into small pieces and still retain the attributes of the whole. A dollar is money, and if it's split into 100 parts, each penny is still money.

In the same way, regardless of whether a malicious user gains illicit access to a million records or a thousand records, they still bear representative values. Further, because there is such a strong secondary market, the data can be traded back and forth with relative ease. It is not an immediate concern, but it is worth asking about the source of the data an organization purchases to be sure that they aren't supporting malicious users.

There are two issues at play: First, any data is a target. If nothing else, it can be distributed and used for analysis purposes or sold to others. It's possible to consider that a lot of data is not sensitive data. But that would miss the central point that if the nonsensitive data is at risk, it's likely there's a security risk around the sensitive data as well. In addition, what constitutes sensitive data is a bit murky, as will be covered in the chapter about data processing.

BOX 10.2   Target Breach

In 2013, Target suffered a huge data breach (Krebs, 2013). It was one of the biggest breaches of the time (or at least that was publicly discussed). Tens of millions of customers' credit card data was compromised. In this case, *compromised* is a polite euphemism for "a criminal copied it and now has access to it." In a bit of macabrely amusing turnabout, they had stolen more credit card data than the market could bear. Anecdotal stories told of desperate attempts to sell the data online at hugely discounted rates, only to have no buyers.

The other issue at play is the idea of data permanence. Once data is created, it's difficult to ensure that it can be removed. Consider three simple examples:

1. An employee copies data onto their personal computer (either according to or against organizational policy) and then loses that computer. Or, possibly, they upgrade the hard drive and discard the old hard drive without securely erasing everything on it. Where did the data go?
2. Two campuses of an organization (or, possibly, two retail locations) are connected via leased connections owned by another company. Suppose a law enforcement agency or a malicious user is tapping into a node in between those two sites, analyzing all of the data.

BOX 10.3   SCIF

The military has three broad levels of security clearance: confidential, secret, and top secret. In general, having a level of security clearance means you are trusted to know and not improperly share data of the same level or lower. There are various rules meant to reduce the problem of data permanence. For example, there was a time when top secret documents could neither be digitized nor photocopied, which ensured that there was only a single copy of that data available.

More restrictive than top secret is data that is SCI (sensitive compartmentalized information). This is, reductively, where the idea of "need to know" comes from. Not only does SCI data require the appropriate level of clearance, but it also requires notation of the specific field (that is, someone assigned to Pacific Command likely won't have any reason to access data in European Command's SCI). This is countered by SCIFs, or sensitive compartmented information facilities. SCIFs are interesting places: Imagine giving a group of paranoid security experts unlimited time to think of any possible attack vector ranging from plausible to fantasy levels of science fiction and then allowing them to take steps to prevent those vectors.

At one point, SCIFs confiscated some toys that entered the facility. The concern was that technically a "Furby" was a recording device and could therefore be used to cause insecurity. This concern is both valid and ridiculous at the same time, which is possibly the best summary of modern information security.

---

3. A company leases a cloud company to store large amounts of data for them. Since there's no way of knowing where the physical location of the data is, there's no way of knowing the security. Suppose that the cloud company switches subcontractors and the old subcontractor doesn't delete the data. Suppose the cloud company subcontracts out their backups with a separate subcontractor. All of this is invisible to the original company, who may have no idea about the number of extant copies of the data.

There are no easy answers to the issue of data permanence. Military classified servers go through extensive security processes, even going so far as to develop their own internet separate from the internet called SIPRNet (Sip-ehr-net, secret internet protocol router network, which is complemented by NIPRNet, the nonclassified internet protocol router network). High-level security officials perform secret meetings in person without using digital devices at all. These are the extreme ends, but it's important to recognize that once data is produced, it is likely relatively permanent. As a result, every organization needs to have a data management policy, likely as part of their information security policy.

SIDE QUEST: DATA SCARCITY

In the early days of computers and 8-bit video games, there was a problem with data scarcity. Because the actual physical medium was physically storing electricity or magnetic charge, it could store only a certain amount of data. So, for example, when Link was exploring around Hyrule and collecting rupees, his wallet could hold only 255 rupees. This was because the programmers were concerned about how much space a specific game save might take, so they limited it.

However, there is little excuse for that in the modern computing era. This is an important note because, for the most part, space is cheap and free. There's little reason not to acquire as much data as possible and then store it indefinitely. There exist very large data companies

---

BOX 10.4   Dr Who

One of the great tragedies in television broadcasting history is that some of the early television shows that were broadcast were not retained. For example, a large number of classic episodes of the British cultural icon Dr. Who are completely absent. Restorers have gone so far as to try to piece together episodes from rare home recordings spliced with still drawings voiced over by actors.

This happens for a variety of reasons: Sometimes the celluloid wasn't stored properly, or there were routine fires or other hazards. But the one that flabbergasts modern historians is that much of classic television from the early days of broadcasting was just taped over. Film was expensive, and television broadcasts were considered a one-time feed, without any consideration that people in the future might want to retain those bits of history and nostalgia. Modern technology has largely ensured that flaw won't be repeated, but it bears considering: What other mistake will modern technology make that will have future historians shaking their heads in disbelief?

(such as Google) who need to come up with creative ways to store their data. However, for most companies, data storage should be cheap enough to be used relatively flagrantly.

This "unlimited" data standard comes with a few catches. Moore's law, Nielsen's law, and the variation on Kryder's law provide some concern. For example, if the price of processing halves every 18 months, but the price of storage halves every 12 months, there's an exponential growth in the difference between the ability of a computer to process data versus store it. This is sort of like recording 36 hours of television a day. No matter how much TV a person watches, they won't ever be able to catch up. There are a number of workarounds, but none of them are ideal. They'll be explored in further detail in the chapter on decision support systems.

BOX 10.5   Panopticon

There is no modern conundrum, whether technological or not, that doesn't have a precursor historically. The issue with storing too much data and not being able to process it strongly reflects the concept of a panopticon by Jeremy Bentham. This was intended to be a challenge on how to design a prison such that a single guard could monitor a large number of prisoners. The solution is, essentially, a bit of trickery using one-way glass so that prisoners can't tell if they are being monitored at any given moment. The assumption is that the prisoners will always act as if they are being monitored.

BONUS LOOT: BUSINESS FUNCTION—SALES

Sales is arguably the most competitive business function. It's easy to measure the performance of salespeople simply by comparing their productivity with each other. It's easy to measure the value of their clients using simple metrics.

As a result, sales departments tend to be on the cutting edge of most decision support system implementations. For example, CRM (customer resource management) was originally a sales tool to manage customer contacts. Eventually it developed into an entire system that was genericized to a mode of interacting with customers. But, at its core, it's still focused on providing sales staff with what they need to ensure they have the best possible chance of making a sale to a customer.

A typical sales-oriented DSS has a list of clients, along with a history of every single contact made with that customer. This includes bills paid, services/product ordered, automated systems calls, human-staffed call center calls, and a summary of everything from each of those. This constant evaluation of every single person leads toward that competitiveness.

The good news is that it's easier now than ever before to be a good salesperson. The principles of sales haven't changed in thousands of years except by refinement. But with support tools, it's possible to get by at higher levels of productivity without significant experience.

BONUS LOOT: RESUME BUILDERS—ACADEMIC/PROFESSIONAL PAPERS

One of the most effective ways to both train your mind and to represent that training to the outside world is to contribute to research. How much it matters differs by industry. However, there is a certain prestige in being able to point to a publication—it is a stamp of approval from an outside agency who agreed that what you had to say was not only valid but so profitable that they couldn't afford not to publish it.

A pattern of publication in certain fields will probably narrow down the applicability of your resume to those fields (but increase its effect). However, a single publication will always be an effective way of expressing your ability to think critically, communicate effectively, and produce a professional deliverable. If you do not have any publication attributable to you, you should always be looking for situations to change that.

If you are not comfortable producing a paper yourself, it is always a valid solution to seek one or more partners to do so. Producing a paper is a large undertaking, and it's still impressive to be part of a team production (and, ostensibly, more so as it shows the ability to work in a team). Potential places to look for partners include professors who want to work with their students on research; classmates who write well but can't come up with a good idea; classmates who come up with good ideas but can't write well; classmates who are good at organizing thoughts and structures; work colleagues who have ideas but can't express them; and work colleagues who can express your ideas.

There are typically four categories of publication. In order of most to least impressive (from an academic perspective), they are academic journals, trade journals, news outlets, and other. Academic journals typically have a high requirement for publication and are frequently more interested in proving underlying theory than in solving a specific problem. Trade journals tend to have a similarly high requirement for publication but accept discussions on specific problems and welcome authors with practical rather than academic credentials. News outlets have a lower academic standard, but with a strong enough record behind them that they are typically able to provide a substantive indirect recommendation. Finally, be careful about publishing in any other source, as there are a lot of places where the corollary is unwelcome (for example, if their advertisement is associated with extremist positions of any kind).

When looking for ideas on publication, there are also a number of options available. One can always ask, "Do you have any ideas that I can work with you to publish?" Similarly, the most effective papers are ones that solve specific problems (whether theoretical or practical), so practicing developing a problem statement is effective. Observation is a key skill in finding problems that need solving; look for people who repeat a task or who express frustration at a task. Finally, it's important to keep current with the target industry, as reading published papers or news stories in the industry can spark both creative problem finding and creative problem solving.

BONUS LOOT: SOFT SKILLS—ASKING THE RIGHT QUESTIONS

There is a missing step in what's been covered so far. How does data go from data to information? In the modern era, that process is focused around analytics. Analytics obviously derives from the same source as analysis and is the process of analyzing data to produce information (or more data).

There are three levels of analytics. On the lowest level are the modelers who take the math and the theory and produce the math that makes the rest of the analytics possible. The next level is the data analyst who cleans data, puts data into the system, and produces basic reports from the data. And at the top level is the business analyst who takes the results from the data analyst and presents it in a way that makes the most sense to their audience.

But the most important part of this process is that of asking the question. The right question is the difference between a successful analysis and a poor analysis. A good business analyst will be able to understand what a nonanalyst is asking and phrase the question in a way that will give the data analyst the best chance to answer.

However, like most areas where the nonexpert is dealing with the expert, it helps to meet the expert halfway, so it's important to know the best method for crafting questions. Going into detail is beyond the scope of this chapter, but here are some basic suggestions: Study formal logic, as the difference between "not" for a technical and nontechnical manager is very different; structure questions with one specific answer per question (an analyst would always rather get multiple questions than one question that tries to do too much or is too vague); and ask for feedback on how your questions can be more helpful.

BONUS LOOT: CERTIFICATIONS—TABLEAU

Data visualization is its own field and has its own ins and outs. Tools in analytics tend to be split into three areas, one of which is visualization. This will be covered in Chapter 16; however, one of the tools for visualization is called Tableau. Tableau is a very interesting tool because it's designed to accommodate what's called "no-programming development." This is, at its core, a simplified form of visual programming.

Tableau can become very complex, and rigorous training in it is possible. However, at the other end, simple tasks can be done by, essentially, giving the Tableau program a set of data in a recognized form (web data, Excel, tables of almost any format) and letting Tableau choose the best presentation on its own.

From this point, Tableau has options to link, mask, highlight, or extrapolate data. There are a number of tools available. Just jumping into Tableau is not a substitute for a full education in analytics and visualization, but it does provide many impressive looking visual displays that would have been impossible to produce in real time just a few years ago. And the key is that it does it easily.

Further, because it's easy to understand what Tableau does (boring data goes in, pretty picture comes out), a lot of executives are being sold on it as a platform. This makes Tableau a popular technology in the market right now. More rigorous certification options are available, but there are also teaching workshops being offered in a large number of municipalities. It's worth checking into, as it's certainly a nice resume booster.

REFERENCES

Krebs, B. (2013, December 20). Cards stolen in Target breach flood underground markets. https://krebsonsecurity.com/2013/12/cards-stolen-in-target-breach-flood-underground-markets/

Data Processing

VOCABULARY

> Aggregation

> OLAP

> Confirmation bias

> Correlation

> Causation

> Oversummarization

> Pandering

CONCEPTS

> Data versus information

> Dashboards

> Feature creep

> Logical fallacies

MAIN STORY: DRIVING PRINCIPLES

1. Data can be processed to produce general purpose results or to answer specific questions.
2. Logic errors are easy to introduce into the process of turning data into information.
3. Data processing is about telling stories.

SIDE QUEST: ANALOGY—A HOUSE

In Texas, the fastest way to make a buyer lose interest in a house or to tank the house's value is to have foundation problems. Modern foundations are comparatively easy to fix, and modern foundation fixes are as good as new. But, for some reason, the idea permeates through Texas culture that if a house has ever had any foundation problems, it's going to fall over at any moment.

But underlying any decision about whether a foundation problem is problematic or fixable is a basic understanding that foundations are key to the structure of the whole house. Earlier, the distillation model was presented as a way of conceptualizing the process of going from data to information to decisions. But a house is also a good metaphor to use, emphasizing different aspects.

The foundation is data. Deeper footings, deeper piers, thicker slabs, higher-quality concrete, and careful site preparation all make a foundation stronger. There are probably attributes that can be shared between the metaphor, but that's tangential. The stronger the foundation, the more secure the house.

The house, which represents information, sits on the data. Each room in the house is still built on the data, but they serve a different function. Information, similarly, can be analyzed differently to pull different views and purposes. There's even a secondary metaphor about how second-story rooms can be built on top of the first-story rooms, suggesting that information can form the data foundation for other information purposes.

Finally, there are people who have to make decisions about how to use the rooms of the houses. A kitchen is the perfect place to create a meal. An office is an excellent place to write a textbook. But ultimately a person is going to have to make the decisions about how the information should be used.

MAIN STORY: INFORMATION UTILITY

Suppose a tourist arrives at Heathrow Airport, visits one of the ubiquitous visitor help desks, and says, "Give me some data about London, please." A very likely response is going to be a fact sheet listing population, square mileage, major roadways, distances to other major cities, political figures, and so on. How useful is that going to be for the tourist?

In the realm of information systems, the idea would generally be that the tourist should say, "Give me some information about London, please." Suddenly, this becomes much more personal, as the response moves more toward, "Here are some things you should know," "These are the things that most tourists find useful," or "You can get there by getting on XYZ bus."

But common sense suggests that's still not a very useful answer for the tourist. The distinction between data and information is that data is facts, but information is useful. Those bits of information are generally useful. However, the tourist may have questions like, "Where's the nearest bathroom?" "How do I get to my hotel?" or even, "I'm vegan and I'm craving something Mediterranean, but my credit card won't work internationally. How can I get some cash, and where would be a good place to eat nearby on my way to the business function I'm attending?" Suddenly, the answers to these questions are much more directly useful to the tourist.

BOX 11.1   Utility

Utility is the ability of something to be used in a beneficial manner. *Usefulness* is a synonym for utility. It is a relative term: A steak has utility to an adult but none to a toothless infant. *Utile* is the adjective, and *utility* is the noun; that is, something is utile, but it has utility. Economics has a technical definition of utility and a measurement, in utils. However, for broad, general discussion of utility, it's frequently enough to note whether utility exists or whether one situation has more utility than another.

The first distinction regarding information being useful is true. But there's a qualifier: Usefulness is relative. What this means is that in order for data to be processed into information in a manner that's useful, it typically needs to be qualified into an answer. For example, given the population of every city in a state, processing that data into the total number of people who live in a metropolitan area is probably useful for state planning purposes. But if the particular committee that commissioned the analysis needs to figure out which cities are growing the quickest, the information isn't useful.

This leads into the first of two ways to process data. In another context, this is tangential to supervised data mining. Essentially, a question is asked and the data is aggregated and calculated in such a way as to provide information that relates to that question. For example, map apps offer several different filters. Typing the word *restaurant* into the search function gives the option of ranking the results by distance, by estimated cost, by rating, or by filtering according to different types of restaurants. A person who is looking for cheap pizza may miss a suitable option when scanning through all of the other types of restaurant or costs.

Note the word *aggregation*. Frequently, in information systems, data processing is related to different forms of aggregation. Aggregation is the process of substituting a summary or representative value for many individual values. Examples are means, modes, maximums, and standard deviations. Different values represent different aggregations.

The second primary way to process data is to identify all related aggregate values to a particular topic. This way is tangential to unsupervised data mining. The end result of this sort of analysis is typically a large list of unhelpful results. For example, when finding the average amount spent on groceries, a retail chain might notice that customers who purchase generic label products spend less money than those who purchase name brand labels. While that may be true, it's likely unhelpful since it's also self-evident that people who buy less expensive products spend less money. As a result, the follow-up step is to look through the list of results and find the aggregate values that are useful and related to answering a specific question.

BOX 11.2   Qualitative Data Processing

The type of data processing discussed in this chapter largely focuses on quantitative analysis. The term *quantitative* means that it focuses on the numbers and typically results in aggregate values. There is another form called qualitative analysis. Qualitative descriptions of data seek to capture essential qualities of the data and frequently consider each piece of data separately. Computers do this process poorly (although they are getting better).

The most rigorous form of analysis uses both qualitative and quantitative methods and is called mixed methods. Identifying appropriate methodologies and pairing them with computer-driven quantitative analyses is a skill that can benefit every professional, but it is outside the scope of this text.

Both methods are used frequently. The first one is obvious and straightforward: Ask a question and try to discover if the data demonstrates an answer. The second one, however, frequently leads to unexpected results that the analyst would not have noticed with the more specific target of the first method.

SIDE QUEST: DATA VISUALIZATION

One of the most important parts of data processing is to display the data in some manner. One of the most useful advancements provided by technology is the ability to demonstrate data more easily. The easiest way to consider the difficulty in visualizing data is to consider multidimensional data. For example, a two-dimensional table compares two factors. Across the top, it might list every branch of a fast-food franchisor. Down the side, it might list months. And in each cell, it lists the total revenue for each branch that month.

This is a great chart, for what it does. But what happens if the executive team wants to see the net profit of each branch? What if they want each branch, but they want them broken up by product category rather than time? Historically, this would have meant printing a new chart, because there's no way to show these extra variables in a two-dimensional chart. This is a successful approach, but it means that any cross-referencing has to be done manually by flipping pages back and forth.

The classic tool that's used in this situation is called an OLAP cube (online analytical processing). OLAP first became popular in the 1970s and is still widely considered the only useful method for interacting with data. There are a number of replacements and successors, but none have added enough benefit over the original model to have been adopted widely.

The easiest way to present multiple dimensions of data in a two-dimensional chart is to just cram the new variables into one of the dimensions (for example, the rows might be labeled (1) January – Revenue, (2) January – Profit, (3) February – Revenue, and so on; and the columns might be labeled Location 1 – Breakfast Foods; Location 1 – Entrees, Location 1 – Sides, and so on.). The problem is that how they're crammed into the chart is frequently arbitrary, compromises readability, and either duplicates information or removes some of the aggregate values.

OLAP presents this chart but does so in a way that allows for collapsing and expanding the extra variables. The axes are typically assigned a major variable and one or more minor variables. The minor variables can then be expanded in real time or collapsed if unimportant. For example, the table might start with only showing the total profit from each branch, but if Location 1 is making the lowest profit, it could be expanded to show all of the product categories in order to see if that might be the cause. Typically, a good OLAP program will have the option to—in real time—reorder variables, change the degree of aggregation, and hide columns or rows according to a threshold.

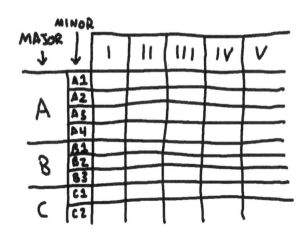

FIGURE 11.1 *Simple OLAP example.*

As a result, OLAP is useful not just for a chart that wants to show four variables in two dimensions, but it can frequently accommodate dozens of variables, most of which start out hidden. The process of exploring these variables and expanding on individual values is called drilling down into the data, which is the origin of the term *data mining*.

MAIN STORY: TIMELINESS OF DATA PROCESSING

There are several scopes of data processing and presentation that are useful, and they follow in a pretty straightforward manner. The first is to summarize the data that supports the answer to a specific question. For example, a company might ask, "What is the best location to open a new site?" One approach might be to analyze key aggregate values from all existing sites and identify which ones are successful. A subsequent analysis might evaluate what metrics apply to the most successful sites that might relate to the purchase of a new location. Finally, another analysis might look at all available locations and rank them based on how they relate to the metrics identified in the previous step. The output would then be charts representing the findings in each of the three analyses. This is a very targeted approach to presenting the results of data processing: It answers a specific question and highlights those specific answers.

The second method tends to be a more broad spectrum analysis. Ahead of time, a determination would be made as to what metrics are important to a particular type of report. For example, it might be the CEO's daily briefing, a data sheet distributed to all department heads, or a weekly employee report for midlevel managers with many operational direct reports. The idea is that the report can be developed ahead of time, and as new data is put through the ETS process, the report can be generated periodically (typically daily, weekly, monthly, or quarterly). Since the developers of this report can't know what will be important in the future, they include everything relevant and trust the recipients of the report to be able to review it and identify the values that are important to them. The most classic example of this is the stock report that appears in almost every major newspaper: Most of the stocks won't change much day to day, and the editors can't know which stocks will be important to any given reader, but the readers can easily scan through and identify the stocks that are of interest to them.

Finally, there's a newer scope of data processing. The first case was essentially on a case-by-case basis to solve a specific problem. The second case was a brute-force presentation of all relevant aggregate values. But, in many cases, it's possible to adequately address both of those areas. This is what an OLAP cube attempts to do, and it typically does so in the most effective manner for tables with a high dimensionality. But Tableau or Microsoft's PowerBI are also attempts to do this. A relatively new term for this is *dashboard*. A dashboard takes data, frequently in real time, presents it in a manner that shows a wide variety of aggregate values, and frames it in a way that answers specific questions. A good dashboard will have several pages, each of which is a dynamic presentation of data in a slightly different angle or viewpoint.

MAIN STORY: STORYTELLING

These newer styles of presentation are called dashboards in an effort to represent the idea of viewing a lot of information all at once. It's intended to be the same as a car's dashboard, which has a number of instrument panels that an experienced driver can take in instantly. Just describing why it's called a dashboard explains why they are becoming so popular, and in turn it brings the process full circle, back to both the targeted and the broad presentations of data.

Remember that none of information systems has real meaning without the people on the right side of the seesaw model. They interact with the outside world. People engage in process and use the data to make decisions. It's those people who have to be targeted.

Data processing is not about numbers, data, hardware and software, or almost anything else. It's about telling stories. Everything else is a vehicle to get there. Why does a person buy a name brand product instead of the generic that's probably produced in the same factory? They heard a story in the advertising and it convinced them to buy the name brand. Why do people increasingly choose not to smoke tobacco? It wasn't until the antismoking campaigns stopped using statistics and started telling stories. Why do people smoke tobacco? They like the image it presents and therefore the story it's telling.

In order to have an effect in the real world, data has to tell a story.

Data processing is, ultimately, the method that produces that story. So a dashboard should lead the user from one result to the next, allowing them to understand intuitively what the numbers are saying about a real-world situation. The easiest way to lose a person's attention is to forget that they have an attention span and just give them all of the information available. There is so much information that it just becomes noise, loses its utility, and in a sense reverts back to data.

Both the specialized report that answers a specific question and the broad report that gives all of the information available can benefit from this. They need to tell a story. In the example about finding a new site for a company, the report isn't just three tables pasted into a document. In order to be effective, it needs to lead the eye, highlight the most important bits of information, and include prose descriptions (either written or verbally presented) that take the reader on the same journey that the author went on to come to a conclusion. Similarly, it's no longer enough for a weekly or monthly report to just give the numbers; there are so many more tools available for presenting the information that they should be taken advantage of.

One of the things that will always be in high demand is the need for someone to explain why the data or the information is important. Computers do a good job of processing the data, but people give it semantic meaning.

SIDE QUEST: FEATURE CREEP

Feature creep is a fundamental problem with data processing that is shared with almost all development tasks. Feature creep occurs when the initial goal of a project is subsumed by "wouldn't it be nice if …" It's deceptively easy to take a clean and well-designed interface and degrade its utility by trying to add useful features.

This section is a clean and easy place to discuss feature creep, because the output can be visualized. Imagine a fact sheet that is intended to come out on a one-page spread, but there are many stakeholders in the process. Politics would be an excellent example. Campaigners might choose to develop a simple flyer that expresses the details of their cause, why readers should vote a certain way, and what the intention is.

But politics is also a cooperative endeavor. Campaigns typically have ties with other ventures and are frequently short on funds. So it may seem like a good idea to join forces with another group to get two issues onto the same sheet, but the plain fact is that the single sheet only has so much space—what's well designed and compelling for one issue may not be well designed or compelling for two. What was initially intended to address one goal resulted in a product that was less than ideal for two goals.

Feature creep in industry is very similar. A web designer might contract with a client to put together a website in 6 months. Three months into it, the client may have attended a sales presentation and decided that it was vital to include some new feature. This new feature shouldn't just get "tacked on" to the end of the web design project. To properly be included, it should have been included in the central planning.

One extra function is likely not a project-breaking problem, but it's a slippery slope from one new feature to a dozen new features until the after-the-fact additions become more substantive than the original goal. As an aside, this is also one of the key reasons security is frequently lacking in process and software: In an effort to satisfy stakeholders who want extra features without proper planning, security is frequently one of the easiest areas to gloss over.

The best analogy to this is safe driving on the highway. Everyone has driven down the highway and suddenly realized they're in the wrong lane to take their exit. Safe driving would suggest that an extra five minutes to take the next exit and reroute is the best solution to an unplanned situation. Driving across three lanes of traffic and just barely making it onto the exit is also a solution, but succeeding at it is almost entirely a matter of luck and will eventually result in catastrophe. In the same way, completing the original project and then developing a new plan for the next version is probably a better solution than trying to produce a poorly designed product that has the extra features at the outset.

MAIN STORY: LOGICAL FALLACIES

If data processing and presentation are all about telling a story, then it's a narrative. And it becomes important to safeguard the premise of this narrative for two reasons. The first is that most people have an intuitive understanding of logic errors. If they can't point them out explicitly, they still become less trusting of the conclusion if they feel misled on the way. The second is a moral imperative. Changing the structure of the discussion away from the objective data to a narrative instead of the empirical numbers is an act that implies an adherence to what that data showed.

There are a few logical fallacies that are very common and should be given attention:

- Confirmation bias: Researchers and analysts very frequently find the answers they want to find. Since researchers and analysts are fallible, this sometimes means that they took shortcuts with the process or misinterpreted results or summarized conclusions in favor of the desired result. This is not always malicious; it's frequently a benign process that stems from human expectations that what we want to happen will happen.

- Correlation and causation: When two things happen in a related manner, they are correlated. But it is not always provable which one caused the other, or even that they weren't both caused by outside influences. Word use that implies causation frequently needs to be avoided.

- Oversummarization: Typically data analysis comes away with very specific conclusions. It takes a wide variety of support to be able to make general statements. However, it's easy to jump to unwarranted conclusions when summarizing data. It's important to make sure that each claim flows from one to the next.

- Pandering: One of the benefits of the computerization of data analysis is that the data is fixed and available for everyone. This prevents the pressure for subordinates to come to the same, possibly incorrect, conclusions of their superior. However, the more the results of data processing are handled and arranged, the easier it is to insinuate or include conclusions that the audience wants to hear.

BONUS LOOT: BUSINESS FUNCTION—PROJECT MANAGEMENT

Modern project management has bifurcated to a certain extent. While the basic tools that are used are very similar and expertise in project management has a certain capacity to transfer between industries and project types, there are still some differences based on industry culture that change the practical realities of project management.

On the one hand are what would be the more practical, tangible projects such as building highways, general building contractors, and civic planning departments. These tasks all share the same basic premises of project management. But at the same time they're unique since it's possible to see and touch the final and in-process projects. When a highway is being built or renovated, measuring completion rates is effectively as simple as driving along the highway. When building a house, the walls are rising. The management of the operational roles in these projects (the people operating the cement mixers, framing the building, or testing the integrity of newly laid pipes) tends to be more cut and dried. It's not simpler, per se; however, it is a more direct approach.

In information systems, projects tend to be a little more ephemeral. They're only as real and tangible as the scope of the project. For example, developing a new software system for an HR training platform doesn't have a fixed start or stop point. There are times when it makes sense to develop a process and then improve on it over time, which tends to lead toward more permanent "project" managers whose projects don't have a fixed start or completion point.

This tends to lead toward lost facilitators without specific targets and guidelines. This is important to recognize, because these roles aren't always going to lend themselves toward simplistic standards of success. (For example, how does one measure the success rate of a project manager for a security company? Failure is easy to measure, but success can't be listed as just "not failing.")

The two most functional ways to address these are to make sure that every project or process has an individual who is directly responsible for its successful functioning—if there's a problem or if consultation is needed, it's immediately apparent who should be contacted. The other side is that while historical metrics for job performance may not apply, effort should be taken to identify what can be used as some form of metric.

BONUS LOOT: RESUME BUILDERS—SELF-PROMOTION

One of the most difficult parts of producing a resume is finding the right tone, attitude, and volume. While it's appropriate to make funny cartoon voices with a group of kids, it's probably not appropriate at a funeral. Developing the ability to write like a resume writer is a skill that takes time and practice. It is a good idea to try writing several resumes from scratch. Offering to help other people write their resumes (and selfishly taking away their chance to practice on their own) is a good step. Similarly, writing several personal resumes for different industries, job roles, or aspects you want to highlight is a good idea. The most effective activity is spending some time reading successful resumes in your field to get an idea of the tone and the patter. There are certain combinations of words that mean something in one field but are nonsense in another field. That's an important mode of writing to acknowledge.

Attitude is another aspect of self-description that's hard to master. Most people tend to be either self-deprecating or overly boisterous when talking about their accomplishments. There are few people who are naturally able to hit exactly the right attitude for self-description. It's possible to spend some time experimenting with attitude and determining what others are looking for, but a good place to start is to consistently consider how every statement helps the person reading. If you're applying for a job, you want the person reading the resume to see every line and think, "This person would be such a great help to me!" No matter how impressed you are with how you did something or even whether you did it, consider whether the reader will feel better about themselves by having read it. Because, in the end, you're not trying to impress you, you're trying to impress your reader.

Finally, volume is important. Volume is difficult to pin down because everyone has a different idea of "right." The British and European model is the curriculum vitae (CV; literally, "an ordered list of my life"), which lists every single detail for the entirety of a person's work history. The Japanese model is much more constrained. Specific duties or accomplishments are almost never boasted about, just a simple listing of where and when. The American version tends to be much more free form, but people differ in their preferences for level of detail. Typical rules dictate that experienced individuals should have two-page resumes, new professionals ought to have one-page resumes, and some specific industries should list everything. Your level of detail should attempt to fit that length (include less if there are more jobs; include more if there are fewer jobs). You should limit the time frame of your resume to what is appropriate to the job you're applying for (nobody wants to hire based on technology skills from the 1990s) and consider whether a particular job or duty would be related to the duties of the job you're applying for.

The simplest solution to navigating through self-description is to create a new resume for every job you apply for. Each resume should filter through a centralized CV-style listing of everything you've done or been a part of and should be included only if it seems relevant to what you'd be doing in the new job.

BONUS LOOT: SOFT SKILLS—ELEVATOR PITCH FOLLOW-UP

Elevator pitches are great. They're a 30-second distillation of what to say about a topic. But then what? Suppose that a person says, "Wow! You've got my attention! I want to learn so much more about that!" An elevator pitch alone isn't enough.

Instead, a comprehensive solution involves a series of elevator pitches. Success relies on knowing how to go through these pitches. An elevator pitch shouldn't sound rehearsed, but it should sound practiced. The difference between these two words in this context is the difference between an insincere model in a TV infomercial and the smooth patter of a three-card Monte hustler, respectively.

The tool that helps most is a set of index cards representing approximately 30-second pitches. The cards can then be arranged on a flat surface to represent branches of a conversation. If the person says, "Tell me more about your target clientele," there should be a card for that. After that, rehearsing various paths through the conversations with a partner is a good approach.

Being able to talk up one's current employment, employer, and colleagues is the sort of skill that will endear one to everyone around.

BONUS LOOT: CERTIFICATIONS—PMI

Six Sigma certification is one brand of project management methodology. There is another brand produced by the Project Management Institute. While Six Sigma certification is offered and endorsed by individual organizations, the PMP certification (Project Management Professional) is developed and controlled by PMI. This distinction is not important from a broad perspective; they're both valuable certifications. But some individuals prefer one approach over the other.

Adherents to the Six Sigma method don't always appreciate being likened to adherents of PMP certification (or vice versa). The reason they both exist, however, is that they are different sets of tools for addressing the same problem of project management. As a result, it's even feasible to get both a Six Sigma black belt and a PMP certification. The relative utility of both is debatable, but it may be a valuable step.

The reason both of these certifications are brought up is that while they are comparatively difficult and time consuming to attain, they have broad interdisciplinary recognition. It will almost certainly never harm a resume to have them, and they are a boon to almost every general business function.

CHAPTER 12

DSS (Decision Support Systems)

PRE-READING CHECKLIST

VOCABULARY

> DSS

> Passive mode

> Active mode

> Cooperative mode

> Presentation layer

> Application layer

> Data layer

> Cyberchondria

> Artificial intelligence

> Data warehouse

CONCEPTS

> Haettenschweiler model

> Power model

> Common DSSs

> stack

> Three-tier model

MAIN STORY: DRIVING PRINCIPLES

1. Decision support systems do not make decisions; they allow humans to make better decisions.

2. Different types of activities are best served by different decision support systems.

3. Care should be taken not to let the DSS's "understanding" get too far ahead of human "understanding."

SIDE QUEST: ANALOGY—COMPUTER SIDEKICKS

Quick, list off every pop-culture reference where the protagonist has a magical machine of some sort that provides them with insight into their current predicament. David Hasselhoff had KITT in *Knight Rider*. Every character in every Star Trek has an omnipresent computer that speaks techno babble. Ash Ketchum has his Pokédex. The astronauts in *2001: A Space Odyssey* had the HAL computer. There are dozens of examples of characters needing something extra to inform them about the world around them and help them make good decisions.

One of best examples is Professor Xavier with Cerebro. Professor Xavier is a talented superpsychic mutant who can read people's minds, move stuff with telekinesis, and whatever other powers the comic book plot needs at any given moment. It's important not to discount the fact that he's already well trained in using his mutant powers.

With Cerebro (a sort of helmet computer whose origin is only loosely explained), however, he can read the mind of everyone in the world, communicate with anyone he needs to, and move all sorts of stuff. It's not just "what the plot needs," it's "what the plot needs, but all over the world." This well-trained psychic is able to exponentially multiply his effectiveness with the assistance of this fantasy device.

What's exciting is that a lot of this sci-fi ephemera is starting to have real-world counterparts. For example, the tricorder (a sci-fi medical scanning device) from the original *Star Trek* has fascinated medical researchers for years, and they have been able to recently develop limited prototypes to duplicate it (Belfiore, 2018). The Pokédex is such a novel concept as an authoritative listing of everything known about Pokémon that zoologists have put one together for real-world animals (Silverman, 2016). Augmented reality devices are becoming common, allowing people to identify astronomical objects (Corpuz, 2020), translate foreign languages (both written and spoken) in real time (Google, n.d.), or even play video games in real-world spaces.

MAIN STORY: WHAT IS A DSS?

The entire category of software, hardware, and communications tools that are devoted to making good decisions is called "decision support systems." It should, properly, include the people and processes as well. However, because the industry typically views a DSS as a package that can be set up in any organization, it shouldn't be viewed as a full information system. However, within the organization and over time, it should be incorporated into the full range of components.

There is not an agreed-on definition for decision support systems; however, there are some frameworks that typically help create broad yet distinct classes. The two most helpful are the Haettenschweiler model, which focuses on the modality of the DSS, and the Power model, which focuses on the composition of the DSS.

The Haettenschweiler model (Gachet & Haettenschwiler, 2003) comprises three modes:

- A passive mode DSS provides data to help make a decision but doesn't make any recommendations. An example might be a system that helps to filter resumes based on predetermined rules but otherwise just presents everything that meets the basic standards.

▪ An active mode DSS provides a suggested decision and provides the data only as a support to that decision. An example might be a system that sends notifications of new products based on similarity to previous consumption behavior.

▪ A cooperative mode DSS provides an iterative series of interactions to come to a conclusion. The most classic example is any variation of an expert system such as one that asks questions like, "Where is the pain?" and narrows down the kind and frequency of the pain to provide a medical diagnosis.

The Power (2002) model has five types of DSS that support the ability to make decisions based on what the system is composed of.

▪ A communication-based DSS allows people to communicate with each other and therefore make stronger decisions.

▪ A data-driven DSS provides tools to allow the manipulation of data to come to new conclusions.

▪ A document-driven DSS emphasizes access to, retention of, and organization of documents of varying types.

▪ A knowledge-driven DSS provides ways of recording difficult-to-record data like a person's expertise over a career of performing a certain job.

▪ A model-driven DSS provides outputs based on mathematical and statistical models in a way that abstracts away the base data manipulation.

BOX 12.1   Power's Text

Power's text (*Decision Support Systems: Concepts and Resources for Managers*) is a good target for reading more about support systems. It's on the technical side, but since it's posted publicly it's good to reference for specific ideas. It also has some examples of alternate takes on some of the same concepts in this text. For example, Power references a successor to the Anthony triangle that has four layers rather than turning it into a ternary.

The point of these two models is not to provide a list of topics that have to be memorized. These models provide a convenient set of options when structuring roles and processes. Across an organization, it's likely that each of the five compositions should be addressed in some fashion. And any given role should decide what mode of decision making is most appropriate and which of those compositions should be accessed. Both models can feasibly be used in conjunction with each other when determining which is the best approach.

> ### BOX 12.2   Expert System in Fiction
>
> Check out Steven King's (1980) *Firestarter* for a fictional interaction between a person (an excellent example of the evil spy trope) and an expert system. It's eerie and probably a little pie in the sky. Skip the film.

SIDE QUEST: DSS EXAMPLES

The number of decision support systems is expanding all the time. Further, routine tasks add DSS capabilities on a frequent basis. Here is a sample of common DSSs:

- Expert system (cooperative, knowledge driven): The most common example of this is WebMD, which is a classic website for identifying user illnesses. However, alternative versions exist and are frequently employed by hospitals to support doctors or give them potential alternatives for investigation.
- Wiki (passive, document-driven): Wikipedia is only one wiki. Other examples are Wiktionary, Gamepedia, or Wikispecies. These are all places that allow for users to store documentation about a general or specific topic for others to look up as they choose.
- Help (active, communication driven): Most modern websites for services that have a log-in are beginning to utilize a website chat function. This cuts down on phone calls, increases response time, and typically increases user happiness, but it still takes time. As a result, sites are frequently using systems that try to interpret the user types and automatically provide catered answers to their questions.
- Mapping (active moving toward cooperative, model driven): Modern mapping software uses an algorithm to interpret satellite images to create roads. Then, based on user data, the app will frequently update traffic patterns in real time. As a result, when a person asks it where to go, it can automatically identify the fastest route based on current conditions.
- Online video games (passive, data driven): As odd as it may seem, modern online video games share a large amount of similarity with decision support systems. They are data driven in that they are just a series of defined data objects and the user chooses when or where to interact with them.

MAIN STORY: DECISIONS AND THE THREE-TIER MODEL

Because decision support systems are complex systems, it's useful to return to the divide-and-conquer design method from Chapter 4. Remember that the impetus behind it is the opposite of gestalt: The difficulty of each part is much less than the difficulty of the whole. For example, one of the reasons OSHA requires employees to be notified that heavy items must be carried by two people is because the total difficulty for two people is much less than the difficulty for one person. The amount of work accomplished is the same—moving an object from one place to another—but the cost in effort and risk of injury is substantially lowered.

In the same way, complex processes and systems benefit when they're given a structured method of division between portions. One of those most common types of model for doing this is called a stack. In a stack, a large system is divided into smaller parts, and those parts are stacked on top of each other. If the stack has seven parts, part 1 can interact only with part 2, part 2 can interact only with parts 1 and 3, part 3 can interact only with parts 2 and 4, and so on.

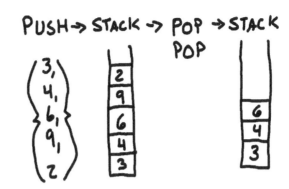

FIGURE 12.1 *Stack example.*

BOX 12.3   Stacks and Queues

In computer science, data structures are what programmers use to organize their data. There are two simple structures that everyone learns: stacks and queues. These are both used to keep track of sets of things (for example, milk put into a cooler at a grocery store). In a queue, the first thing to be assigned to the queue is also the first thing that is scheduled to be removed from the queue. In a stack, the most recent thing to be assigned to the stack is the first thing scheduled to be removed. A grocery store should use a queue structure for putting out its food: New milk goes behind the old milk in the display rack. On the other hand, receptionists frequently use a stack structure: Older calls get put on hold when a new call comes in so that the line isn't left unanswered.

Why does this limitation help? Why isn't the system designed so that every part can interact with every other part. Practically, it's because the system is complex, and in an effort to simplify it, the lines of communication are simplified. It's easier to grasp the role of part 2 if it needs to have processes for handling input and output only to parts 1 and 3. Alternately, if every part could interact with every other part, there would be 21 different lines of communication that need to be structured. By structuring the system so that each part interacts only with its adjacent parts, there are only six lines of communication that need to be structured.

On paper, military rankings are structured like this: Privates interact with their NCOs (noncommissioned officers). NCOs interact with their OICs (officers in charge). OICs interact with their superiors. Lieutenants typically interact only with NCOs and captains. Captains tend to interact only with their lieutenant subordinates and their commanding major. And so it goes up the chain of command. (Of course, in the real world this is not so simple. Lines jump these rankings all over the hierarchy. And in a real-world stack there might be good reasons to make exceptions, but the exceptions don't define the intended structure.)

One of the most ubiquitous stacks is the three-tier model. Originally, it was a network model for networked applications. However, it was so useful in separating very distinct parts of an application that it has become the de facto standard for even standalone applications. It is becoming more common in real-world situations as managers realize that the structure has always been implicit, even if it wasn't acknowledged.

The three-tier model has three layers: the data layer, the application layer, and the presentation layer. The data layer is where the data set and the data exist. The application layer is where the processing happens. And the presentation layer is where the interface with the user exists.

- The presentation layer exists to take user input and pass it on to the application layer in a recognizable format.
- The application layer processes the user's input and sends a request for any needed data to the data layer.
- The data layer responds to the application layer with exactly the data requested in the format requested.
- The application layer processes the data to produce an output and sends it to the presentation layer.
- The presentation layer formats the output in a standard and clearly readable fashion and presents it to the user.

This structure has a lot of benefits, especially with the recognition that there's an implicit 0 layer: the user, who can interact only with the presentation layer. This structure provides a large amount of the security in modern applications (it is not a substitute for proper information security, but it is a component). Users cannot accidentally send improperly formatted requests to the application layer and break it, accidentally or intentionally, because the presentation layer will filter improperly formatted requests. Users cannot interact directly with the data, possibly introducing errors or gaining improper access to data. The application layer doesn't need to worry about formatting; it can just process the data appropriately.

The second big benefit to this three-tier architecture is that it is severable. Suppose that a company makes a significant investment in a new website using the three-tier architecture and they need to recoup that cost over a period of 5 to 8 years. Fashions and styles for visual displays like websites do not stick around that long. However, since the input and output to the application layer is formal and structured, a new presentation layer can be developed without changing the other two layers. Similarly, a company could develop the presentation and application layers as a general structure and then sell them to other organizations that already have databases.

This three-tier architecture is going to become more common and explicit in nontechnical management structures as time goes on. But it's also a good representation of stacks, in general. The two big benefits listed apply to any stack, customized to that particular application. Most importantly, however, as long as there's always a top-level presentation layer (or a synonymous name) responsible for accepting user input and formatting the output, it separates the user from having to know the technical details of the application.

MAIN STORY: MACHINE INTELLIGENCE

The secret to a good decision support system is its illusion of clarity. For decades, slightly sketchy late-night infomercials have sold foolproof systems for investing in stocks, real estate, or some other vehicle of questionable legality. They promise that the system analyzes 1,001 sources of data and then presents the user with a clear and guaranteed recommendation for investment. But if that were the case, why wouldn't the system be used everywhere? The reality is that they only provide an illusion of clarity.

Stock investment is a complicated subject, and the 1,001 sources of data the application uses in its analysis can't possibly all agree so fully that a clear and direct recommendation can be given as a one-size-fits-all solution. More than likely, it is masking its internal thresholds and assumptions for the sake of clarity, presuming that the user isn't well versed in the nuances of investment (a fair assumption, since the user is taking investing advice from a late-night infomercial salesperson). But, again, investment is complicated. The recommendation can be simplified; however, without a base level of understanding, its accuracy is reduced to trying to divine meaning from the pattern of heads and tails in coin flips.

The point is that modern decision support systems are fantastic tools. They are literally bringing to life things that were fantasy just a few years ago. But they're just tools. They may have a deceptive anthropomorphism, but it's important to remember that they're just tools. They don't convey expertise to the user; the user has to have that expertise before using them.

In this case, the contranegative is also true. If a user doesn't have expertise, the utility won't convey anything to them. Some examples might include the following:

- Web-based medical expert systems: There is a new term being used in the medical community, *cyberchondria*. These are normal people who develop symptoms of hypochondria (an otherwise healthy person who is convinced that they have contracted an illness) because they read something on the internet that implied their minor symptom was a major symptom. While individuals are ultimately responsible for their own health, anything beyond minor problems requires a trained medical diagnostician.
- Artificial intelligence: There have been the beginnings of discussions on how to handle conclusions reached by artificial intelligence algorithms or machine learning. Data goes in, and an answer comes out. But even if the answer is right, how can it be put into context without knowing how that answer came about? For example, one class of artificial intelligence algorithm is called a neural network and seeks to simulate an early model of brain connectivity. What's interesting about these is that they're formed of a series of "neurons" (just data structures that represent neurons). The input and output neurons are human readable, but the intermediate neurons are effectively impossible for humans to interpret.

■ Driving errors: There are thousands of anecdotes about people getting lost when following automated driving directions. In Australia, one mapping app sent people through the middle of a desert with no road resulting in numerous calls to emergency services as people got stranded hundreds of kilometers from a gas station. Some websites promise to find an address for anyone. However, when it can't find the address, it offers the geographic center of the country the person lives in as its best guess. There is a farm in the geographic center of the United States that complains about the number of wrong address visitors they get every month. Otherwise, people have driveways, unpaved alleys, parking garages all mistakenly identified as roads. The damage unwitting drivers cause to the owners of those location is substantial.

This is not a call for an immediate technophobic reaction. Again, decision support systems are excellent tools, but they absolutely require training and at least a basic knowledge of the fundamental aspects of the decision being supported before they should be used.

SIDE QUEST: DATA WAREHOUSES

Data warehouse is the term for any large database. Properly, data warehouses and databases are constructed differently, with databases having less data and more structural complexity and data warehouses having more data and less structural complexity. But, for the most part, we consider something to be a data warehouse if it's intended to collect data indefinitely, not be used for real-time calculations, and is subjectively larger than an average database.

A data warehouse is substantially larger than the average database. For the most part, an average database is going to hold operational data. Remember, as of the time of writing, the average hard drive was measured in terabytes. A large organization might have terabytes worth of data, but more than likely it will have data in the gigabyte range. A small organization will have a database in the kilobyte to megabyte range. Small general-purpose warehouses start in the terabyte range and move up to the millions of terabytes (exabyte) range. Remembering that hard drives are measured in the terabyte range, that active memory is in the gigabyte range, and that a processor could likely read less than a gigabyte a second, a process would take in the range of hours to even read through a moderately sized data warehouse, without making any calculations.

A data warehouse is typically not used for real-time calculations since a "real-time" calculation typically needs to occur within a few minutes or so. For example, an analyst might need the answer to a question, but there may be a mistake in the question itself. The analyst would need to know within minutes that there was a problem rather than wasting the whole day waiting to find out. Typically, the range for what's considered "real time" varies by industry and application: In video games it's virtually instantaneous, in weather forecasting it's in portions of an hour, and in large simulations it's measured in multiple hours. However, within an industry and application, the range tends to go down over time (consider a weather forecast; for example, the *Farmers' Almanac* predicted weather on a yearly cycle, then came news predictions over the course of days, and now there exist apps that provide predictions in 15-minute increments).

Finally, a data warehouse is almost always a storage medium, not a calculation medium. It can't be a hard rule, but operationally most data warehouses are considered write-once media. That is, once it's been written, it doesn't get changed. It's not worth the time and operational interruption to fix one factual error out of trillions of facts. For the most part, it's assumed that the rest of the accurate data will dramatically outweigh any errors.

The question then becomes "If a data warehouse is primarily used for storage, not for real-time analysis, and is too large to work with, what's the point?" This is where data marts come in. Typically, a data mart is a subset of a large data warehouse; however, a data mart is small enough to be worked on in real time. There tend to be three primary methods of using a data mart. Sometimes, a user needs to use a data mart as a substitute for the larger data warehouse. In that case the user will clone a sample of the larger data warehouse to run tests in real time on the data to confirm that the calculations are correct before running those calculations on the entire data warehouse. Alternately, a user might create a temporary data mart taking all of the data within certain constraints (e.g., only data from 1996–1998 in Dallas County, Texas) and run their calculations on that. Finally, there are frequently semipermanent data marts that exist in some context like "all data for the last month" or "historical data for a certain location" that are used in operational calculations. These last aren't updated in real time; rather, they are updated to the latest data overnight or weekly or monthly or on some other fixed schedule.

BONUS LOOT: BUSINESS FUNCTION—CONSULTING

Modern consulting is exactly the same as it has always been. However, in many ways it's also evolved to look very different behind the scenes. Traditionally, hiring a consultant involved having an industry expert show up at a business, interview employees, observe operations, and then make recommendations to improve efficiency.

And for the most part, that's still the ideal for how a consultant should work. However, most industry experts have the data available to them now to realize that there are only a very few proven, universal strategies in any given industry. Further, few companies are adhering to all of those proven strategies. The modern consultant's recommendations are frequently a foregone conclusion: It will be one of the areas they've pre-identified as being a proven strategy.

Many consulting organizations have developed standardized tools (or even form letters) that they cater to the specific company, but the particulars are frequently fairly cookie-cutter. This is beneficial for new entrants to the consulting field, as any previous observations along the lines of "companies that do X tend to be successful" is enough to get started. If a new consultant can identify metrics to determine whether a given company is doing X and can develop specific action steps in order to achieve X, they've got a good start on the basics of consulting.

On the flip side, this means that companies should also be careful. There's very little point in hiring a consultant if the basics aren't already being done. Always double-check the basics before looking for advanced solutions. There's wisdom in starting from the beginning in any self-evaluation.

> **BOX 12.4   Foundations**
>
> As one residential engineer said, "Sure, I can come out and take a look at your foundation. But I gotta be honest, I'm just going to tell you what everyone else has told you: I can't get under your house to look and you should hire someone to dig out your crawlspace. And then I'm going to charge you $700 and go back home."

BONUS LOOT: RESUME BUILDERS—WEBSITES

If professional self-improvement were broken down into two categories, they would be skill development and networking. For example, when trying to leverage current experience into a higher-level job, a professional can either demonstrate they have the skills needed for the promotion or they can network with others in an effort to have their expertise recognized.

There is one activity that can do both of these things at the same time: website administration. In this case, "website" will be used, but it could apply to any number of platforms: LinkedIn, Facebook group management, YouTube video creation, forum administrator, community manager, and so on. Creating a centralized location for people in a particular industry or hobby group to congregate has three large effects:

- Running a website or its equivalent is hard work. In a lot of ways, it's an entrepreneurial venture, requiring the self-discipline and jack-of-all-trades mentality that an entrepreneur needs. The site doesn't have to be the biggest. Even a moderate amount of success is impressive and worth boasting about.
- The people who congregate on such sites aren't just there to talk. They're also looking out for themselves. Finding that the administrator is available for communication will cause those users to be more likely to express interest in a more formal collaboration.
- It's not worth doing unless the subject matter of the site is actually interesting. In that case, there is not a loss scenario, since the development of the skills to run the website and networking with the people on the site are both done in an area of interest.

Some people are comfortable cold-calling for new job opportunities or are naturally able to turn every social interaction into a networking opportunity. But for people who need to slowly ease their way into the process in a comfortable and familiar setting, developing a website and building the community that surrounds it is a solid mechanism.

BONUS LOOT: SOFT SKILLS—FEATURE CREEP MITIGATION
By Fawn Walker

Feature creep is the tendency of project requirements to exceed what was initially projected. It happens when users keep adding additional features to their wish list or when engineers see something new and great that they think they need to work in before the project is complete. Feature creep can cause projects to be delayed, go over budget, or even derail them completely (McMahon & Harris, 2020). Failure to make deadlines can also create a loss of business opportunities, and nearly all software failures can be traced to poor software project management (Pfitzinger, 2012).

Even an iterative methodology, such as scrum that attempts to incorporate change, requires that changes be included in a controlled manner. Scrum methodology involves a series of sprints during which clients are not allowed to interrupt or interfere. Any changes to be made are considered after the sprint is completed. Interference during a sprint could be by a client or even a product owner or scrum manager, unfamiliar with the scrum process, who asks for regular project updates as if they were using a traditional methodology. In fact, in one study, 50% of the projects they investigated had significant issues due to senior management not understanding the scrum process and believing that, as an agile process, they could incorporate change at any time. In other cases, senior management put pressure on the scrum team to shorten its time estimates or to make multiple sprints on multiple projects at the same time (Tanner & Mackinnon, 2015). As discussed earlier in the textbook, when you hire an expert, you need to trust their judgment.

Some ways to mitigate feature creep in traditional methodologies include having a knowledgeable product manager and a team that meets frequently and discuss their progress, including the need to avoid scope creep in all but the most critical issues (Doll, 2001).

Other ways to mitigate feature creep in more traditional methodologies are to ensure that the purpose of the project is clear from the beginning, priorities and deliverables are understood, and the project's critical path is charted and monitored. Any change requests should have a formal process and, if warranted, be scheduled during the proper time (Ray, 2013). Project management recommendations are to define the scope; log any changes that end up being required; notify stakeholders if changes cause deadline problems or need additional resources; monitor the team to ensure they are on track (and not making any changes themselves); set priorities; and, above all, avoid traps that begin with "Well, while you're in there …" "All you have to do is …" or "Hey, it will not take that long."

BONUS LOOT: CERTIFICATIONS—COLLEGE

For a moment, consider a person who is a prodigy. They fly through school and graduate from college at the age of 12. How valuable was their college education? Likely they were self-taught in most of the concepts because there's no way they were lectured fast enough to get anything out of class. On the flip side, consider someone who spent 20 years to get their 4-year degree. What is the value of their degree compared with their practical experience? College degrees have value and merit, but it's important to put them in scope when making hiring decisions.

However, there is also an option at colleges for a "certificate" (not quite a certification, but the root is the same). Certificates tend to be between 12 and 30 credit hours of study (or between 4 and 12 months). They have value because they can be obtained more quickly than a full degree in a subject and can apply to much more granular fields. A full degree needs to have enough people to justify it. But a certificate can be put together from parts of an existing degree until it has enough students to warrant specialized courses.

However, college certificates are frequently a costly option, so what's the trade-off to justify that cost? Effectively, it comes down to acceptability. Almost everyone recognizes what one college class means (by ACE standards, approximately 48 hours of supervised study; Wikipedia, 2020), and that tends to hold sway for longer than other certification types might.

REFERENCES

Belfiore M. (2018, February 26). This real-life tricorder is aiming for store shelves. *Bloomberg*. https://www.bloomberg.com/news/articles/2018-02-26/this-real-life-tricorder-is-aiming-for-store-shelves

Corpuz, J. (2020, March 31). 15 best space watching apps. *Tom's Guide*. https://www.tomsguide.com/us/pictures-story/752-best-space-watching-apps.html

Doll, S. (2001, March 13). Seven steps for avoiding scope creep. *Tech Republic*. https://www.techrepublic.com/article/seven-steps-for-avoiding-scope-creep/

Gachet, A., & Haettenschwiler, P. (2003). Developing intelligent decision support systems: A bipartite approach. *International Conference of Knowledge-Based and Intelligent Information and Engineering Systems*, 87–93. https://link.springer.com/chapter/10.1007/978-3-540-45226-3_13

Google. (n.d.). Google Translate. http://translate.google.com

King, S. (1980). *Firestarter*. Viking Press.

McMahon, M., & Harris, B. (2020, July 30). What is feature creep? *Wise Geek*. https://www.wisegeek.com/what-is-feature-creep.htm

Pfitzinger, P., (2012, October 15). Marathon race-day nutrition and hydration. *Runner's World*. https://www.runnersworld.com/advanced/a20814001/marathon-race-day-nutrition-and-hydration/

Power, D. (2002). Decision support systems: Concepts and resources for managers. *Faculty Book Gallery*. https://pdfs.semanticscholar.org/9939/47b09837c0a94e8b7bf869f104ec11fde32c.pdf

Ray, S. (2013, May 1). Ways to avoid scope creep. *Project Manager*. https://www.projectmanager.com/blog/5-ways-to-avoid-scope-creep

Silverman, L. (2016). The app that aims to gamify biology has amateurs discovering new species. NPR. https://www.npr.org/sections/alltechconsidered/2016/08/06/488830352/the-app-that-aims-to-gamify-biology-has-amateurs-discovering-new-species

Tanner, M., & Mackinnon, A. (2015). Sources of interruptions experienced during a scrum sprint. *Electronic Journal of Information Systems Evaluation*, 18(1), 3. http://ejise.com/volume18/issue1

Wikipedia. (2020). Course credit. https://en.wikipedia.org/wiki/Course_credit

Analysis and Design

The first two parts of this text cover the details of information system operations. The seesaw model is the framework for detailed study of the parts of information systems.

Part III consists of three chapters with the ultimate goal of answering the question "Where do information systems (or other solutions) come from?" For most part, the answer is "We studied the problem systematically and came up with the following requirements." The systematic study process is defined in Chapter 13, the systems development life cycle (SDLC). The activities required to participate in the SDLC are called analysis (Chapter 14) and design (Chapter 15).

Systems Development Life Cycle

VOCABULARY

> Analysis
> Design
> Testing

> Implementation
> Maintenance
> Prototyping

> Effectiveness
> Efficiency

CONCEPTS

> SDLC
> Economies of scale

> Vertical integration
> Diseconomies of scale

> Brook's law
> Agile methods

MAIN STORY: DRIVING PRINCIPLES

1. The SDLC is the basis for almost all process improvement and assessment methodologies.
2. Identifying problems early saves time, money, and reputation.
3. There are other successors to the SDLC that should be considered.

SIDE QUEST: ANALOGY—WATERFALLS (CASCADES)

Imagine being in the Alaskan wilderness, rushing down a cold, crisp stream in one of those big, yellow, inflatable rafts. The river is running quickly, but not dangerously. But the reason you're on this particular river, at this particular point, is that the spring floods make a set of whitewater rapids sections that are particularly exhilarating to traverse. You might be a little trepidatious, but you believe that you're going to have fun over the next 5 days.

However, just because you intend to complete the rafting adventure doesn't mean you have to. Suppose you realize you forgot necessary medication. You forgot to bring a paddle or food or change of clothes. You develop a blinding headache. A small hole gets torn in the raft. A large hole gets torn in the raft. It turns out that the rapids aren't as interesting as they were supposed to be. It turns out that some of the rapids aren't just exhilarating, they're dangerous! One or more of these issues may arise, and there's always the possibility that all of them happen. And then you're just out of luck.

The point is that, at any point over the next 5 days, you could get off the boat. Some unintended issues are more problematic than others: A small hole in the raft is manageable, but missing needed medication is dire. However, every moment you stay on the raft is a moment further from your starting position (where you presumably left said medication).

The obvious connection is that if you spend the next day in the raft and then head home, you're losing 2 or more days. Not only that, but getting to the end of the 5 days of rafting means you likely have transportation waiting to pick you up. Bailing early possibly means a long and exhausting walk back.

This is the premise of what we call the waterfall methodology. There are any number of variations on the base model, but the primary point is that identifying problems sooner rather than later typically results in magnitudes of savings in time and resources. Almost all systems design keeps this method in mind, both in the systems design itself and in the processes that are being designed.

So far, the analogy's been all about the rafters though. What about the water itself? First, it's on one elevation, and then it slowly moves to a lower elevation. And when it finds a rock in its path? It moves around it. And when there's a waterfall? It goes over and keeps going down.

That part of the analogy is boring, but the idea is still sound. The water is going on its path. It doesn't just stop. And that's another of the basic design techniques that good systems designers use: cascading faults. When there's a problem with a process, the process itself should try to recover. Failing that, it should try to continue down a different path. As a last resort, it should fail in a way so that the next time the process occurs the error can be fixed ahead of time. But the key is, things don't just stop and fall apart; they continue as effectively as possible.

MAIN STORY: CASCADE MODEL AND SDLC

The SDLC stands for both the systems development life cycle and the software development life cycle. In information systems, the primary focus is obviously on systems. However, they are both traditional methods of software development. The software development life cycle is still taught, but it is not used very often. The systems development life cycle is still effectively used for a variety of reasons, largely because programming and process design

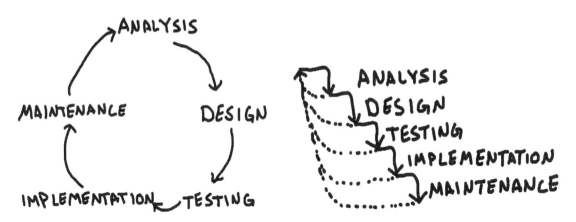

FIGURE 13.1 *SDLC.*   FIGURE 13.2 *Cascade methodology.*

are not the same thing and because governments and corporations do not move as quickly as small teams of programmers.

The SDLC is, essentially, a flowchart that moves circles across five different stages. The SDLC is also frequently referred to as the waterfall (or cascade) methodology. Doing so loses the cyclic nature but gains the emphasis on each step being more substantial than the one before. The question is supposed to be along the lines of "When going down a series of cascades, if you forgot your tent at the top, when is the appropriate time to stop and go get it?" The answer is "As soon as possible; climbing back up a mountain is hard work!" The same thing happens in the cascade methodology. Realizing that there are fundamental problems and returning to the beginning is cheaper, less time consuming, and the best option at each stage of the process. For example, realizing during the prototype phase that a particular computer configuration won't actually meet the needs of users is better than coming to that conclusion during the implementation phase.

Properly, the SDLC is the easier model to use; the cascade is really just there for the purpose of illustrating that each step is more expensive than the previous one. However, it is still occasionally used by managers who prefer that emphasis. The cyclic nature is important, however, as all modern systems processes should be considered cyclical.

SIDE QUEST: EACH STAGE OF THE SDLC

The SDLC has five phases, each of which need to be addressed in detail:

1. Analysis
2. Design
3. Testing
4. Implementation
5. Maintenance

As a side note, in cooking there are what are known as "mother sauces," because they're what all of the other sauces derive from. This SDLC is a sort of "mother cycle" for a large number of other cycles. They may combine, expand, or emphasize different stages. But they are all still variations on the SDLC. This is true for almost every industry, and it would not be a huge stretch to say that understanding the developmental life cycle of a given industry is the key to understanding that industry.

ANALYSIS

Process title:	SDLC Analysis Phase
Responsible party:	Systems analyst
Process goal:	The SDLC analysis phase intends to take an inventory of the current situation within the scope of a particular aspect of a process, workflow, or organization.
Input:	A detailed description of a problem.
Deliverables:	A description of what the current situation is in such a way that the form of a solution is implied.

Steps:

1. The first step in the analysis phase is typically creating this process description. If it exists, it needs to be checked. If it doesn't exist, it needs to be created. At this point, if it's noticed that the process is redundant or not effective, then it's better to stop the process altogether rather than continue through the SDLC with a process that is not beneficial.
2. Everything that's part of the process needs to be inventoried and the parts' relationships diagrammed. There are tools to do this, but that goes into more detail than we need. Typically, a rough diagram is satisfactory.
3. Identify any problems in the routine operation of the process through examination of the diagram, interviews with the workers, or analysis of any pertinent metrics.
4. Describe what the process should be doing that it isn't. For example, when considering the computers issued to employees, every 3 to 5 years the answer will typically be some variation of "The computers need to respond to the employees faster and be more compatible with modern software." For highway construction projects, the answer is frequently, "The roadways need to increase safety parameters by using modernized surface materials and routing options."

DESIGN

Process title:	SDLC Design Phase
Responsible party:	Systems designer

Process goal:	The SDLC design phase takes a description of what needs to be happening in a process and designs a solution that addresses that need.
Input:	A detailed description of the solution.
Deliverables:	A new process.

Steps:

1. The first step of the design phase is to evaluate the description of what the solution should look like. At this point, if that solution isn't attainable (a decision generally arrived at through feasibility analyses), per the waterfall model, it would be a good idea to go back to the beginning of the SDLC rather than wait until a later phase when more resources will have been spent on a flawed process.
2. It's difficult to describe how design should work. There are a number of different methodologies attached to it as well as a number of philosophies regarding how it's supposed to work. But it's part mysterious black box and part persistence.
3. The process should be diagrammed in a formal manner appropriate to the industry. In a pinch, a documentation of steps like this will work for simple processes.
4. The process should be double-checked to ensure that it will accomplish the stated goal of the process as well as address the solution description produced in the analysis phase. Generally, the stakeholders should agree on the process design; this condition (and process) is called buy-in.

TESTING

Process title:	SDLC Testing Phase
Responsible party:	IT, operations, a process redesign committee, or whoever else is appropriate
Process goal:	The SDLC testing phase is an attempt to identify whether a given design will, in fact, be usable in practical setting.
Input:	A designed solution.
Deliverable:	A working test version of the solution.
Options:	The testing phase varies greatly in its execution. Obviously, a pilot testing a radio that operates on a new form of radio wave modulation is going to engage in the testing phase very differently than a construction company testing a new form of sidewalk concrete. However, there are some basic testing methods that will be used in place of steps for this process.

Steps:

1. Prototyping. This is almost always the correct method to use. In the prototyping method, one or a few of the designed solutions are put together and tested. For

computer upgrades, this may mean upgrading one or two computers and testing to see if the upgrades work, followed by a broader test across, say, 1% of all computers at an organization.

2. Cutoff. This is the formal term for no prototyping phase to speak of. Once a new process is designed, it's implemented, and everyone has to use the new version. This is never the correct way to approach it.

3. Phased. In the graduated method, rather than using a small sample like in prototyping, an organization typically enacts the new design in slices of the company. For example, when a roadway is being replaced, it's typically not feasible to replace a single 1-inch-wide strip of the whole road. The road is typically broken down by lanes, and each lane is replaced at a time. Typically, the biggest hurdle in this method is in the large number of resources lost if the testing fails.

4. Simultaneous. In the simultaneous method (sometimes called parallel), a full rollout of the new design is put in place that runs alongside the previous incarnation for a specified period of time. The result is that there are two systems doing the exact same thing. This is typically not an ideal solution, as it tends to result in large amounts of duplication and runs the risk of actions occurring on the old system but not the new one (or vice versa) resulting in poor decision making.

5. A/B. For very small changes, for example to a web page, many companies use A/B testing. Rather than checking to see the performance of the change, they are actively monitoring how clients in the A category perform compared to those in the B category.

6. Graduated. Rather than transition from an old design to a new design by amount, one method of testing does it by function. So, for example, if a company were switching from one Office Suite to a different Office Suite, they might migrate everyone's email over. And if that worked out well, they'd migrate everyone's web browsers. And if that worked well, they'd continue, application by application. This typically draws out the process and runs the risk of not identifying a problem until the very end when it's too late to un-implement all of the changes heretofore accomplished.

IMPLEMENTATION

Process title:	SDLC Implementation Phase
Responsible party:	Typically the same as the testing phase.
Process goal:	The SDLC implementation phase intends to duplicate a success at the prototyping phase across the entire scope and to implement any changes identified during the testing phase.
Input:	Recommendations from the testing phase.
Deliverables:	The solution has been implemented.

Steps: Again, the precise steps are difficult to generalize for an implementation project. WiFi, ethernet, and fiber optic cables all require different skill sets even though they're in the same industry. However, for the most part, there's a push and pull between implementation and testing, with some people preferring more or less testing than standard. A good standard to follow is that there can't be too much testing, and that phasing a rollout in ever-increasing test cases is rarely problematic (for example, 0.01% of the population gets prototyped, then 0.1%, then 1%, then 10%, before final implementation).

MAINTENANCE

Process title: SDLC Maintenance Phase

Responsible party: Users, supervisors

Process goal: The SDLC maintenance phase intends to continue the operation of a process with minimal reduction of efficiency or effectiveness until the next regularly scheduled iteration of the SDLC.

Input: Expected lifetime of implementation.

Deliverable: New problems that need to be solved.

Steps:

1. There's only really one step to the maintenance phase, and that's to use the implemented process appropriately. Everything wears out over time, and there is a consistent, constant improvement in almost all factors across the industry, so eventually the process will need to be reevaluated for relevance. But until then, it's estimated that 90% of the systems development life cycle is in the maintenance phase.

2. One important note, however, is that a second step is also important. Keeping metrics during the maintenance phase allows for the subsequent cycle to improve on any given solution by having real operational data to analyze and look for patterns that might indicate areas to improve the efficiency or effectiveness of the process.

SIDE QUESTS: NEW OR REVISED PROCESSES

There is a difference in design approach between new processes and existing processes. Existing processes should have a wealth of information behind them. If the process were operating in a healthy system, it would have data collected about its efficiency and effectiveness. In that case, revising the process would simply be a matter of either finding situations where the process was inefficient/ineffective and improving those areas or finding situations where the process was particularly efficient/effective and deciding how to make those situations happen more often. An example might be the quarterly review of assembly lines.

If one of them is running slowly, then it's likely that a component of that line just needs to be serviced. On the other hand, someone might notice that the line closest to the loading doors is running more efficiently with fewer errors and suggest that all of the assembly lines might do similarly if the operating temperature were lowered a few degrees.

In a new system the designer is essentially operating blindly. There is intent and goal, but there is no past data to operate on. This is why the modern environment has such a heavy focus on continual improvement (CI). It's okay for a completely new process to run poorly for a short portion of its life span—as long as it's constantly monitored for efficiency and effectiveness. As long as it's improved regularly. As long as a lack of improvement leads to more intense analysis. There is a long list of "as long as" that can apply.

Taking a step back from this twofold split between "new" and "revised" processes, there's a deeper question to ask: Should an organization create a truly new process? For example, if a console video game design company decides to expand into the mobile games market, is that truly a new process? Or is it a revision of the old processes to account for new and changing situations? It is generally a good idea to identify the areas that the company already operates successfully and attempt to duplicate them in the otherwise "new" process?

If there is no aspect of anything the company already succeeds at that can be duplicated in the new process, it's worth asking whether the new process is appropriate for the company. If that video game design company instead decided to open a line of overseas pet stores, where is the advantage in doing so?

This aspect of information systems leads into a conversation on strategic management. But, at this point, it's only important to note that information systems, with its focus on fundamental overview of processes and long-term planning, encroaches on strategic management in a number of ways.

MAIN STORY: TIME, MONEY, CORRECTNESS

There exists a long-standing presumption in any avenue of project management (particularly those with competitive bidding): If a project is broken down into three measurements—time, money, and correctness—then it is frequently true that a project can be done on time, under budget, or correctly (any two of the three). This is just an unofficial rule of thumb to be used in evaluating a process; it shouldn't be taken as a firm rule that can't be overridden.

Consider, though, a DIYer who decides to renovate a room in their house on their own. They might be doing it because they don't have a lot of money, and as a result they buy only cheap supplies. In that case, they either need to wait a long time for good supplies to go on sale, or they'll choose cheap supplies that will harm the quality of their product in the long run. Alternately, if they aren't worried about cost, they could do it quickly and correctly, but it will be comparatively expensive.

Similarly, any project or process can typically be categorized in these three areas. Someone with a focused attention to detail is going to take longer on a process than someone whose philosophy is "get it done and move on." Which areas are emphasized or glossed over has a lot of relation to a company's culture and core competencies. For example, fast-food

---

BOX 13.1   TMC Ternary

An argument could be made that the "best two out of three" mentality is a bit shortsighted and that the measurements should be made on a ternary where each corner is one of time, money, and correctness. Then a process falls closer to one or the other corners and the middle is an average of all of them. However, this produces two problems: (a) there's no win state, as it is emphasizing shortcomings in all three areas, and (b) it becomes much more complicated for what are supposed be much more vague guidelines.

---

restaurants are never going to succeed at emphasizing the quality of their food; it's always cheap and fast. On the other hand, putting "executive" in front of a service implies that it's fast and of quality but will likely suffer if it also tries to advertise how cheap it is.

The takeaway from this rule of thumb should not necessarily be "It's okay to fall short in one area," so much as it should be "This is a method of identifying an area that can be improved on."

There are also some related, formalized rules for addressing these issues:

- Economies of scale. For many processes, there is a synergistic effect in producing more. For example, in a factory that produces sheet metal from refined metal, there is typically a fixed amount of overhead: the cost to purchase the factory's land and building, administrative costs for the executives, and some nonoperational functions, lights, internet, web space, logistical transport, and so on. This means that whether the factory produces 1,000 linear feet of sheet metal an hour or 10,000 linear feet, the cost is spread out across production. For many industries, ramping up production results in a lower per-unit cost and time to product without (ideally) sacrificing quality.

- Vertical integration. For many processes, incorporating source or distribution channels will allow for the same sharing of overhead as in economies of scale. For the sheet metal plant, expanding to incorporate the processing of raw ore into refined metal might provide another synergistic effect. However, vertical integration requires much more planning and investigation to ensure that it is decreasing per-unit cost without sacrificing the total time to product or final quality.

- Diseconomies of scale. There also exist industries for which the opposite of economies of scale exists. For example, an artisan cake baker whose brand is on uniqueness and attention to detail can work for only so long. Taking on additional orders likely means increasing the variable costs, and the increase in those variable costs may be more per unit than the increase in revenue. Industries that are intricate, require a large amount of human interaction, or have fixed timescales tend to suffer from diseconomies of scale.

■ Brooks's law. In software development (and, by extension, related industries) there is an understanding that adding more workers to a project that's already late will not make it go faster. This is for two reasons: The number of people available and the distribution of labor were arranged during the planning phase, and the amount of time it takes to familiarize the new workers to the project is more than the time adding that worker will save.

BOX 13.2   Scaling Economies/Diseconomies

The reality is that economies of scale and diseconomies of scale are the same continuum. Every industry has an optimum production level. Increasing production up to that level will see benefits beyond the cost of the increase in production. And after that point, the benefits will be equal to or lower than the cost. The key is to identify where that point is objectively rather than simply trying to grow for the sake of growth.

SIDE QUEST: EFFICIENCY AND EFFECTIVENESS

There are two ultimate metrics in business and information systems for the effectiveness of any action, process, or project:

■ Effectiveness is primarily a binary (yes/no) measurement to determine whether the goal was accomplished. However, it can be used as a scalar measurement in some cases to determine how effective it was.
■ Efficiency determines the value of the end result compared to the amount of resources expended. This measurement is dependent on effectiveness, but it is not secondary to effectiveness.

Effectiveness and efficiency are the two measurements that should always be considered. When considering effectiveness, it's important to establish goals. When these goals are related to achieving specific numbers, the extent that those numbers are exceeded can also be measured. Examples include President Kennedy's declaration that the United States would land a man on the moon; the process to achieve that was effective. Alternately, NASA's current goal to put astronauts on the south pole of the moon by 2024 could also be measured in effectiveness (i.e., whether it is achieved in 2023 or 2025).

When considering efficiency, the amount of resources expended is vitally important. Going to the moon in 1979 was hugely expensive, with the amount of money allocated to NASA reaching as high as 4.4% of the U.S. GDP in the decade leading up to the landing. Comparatively, the current goal of returning to the moon by 2024 is being planned with budgets closer to 0.5% of the U.S. GDP. To a certain extent, efficiency is not as useful in isolation. It's more useful when it has something to compare to, whether that's a year-over-year comparison, comparing to industry or regional standards, or comparing to pre-allocated resources. Money is the most common measure of efficiency, but time, raw materials, and opportunity costs are also reasonable metrics.

There are a number of different systems of evaluation for processes or tasks: Did the team learn valuable skills? Did the culture of the organization improve? What was the safety rating? However, every reasonable system will include the metrics of effectiveness and efficiency in some form.

MAIN STORY: AGILE METHODS

The SDLC is an older model. It was developed with the presumption (reasonably valid for the era) that any task that requires substantive amounts of planning is going to take months or years to accomplish. As a result, it's what is considered a monolithic model. The task is accomplished in one go, and then there is a possibility of the next version.

Newer iterations of the SDLC introduce some more atomic concepts such as the idea that the SDLC is a cycle; completing the implementation and moving into the maintenance phase implies that there will be a subsequent analysis phase moving into another iteration of the cycle. This is known as the assessment cycle in some industries and the quality improvement cycle in others. Continuous quality improvement is one variation that fills this role.

Another variation of the SDLC is the business process improvement cycle, which is notable in that it's adopted by the Six Sigma model. Rather than the analyze, design, prototype, implement, maintain cycle, BPI uses the terms *define*, *measure*, *analyze*, *improve*, and *control*. Notice that there's less action in this approach. It is more of a meta-cycle (or epi-cycle) that is intended as an observational overlay for other processes. This could be used in each of the SDLC stages to review how the SDLC is working in efficiency or effectiveness. It is also very useful in continuous processes, such as in manufacturing where the SDLC would be too slow or cumbersome (for example, manufacturing plastic bottles at a hundred a minute doesn't really require an analyze, design, prototype, or maintain phase for each different bottle).

Modern successors to the SDLC are typically considered "agile" methods as opposed to "monolithic" methods. The agile method was intended to improve on the SDLC. However, its benefits were pretty obvious, and many of them were subsumed into the industry at large and it largely became genericized (in the same way that *Kleenex* means "facial tissue for blowing one's nose" in common parlance, even though it's technically a brand name). It has largely been replaced as a brand by the scrum methodology.

The agile methodology is intended to avoid the pitfalls of developing a process that takes months or years to come to fruition. Rather than engaging in analysis and development once during the development process, smaller goals are set and the client or end user is engaged in the process on a timescale of weeks in order to ensure that the process has not veered from their goals or that their requirements haven't changed as time goes on. This is especially important in modern industries where entire new technology-based industries have sprung into multibillion-dollar enterprises in just a couple years (for example, blockchain-based technologies or cryptocurrencies).

A variation on agile methodology is called eXtreme methodology (or eXtreme programming). In this methodology, the idea of shrinking the development cycle is taken to an extreme (pardon, eXtreme) degree. In an eXtreme methodology, the development cycle occurs on a daily basis. The intention is that every day, starting on the first day of development, a working product is produced. The working product might be incredibly boring and featureless, but the intention is that if funding dried up or production schedules changed at any moment there would be a product that at least worked even if it wasn't feature complete. This methodology seems to work very well for industries like game programming, app development, or other conceptual models. But it is obviously less beneficial for things like architecture or large-scale projects.

SIDE QUESTS: FULL CIRCLE

Finally, every step in a given process should refer back to the process goal. If it's not supporting the process goal, the step should be critically examined for whether it's necessary (more likely) or if the goal should be critically examined for modification (less likely). Each step should be a direct application of the goal.

Every process should reflect the vision and mission of a department by specifically supporting one of the goals of the department. If it's not an immediate component of one of the departmental goals, it should be examined for fit and necessity (more likely) or the goals of the department should be changed to accommodate the process (less likely). No process should exist save that it solves a relevant problem that is in the purview of the department.

Every department should, in turn, critically analyze their mission, vision, and goals to ensure that they reflect that of the entire organization, that is, broadly, outside of the responsibility of information systems with one exception: The Information Systems Department should be ensuring that their mission, vision, and goals reflect that of the organization as a whole.

Finally, in this section we've been stating "X supports Y" or "A is a part of B." This relationship may be obvious, or it may be more tenuous. However, it's very important that it be explicitly stated. In the entirety of the analysis and design processes, there's a fundamental rule that if it's not written down, it doesn't exist. And this is a vital thing to keep in mind. If nothing else, consider the situation where a central figure leaves the company abruptly; their replacement needs to be able to explicitly see what the connections are, not try to derive them from clues. Explicitly stating, "The process of X supports the departmental goal of Y because it is the first step in the departmental mission of Z," is appropriate and valuable.

BONUS LOOT: BUSINESS FUNCTION—FINANCE

Finance is almost a cautionary tale in the use of information systems to perform job functions. Finance is almost completely driven by quantitative decision making. In fact, in business analytics, *quantitative* almost always means financial analytics. However, for decades, the process of investing has been driven by the speed and accuracy of technological assists in the analytics process.

The first example was the invention of the telegraph. This led to three improvements in the investing process. First, it meant that (nearly) immediate buy-and-sell orders could be made remotely and enacted by representatives locally. Second, it meant that a constant stream of news was available to remote investors. They could see changes with only a delay as long as the time it took to print out the current stock prices (fast) or analyze their movements (not as fast). But that led to a third development: an encoding schema that minimized the amount of printing, which is why stock symbols are such short letter sequences (AAPL is a little faster over telegraph than Apple Inc., but KED is much faster than Kayne Anderson Energy Development), and until recently stocks were priced in 16ths of a dollar.

The next major innovation for financing was the computer, which was effectively a much more robust and fast telegraph. Rather than acting through intermediaries, it was possible for people to make individual decisions on their own. However, for the investing houses, suddenly what was previously a series of decisions made as much on gut instinct as on quantitative analysis became a competition for who had the better analytical models.

Since the computerization of the finance industry, there has been a multilayered hyper-competition between investment groups. This has led to some morbid hilarity in the lengths that they'll go to edge out their competition. The first layer is in the use of more powerful computers to calculate the quantitative predictions faster and more accurately. The second layer is to hire many more quantitative analysts in the hopes that one of them will be more effective at predicting financials (or use better tools to do so).

However, at a certain point, it doesn't matter how fast or good their predictions are: It still takes fractions of a second for the data to get to the New York Stock Exchange. As a result, there has been a measurable change in the cost of real estate physically near the NYSE as investment firms purchase large office suites to house their computational centers. Data may flow at a variation of the speed of light through electric wires, but that means being closer turns fractions of a second into thousandths of a second.

Finally, financial houses are currently experimenting with offensive algorithms. Since every offer, price change, and piece of electricity that flows through the NYSE is input to the various analytics algorithms, it is possible to fake out some of the competition. This is why some analyses of activity on the stock market show repeated offers every millisecond or so to sell low-value stocks at inflated prices, or alternately to buy high-priced stocks for pennies. The offensive algorithms (or rather, the algorithm designers through their creations) are trying to determine whether they can detect any response in the activity of a competing investment firm as a result.

So, to a certain extent, process design, analytics, and a rampant reliance on technology has resulted in a situation in finance where nobody can win by playing the game properly. The best solution, as in almost every situation, is to determine a way to change the game so that the innovator has an immediate first-move advantage that outweighs any incremental advantage by the larger players.

BOX 13.3   Design Thinking

Alan Cooper (1998), in his book *The Inmates Are Running the Asylum: Why High-Tech Products Drive Us Crazy and How to Restore the Sanity*, describes an aspect of software development that deserves consideration. He discusses the relationship between application providers and application users or purchasers. He posits that in the majority of companies, the application providers consist of the engineering or programming function and the business function. He proposes that the relationship could be significantly improved, along with the usability of the products and thus sales, by inserting another group. He refers to this third group as the design group, people who identify what users want so that the engineering group can provide the capability and the business group can speak to viability. Despite being 20 years old, the text offers some insight into relating to end users, as well as the value of brand loyalty. His process of determining user wants is very similar to some of the research from Stanford, along with that of the Interaction Design Foundation, on design thinking. This is also a spiritual successor to the SDLC.

BONUS LOOT: RESUME BUILDERS—COMMUNITY ORGANIZATIONS

One of the things that separates a post-modern business from those of the past is an emphasis on social responsibility. Just like the soldiers at Nuremberg couldn't say, "I was just following orders," postmodern businesses realize that they can't say, "We acted unethically, immorally, or illegally because our primary goal is to make money." Instead, the emphasis has almost completely changed from "increasing stockholder wealth" to "maximizing stakeholder value." Wealth to value implies that there are more important considerations than money, even though money is still important. Stockholder to stakeholder recognizes that a company has a moral obligation to its employees, its stockholders, its suppliers and distributors, its customers, down through to the individuals who live in the community around it (although the various levels of obligation are not the same or standardized). Increasing to maximizing implies that it's not enough for a company to do well; it has to do its best. There is a constant need to improve and ensure that if there are people the company could be helping, it is helping.

And if none of this is true for a particular company, do you want to work for that company? It could be argued that it's a valid decision to work only for certain companies based on their history of returning value to the community around them.

One way to ensure that you are attractive to the sort of company you want to work for is to have consistent and demonstrated community involvement. Obviously, higher levels of responsibility are more impressive than lower levels. But even volunteering at a local shelter that provides meals to people who are food insecure is effective. It's most important to demonstrate time spent and commitment; donating money or goods is typically not enough.

There is one more layer that provides an ultimate resume builder: utilizing your industry-oriented skills to benefit a local organization. Some industries have this requirement built in, such as law or medicine. But for industries where this is not the case, it is patently obvious which employees are societally minded, and organizations that place a high emphasis on social responsibility will be drawn to that. It follows that, for a socially responsible company, a recommendation of someone who was an excellent pro bono information systems consultant from a well-regarded nonprofit organization should carry more weight than the recommendation of someone who did an excellent job for pay from a well-regarded for-profit company.

Finally, this is one of the best ways to transition from one industry to another. Just like people who want to be game programmers should program games on their own time and produce a portfolio, it's much easier for a non–information systems person to demonstrate qualification in information systems by pointing to their volunteer work in the industry. Changing industries is frequently a difficult and frustrating process, but this method is more effective than presenting a complete lack of experience and hoping someone will take a chance.

BONUS LOOT: SOFT SKILLS—ASSESSMENT

This chapter is about the SDLC, but it's also about assessment cycles. Employers want to find employees who are actually passionate about the assessment cycle. Assessments aren't intended to be superficial nodes to regulations or fads; they're intended to identify real issues that need improvement.

However, to a certain further extent, personal assessment is necessary. One of the common questions that people ask in interviews is "Where do you see yourself in 5 years?" They're looking for someone who has a goal, knows the general pattern of how to get there, and is intent on learning what they don't know and addressing those things. But that requires a consistent self-questioning about what's missing.

BONUS LOOT: CERTIFICATIONS—PROCESS DESIGN

SDLC, agile methodology, scrum, and design thinking all have certifications that indicate a person has achieved a certain level of expertise. These are good certifications to have in many different industries; however, there is one big catch: They are platform specific.

Platform implies a certain mode of thinking and adherence to certain tools and methods. Picking one over others is not problematic, but it does sometimes become a limiting factor. For example, a person who becomes an expert at Linux computer systems is more likely to be ignored by a company or department that primarily uses Windows. Even though almost all of the concepts are the same, because the processes are different there's a certain esprit de corps attached to a particular platform and a certain snobbishness that creeps in.

As a result, sometimes it's a good idea to begin in what's considered a "platform-agnostic" approach. This text, for example, is platform agnostic. It isn't taking a side between SDLC and agile, between R and Python, or among Windows, Linux, and Apple. The basics of information systems are, themselves, platform agnostic between both technical platforms and management philosophies. That doesn't mean that specialization can't occur later, just that in many cases it's best to start with broad theory and the basics.

One organization that offers relatively platform-agnostic certifications is ASQ, the American Society for Quality. Whatever the business field, ASQ has a process improvement certification related to it. ASQ emphasizes quality improvement as a design philosophy, and their certifications center around metrics and methods for highlighting the expertise of quality improvement professionals. It's worth visiting their site and reviewing what they have available.

REFERENCES

Cooper, A. (1998). *The inmates are running the asylum: Why high-tech products drive us crazy and how to restore the sandity.* Pearson Education.

Systems Analysis

VOCABULARY

> Process

> Analysis and design

CONCEPTS

> Governance

MAIN STORY: DRIVING PRINCIPLES

1. Simple structures in systems are frequently better than complex structures.
2. The scope and frame of reference for any process should be the process itself.
3. Oversight of any process should have a singular point of contact.

SIDE QUEST: ANALOGY—MARATHONS

Imagine a marathon run by a well-trained, world-class runner. While any marathon is going to take a lot out of any runner, there's a difference between an amateur and someone who has trained to perform in a marathon such that they can expect completion without complication. For the majority of the population, completing the marathon itself is unlikely (and performance assessment would be made in the amount of completion).

We're going to assume that this highly trained paragon of marathon running is reliable and can complete it. But is that enough to complete a marathon? The outcome is unknown. We have to consider many additional influential factors.

A 26.2-mile marathon will likely need route planning that blocks traffic: Someone needs to block the traffic appropriately. This means that they'll need to have the appropriate permits, find alternate routes for traffic, deploy traffic diverting devices, notify other interested authorities (for example, the fire department and emergency rescue), and perform other such tasks.

Someone must be responsible for hydration. A marathon requires a number of way stations along the route that dispense water, have spots for personal hygiene, and provide an on-duty medical professional who can identify problems before they become major ones. Someone must staff each station, someone has to monitor each station, someone has to source the supplies, and so on.

And in the context of our analogy, we'll identify a third issue: medical support. Running a marathon is hard on the human body. At the outset, it's dietetically difficult to consume and store enough calories to support a runner for the whole distance. As a result of these stresses, it's likely for a person to encounter medical difficulties that require immediate medical attention. Someone must be available to visit any given spot on the route and provide first aid until evacuation to a medical facility.

But consider our well-trained runner. None of this is within the runner's scope of responsibility. Traffic planning is caused, in effect, by the marathon runner, and activities happen within the traffic planner's purview before being realized on the marathon route. The planning, operation, and staffing of the water stations are necessary processes to allow the marathon runner to continue along the route, but all of that happens outside the bounds of the route before coming back to affect the marathon itself. Finally, the medical professional takes injured runners to medical facilities and then comes back—out and back, out and back.

The idea here is that the marathon runner we've created is representing some organizational process. Just like this marathon runner is trained and well versed in running marathons, our process must come to completion. But organizational processes are typically complicated enough to require multiple steps or interactions, and they need to operate across several different departments. Information systems aid and often facilitate complicated organizational processes.

But again, the marathon runner feels that running the marathon is the primary task (process). Ancillary steps (tasks) need to be initiated by the primary process. Of course they must be completed in their own frame of reference and then come back to the primary process. Deliverables and action items go out and then come back—out and back, out and back.

MAIN STORY: BACK TO BASICS

So far, there have been some basic definitions lacking. That was partially done intentionally and partly out of necessity. Information systems as a field has a large number of low-level concepts that need to be covered before the big picture can be addressed. The seesaw model is a fine description of information systems, but it's a model from the outside looking in to see what all the parts are. In reality, the parts all mesh together and defy rigid distinctions. Is an employee deciding to use a cell phone to make an emergency call to their supervisor based on the instructions of a process an example of hardware, software, communications, people, process, decision, or data? In a production environment, distinguishing between them is a conceptual tool rather than a rigid prescription.

However, at this point, all of the pieces have been surveyed. Each portion of the seesaw model has been given individual treatment, data has been discussed in much more depth as the primary vehicle for any system to affect a change in the outside world, and the organization as a system has been projected as a set of operational, managerial, and strategic roles. So now, from an inside perspective, information systems can be recast as consisting of its base unit: the process.

Earlier, it was discussed that the left side of the seesaw model was part of information technology, a subcomponent of information systems. The people side was only part of information systems in the sense that people fulfilled a role, not as the people themselves. The part that truly allowed information systems to contribute to the higher function was processes. The systems development life cycle is the base method for developing and refining these processes, but the contribution of information systems can be narrowed even further. The prototyping, implementation, and maintenance stages may act in conjunction with an information systems department, but they really belong to experts in the specific operational field related to them (even installing computers or communications technology requires technical experts, which may coincide with but is still distinct from information systems).

As a result, the biggest contribution to the organization at large is in the SDLC stages of analysis and design. In fact, systems analysis and design (A&D) is its own subfield that crosses many disciplines. However, information systems experts should, effectively, be experts in A&D. Regardless of whether it's quality improvement, information security, training, information technology, or any other subfield of information systems, the overarching goal should be the establishment and improvement of process through formal analysis and design methods.

MAIN STORY: WHAT IS A PROCESS?

The pieces have already been discussed. In Chapter 13, examples of processes (each of the five stages of the SDLC) were provided. Therefore, some higher-level details on the purpose and intent of processes needs to be discussed, dancing around the concept of systems analysis. This dancing around rather than immediately stating it is partly because, in real-world situations, systems analysis methodologies are readily available, and partly because, for those who are not information systems experts, understanding the higher-order shape of a process is more important.

The term *process* implies that something is being changed. A process might be defined as any series of activities where the primary goal is achieved through that series of activities—at the beginning of the series of activities that goal is not achieved, but at the end of the series of activities it is likely achieved. To make things more complicated, there may be multiple goals. This definition implies several things: A process might be considered with regard to both tangible (such as building a car: at the beginning is a pile of steel and rubber, and at the end is a pile of steel and rubber in a specific shape) and intangible items (such as verifying the measurements made by a remote sensor: at the beginning are unverified measurements, and at the end are verified measurements).

The reason we encapsulate a given set of steps into a conceptual process is to provide the conceptual infrastructure to address it. One person might gather sand, another person might melt that sand, another person might oversee robots that cut that sand, and all of these people are separate individuals with their own agency unrelated in any deeper sense. And yet, we need to know that they're producing integrated circuits; we need the ability to conceptualize that process as a whole.

We consider a process in two different frames of reference. From the outside, we typically see a process as a black box; that is, it is singular in its presentation and we don't break it down further. This allows us to consider a series of inputs and outputs as needed to accomplish the process's task. From inside the process, we would consider each of the steps and ways to modify them to make the entire process more efficient or effective.

One important note is that a process does not happen on its own. There is a tendency to assume that because a process is in place, it will just happen on its own. On the contrary, it must be consistently initiated, whether by oversight, action, or just pushing a button (or some combination thereof). This fallacy is particularly prevalent in large organizations where even high-level employees are unable to see all of the parts of a complex process.

In a very real sense, the flow of information from one part of the organization to another satisfies the definition of a process. As a pile of raw apples moves from receiving to the juice factory processing line hopper, that's a process. As a customer support specialist receives a phone call and produces a report that requests a technician visit the customer's house, that's a process. As a customer sees a thing they want and decides to trade money with a cashier to get it, that's a process. Whether it's a physical item or some documentation, the fact that it was produced as output using a fixed series of steps and based on a defined input makes it a process.

SIDE QUEST: INFORMATION FLOW

When an information systems specialist discusses information, they tend to be doing so within a broader framework. Narrowly, an information flow means information itself, the true facts distilled from data. But broadly, by the time any given process reaches a systems person (either an existing process or a proposed one), even tangible items like concrete or apples or money are just icons on a large planning document. For the information systems specialist, everything that occurs within an organization is framed as information flowing from one part of the organization to another.

To a certain extent, information systems (both the discipline and the organizational department) is practically concerned with this information flow. Information should move freely through an organization in its proper channels. Information silos contribute to a knot of problems that reduce the free flow of information to all parts of an organization. A process view says that product is smoothly being brought into the organization, processed effectively and efficiently, and taken out. It's to the benefit of the information systems specialist to consider this product information because it allows the specialist to consider a process that includes both tangible and intangible components and to treat them equally.

For example, if a process has the goal of accepting a shipment of broken, discarded, or waste glass for melting and recovery, there should be a portion of the process that examines the glass to be sure it's acceptable. But if the person who's responsible for that portion looks at the glass and realizes that the shipment consists of plastic pieces, there's a problem. Which is more important in that process: the actual shipment of glass or the notification by the employee that the input is in the wrong format? The process needs both to consistently run successfully.

SIDE QUEST: PROCESS DEFINITION

There are many methodologies available to assist with the development and planning of information flow. However, like any product, the methodologies will come and go over time. It's the basic features they share that are important. There are some basic approaches to process design that will consistently improve almost any process. A full discussion of these improvements is an entire field of study on its own (systems engineering or logistics). However, there are a couple of important points that should be available to everyone.

The most important is to consider each process as a separate entity. It has a defined start point and a defined end point. It has a defined input and a defined output. We've discussed this several times already, but the key is that additional term *defined*. A process can't operate smoothly and effectively without constraints and definition. Consider the following examples:

- A military drill sergeant who says, "You're going to do push-ups until I get tired!"
- A boss who knows what an employee needs to do in order to get a promotion but who is purposefully vague so that the employee will overperform out of desperation
- Writing a research paper whose topic is just "write a paper"

All these examples have in common an ill-defined start, end, or process point. Consider, instead, the following examples:

- A military drill sergeant who says, "Give me 100 push-ups as a response to your unsafe handling of military ordnance"
- A boss who provides an employee with specific target metrics, performance goals, and time frames that allow the employee to appropriately develop a plan to attain promotion in accordance with the expectations of the company
- Writing a research paper whose topic is specified as answering a specific question, with given target constraints such as reference count and word count

Each of these examples could be changed in response to the specifics of the situation. But it should be immediately obvious that there will be a higher success rate in attaining the goals of the process (don't play with guns, perform excellent work, write a research paper, respectively) in the latter set of scenarios than in the former.

Professionals often need to document—as opposed to defining—the elements of a process. A written piece of paper with explicitly stated sections like "Process Title," "Responsible Party," "Process Goal," "Prerequisites" (a form of input), "Deliverables" (a form of output), and "Steps" is a good approach. One fallacy that many people engage in is the presumption that everyone should just know their jobs. But the reality is that even people who know their jobs probably can't interact with each other and agree on precise details.

MAIN STORY: PROCESS CONCIERGE

All processes should have someone assigned to the process who is directly responsible for that process. Consider a restaurant where one of the waitstaff goes home before one of their customers. Who's responsible for cleaning the table? There's almost always a specific process for cleaning the table (remove dishes, wipe table, wipe seats, rearrange seats and table decorations). But who's responsible for cleaning the table of the person who left?

Obviously, everyone benefits from the table being cleaned. There's another table that can seat more customers, resulting in more tips for the waitstaff. Customers are less likely to be pleased with their dining experience if they're sitting next to a dirty table. And yet, there's typically a presumption that one shouldn't have to clean up someone else's mess.

The immediate solution to this is typically a busser. Rather than requiring waitstaff to determine for themselves who should clean what, the process of table cleaning is given a specific role and there is a person responsible for cleaning all the tables. If a table stays dirty for too long, nobody has to ask, "Who is going to clean this?" There's a predetermined answer.

Similarly, all processes need to be analyzed, initiated, operated, completed, verified, maintained, documented, and assessed by someone. The car-buying industry excels at this approach. When a customer sets foot onto a lot, they are immediately interfaced with by the first available salesperson. That salesperson is then responsible for every aspect of interacting with that customer: showing them cars, supervising test drives, negotiating terms, setting up financing, cleaning the car, initiating post-sales satisfaction follow-ups, and so on. There should never be any question of where a customer is in the car-buying process because there is a single person who they have been interfacing with. That person is guiding them through the car-buying process, and that person should know the exact state of the process. One industry term for this is *concierge*.

When we discuss the idea of a "process," we are typically discussing it in one of two ways, depending on context. For example, when a customer named Jim enters the car lot and is approached by a salesman named Michael, that's a different conversation than when customers enter the car lot and are approached by salespeople. The process might mean the concept of a hypothetical situation in which the process occurs (the process definition), which should be broadly assigned to either a position or a department (salespeople in the example). But the process might also mean the specific implementation in a specific instance (i.e., nonhypothetical), in which case there should be someone who's responsible for that instance (i.e., Michael in the example).

As in the process definition, it is a professionally appropriate decision to explicitly associate processes with their concierges. Each role or organization should have a list of the organizational processes they are responsible for. This list can be included with the mission, vision, and mission statements and is arguably just as important. Alternately, each process should explicitly state who is ultimately responsible for its successful conclusion (the "Responsible Party" section of the process definition).

SIDE QUEST: PROBLEM SOLVING

A problem-solving approach to process development is not the only approach; however, it does provide a good model and self-correction for process development. Using this approach, one would assume that every process can do one of two things:

1. Identify a problem
2. Solve a problem

If the process just exists, but it doesn't identify a problem or solve a problem, the question should be, "Why does the process exist?" Any given problem might have several solutions. But if the process doesn't do something tangible (or measurable), the organization likely runs more efficiently without including it. This is true regardless of whether (a) there is a person responsible for the process, (b) it's primarily focused on machinery, or (c) it just produces a small amount of conceptual complexity.

This demarcation between problem identification and problem solving resonates frequently through large numbers of industries. As an example, here's how the demarcation applies to the research fields. In the research fields (reflecting in analytics and business intelligence), there is a distinction between qualitative and quantitative research. Quantitative is a descriptor that presumes something related to numbers (quantity) and typically connotes large data sets and rigid adherence to numerical measurements. Qualitative is a descriptor that presumes something not expressible in numbers and typically connotes words or long-form prose. Note that this distinction is a connotation: The dividing line changes back and forth as the relative capability of human researchers and assistive computer research devices change.

One model of differentiating these two types of research is that quantitative research has a problem and produces data to solve that problem whereas qualitative research produces data to find the problem. Note that the sequence is opposite: In quantitative scenarios, the problem leads to data collection; however, in qualitative scenarios, data collection leads to the problem. Alternately, it might be said that quantitative information is solution driven, but qualitative information is problem driven.

In practice, our demarcation divides processes into two conceptual groups. The first group is responsible for completing actions, performing tasks, and producing deliverables.

The second group is responsible for measuring the efficiency or effectiveness of other processes and setting limits that indicate when a problem might occur.

Extending our model to a manufacturing setting, a quantitative process would be the production of bolts on an assembly line. Qualitative processes would be weighing the bolts, counting the number of completed bolts, and monitoring customer complaints about the bolts. At first glance, it seems like quantitative processes are the more important process, because they're actually doing something. But at second glance, it may seem like qualitative processes are more important because there are so many assessments required by any given task. But, practically, they are both necessary to ensure a process is running efficiently and effectively.

MAIN STORY: SUPPORT FUNCTION

Ultimately, the most important thing to remember is that all of information systems is a support function. Information systems, information technology, process design, assessment, or any of the other subdomains cannot drive an organization. Process analysis and design should work in conjunction with the people engaging in those processes, not dictating what they need to do but describing and offering suggestions.

A company can't run on metrics; the metrics inform and lead to further decision. An information technology department should not tell the rest of the company what can or cannot be done with technology. It could describe technical limitations or offer alternate solutions, but it's important to remember that information technology experts and systems experts are experts in IT and systems, not the functions that are being supported.

Information systems is a support function. It's an important support function, but it's most effective facilitating other functions, not driving or limiting them.

BONUS LOOT: BUSINESS FUNCTION—MANAGEMENT

There are a large variety of tools available for managers, but there are three functions that tend to be of most interest to general purpose managers. Typically, managers want some method of tracking and delineating the processes that their teams are engaged in, then they need tools that provide them with the ability to track the effectiveness and the efficiency of their teams.

The initial tool set for almost every manager is a word-processing document that lists process information in flat text. Alternately, managers tend to create a spreadsheet that includes lists of performance metrics and calculations to create a record of team performance. The problem is that both of these are time consuming and laborious to monitor and update. When a team member leaves, their metrics have to be purged; when a new team member arrives, they have to be manually added.

The next stage that most managers tend toward is a purchased software package of some sort. Since every manager needs to keep track of what's being done and every manager needs to track team performance, there is no end to the software packages available. Unfortunately, choosing among them is difficult.

Typically, one of the most effective ways to make this decision is to have it solve a secondary problem as well. For example, if the team needs a new method of intra-office collaboration, it's possible to select software that also has general management support tools built into it. Most chat utilities include ways of creating those interactions, or there are wiki varieties that produce this functionality.

However, the most effective method for producing these forms of analysis is an enterprise-wide solution. The organization's IT Department should have provided a software suite for general business purposes. Typically, it will include some form of accounting functionality, investment tracking, human resources databases, training, and so on. One of the components (built in or separate purchase) is typically a method to perform the standards tracking that needs to occur over time. The reason this is generally considered the best method is that every team is performing the same way and can therefore directly compare the results of their analyses.

BONUS LOOT: RESUME BUILDERS—GOVERNANCE

Governance is the process of making sure that an organization is doing what it's supposed to be doing and in the manner that it is supposed to be doing it. For a corporation, this typically means having a board of directors who are not direct employees of the corporation but instead are representatives of the stockholders. Their goal is to make sure that the company is making money for its owners and not wasting it.

This task has developed both a boon and a problem in the modern era. Because so much of the organization is information oriented, it means the organization is able to provide an enormous amount of data to its board of directors. On the other hand, because the organization is information oriented, there's frequently too much data and potential issues get drowned out.

Systems analysis is one of the big areas that helps modern governance, as it allows for the assessment cycle to continue. It can also demonstrate where the progress is happening in a manner that can become standardized across departments and processes.

BONUS LOOT: SOFT SKILLS—ADMITTANCE OF FAULT

Fault is a tricky thing. When getting into a traffic accident, the general recommendation is to never apologize for the accident, because it implies fault.

This advice is also often repeated to women (with the biased and unfair assumption that women are more prone to senseless apology): Never apologize. If they're late for a meeting, they should say, "Thank you for waiting for me." Acknowledge, but don't apologize.

However, other schools of thought note that true, heartfelt apology for a specific issue is something that causes other people to increase estimation. When something is small and obviously someone's fault, an apology, working to fix the issue, and correction of behavior tend to go further than a refusal to ever admit fault.

Both approaches are likely viable, but it's important to make a decision about how to handle mistakes. Everyone makes them, but pretending they didn't happen is definitely the wrong solution.

Systems Design

VOCABULARY

> Work breakdown structure

> Atomicity

> ERP

CONCEPTS

> Gantt charts

> Users

MAIN STORY: DRIVING PRINCIPLES

1. A Gantt chart is an industry-standard graph that all professionals should be able to read and produce.
2. It's easier to change hardware than people, but people are more adaptable to uncertain situations.
3. Good process design involves identifying stakeholders and soliciting their input.

SIDE QUEST: ANALOGY—CIVILIZATION

Nature documentaries always have a narrator who says things with gravitas. Every minor twist and turn of the mundane drama of animals interacting with each other gets anthropomorphized in an effort to draw the attention of the viewer. A common refrain is something along the lines of "and, having lost the battle, the forlorn male is banished from the herd. His chances of survival alone are low in this harsh environment."

An organization is a bit like a civilization in microcosm. Throughout the entirety of civilization, there has been a constant tug of war between individual freedoms and safety in numbers. It even goes back to before civilization. Humans are social creatures. Being around others is hardwired into human instinct. However, with intelligence comes self-awareness and the desire to distinguish oneself.

This push and pull is what makes systems design so important. Just like a civilization's laws and rules need to be codified over time in order to smooth out the interactions with a billion individuals trying to distinguish themselves, an organization needs to have its intentions, processes, and goals designed and structured in such a way as to objectively orient its members.

MAIN STORY: GANTT CHARTS

In systems analysis, there are some basic tools that can be used across most industries. The same thing happens in systems design. Designing a system and designing a process can be generalized across industries. There are a number of design methodologies available; however, one of the simplest is a Gantt chart. This chart was developed by Henry Gantt, who lived from 1861–1919. It's a pretty old category of chart, but it's still ubiquitous.

The first step to creating a Gantt chart is called a work breakdown structure (WBS). A work breakdown structure contains the logical divisions of a task, preferably three to five but definitely fewer than a dozen (depending on the type of work). These steps are then listed and numbered roughly in order of typical completion. This is not a hard requirement, as it becomes impossible in more complicated processes. But generally, listing the work breakdown structure chronologically is the easiest.

Each of these steps is then broken down into their logical sections as well, and these will be listed in a numbered list as hierarchically subordinate to the first set of steps. Each of these substeps would then be broken down further and further. Every step can be broken down further into infinite levels of micromanagement. However, the appropriate stopping point is the point of "atomicity." Atomicity implies something can't be broken down any further, but in this case it means that it doesn't make any sense to break it down any further.

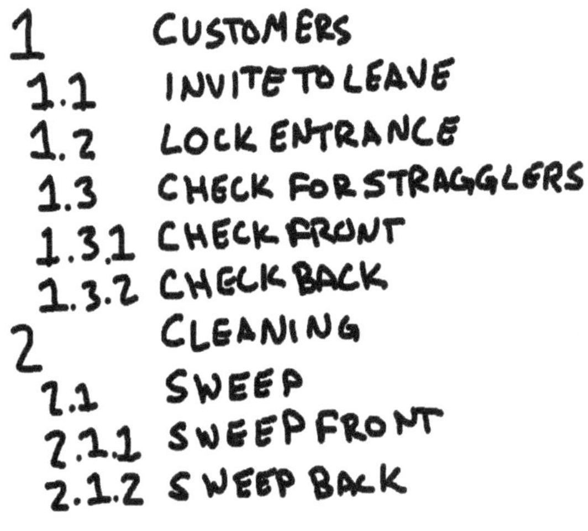

A work breakdown structure is, in itself, a useful tool. Two examples of when a work breakdown structure is appropriate are repetitive tasks and tasks of uncertain duration. End-of-day closing

```
1      CUSTOMERS
 1.1    INVITE TO LEAVE
 1.2    LOCK ENTRANCE
 1.3    CHECK FOR STRAGGLERS
 1.3.1  CHECK FRONT
 1.3.2  CHECK BACK
2      CLEANING
 2.1    SWEEP
 2.1.1  SWEEP FRONT
 2.1.2  SWEEP BACK
```

FIGURE 15.1 *WBS example.*

> **BOX 15.1   Atomicity**
>
> Atoms are the smallest unit of an element. Breaking an atom of copper down any further makes it not copper any more. This concept of the "atomic level" occurs frequently in information systems and computer science. It denotes when something is the smallest unit in a task that has units of varying sizes. For example, an atomic transaction in a database means that it's something that can't happen by parts (for example, writing half of a new entry into a table doesn't conceptually make sense). An atomic-level instruction in a machine is one that has been hardwired into the processor as one of the basic instruction sets.
>
> In information systems, an atomic-level process is one that is a logically consistent event that has no cohesion if broken down further. For example, if a building contractor was bricking the side of a building and planned for it to take 10 days, it might make sense to break "brick side of building" into 10 individual tasks. But since they're all the same routine and monotonous task, it likely doesn't make sense to break it down any further than "a day of brickwork."

processes at a restaurant are an example of a repetitive task for which a work breakdown structure is appropriate. The closing process could be broken down into

1. customers
2. cleaning
3. stocking
4. cash registers
5. locking up;

then it could be broken down further. There's not much need for more structure than this, since all of the tasks need to be done and there ought to be a structure to know if they've been done. Order and timing are less important.

Similarly, even for project tasks, a work breakdown structure is useful when the task is ill-defined, the breakdown is ongoing, or the timing is not determined. A good example of this is in game design. Many game design companies put together an internal wiki with a still-developing work breakdown structure of all the parts of the game. Employees are then responsible for noting which portions of the work breakdown structure they've worked on during the day and marking off tasks that have been completed, tasks they'll work on next, and so on. Largely, it just gives structure to what may not be tasks that have clear structure.

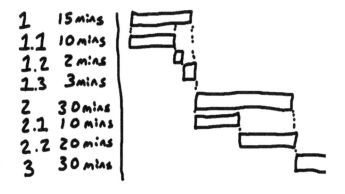

FIGURE 15.2 *Gantt chart example.*

The difference between a WBS and a Gantt chart is that a Gantt chart has two extra requirements:

- An estimated time for each atomic task: Where does this estimate come from? Typically it's based on how long the task has taken in the past. If it's a new task, it's based on industry standards. If there are no industry standards, it's based on someone's expertise. If no one is expert in this area, it's a broad guess based on common sense (along with a recommendation to find someone with some experience in the task to aid in planning).
- Each atomic task needs its set of prerequisites: The majority of tasks will just have a prerequisite of the task before it: 2.7.8.9 cannot start until 2.7.8.8 has completed. However, not all tasks will be sequential. Some may have more than one prerequisite, and others may not have any prerequisites at all.

From here, the Gantt chart is drawn on a theoretically infinitely wide chart that is just tall enough to hold a list of each task. The work breakdown structure is listed on the left side (traditionally, this is not in outline format, rather each task is numbered (e.g., 3.5.6.2.4)). On the right should be a bar for each atomic task of proportional length. The chart's Y-axis represents the WBS and the X-axis represents time. The rule is that each task's bar cannot start (the left edge of the bar) before the end (the right edge of the bar) of all prerequisite tasks. Each higher nonatomic task's bar is then the length between the earliest subtask's start and the latest subtask's end.

Practically, this is a silly list of instructions on creating a Gantt chart. The reality is that a program like Microsoft Visio or one of the many free online utilities should be used. Given a work breakdown structure, task times, and prerequisites, the Gantt chart will automatically be developed.

Creating a work breakdown structure or a Gantt chart for each portion of a process is an appropriate part of the systems design process.

SIDE STORY: THE SYSTEM PROCESS

Many organizations suffer from a complicated intermeshing of a set of holistic processes that developed over time with no governing or planning effort involved. This makes it difficult to track down the status of a given process. For example, in a custom manufacturing industry, there's frequently a large divide between the production floor and the operations staff. The operations staff knows where the order is, and the production floor knows where the production is; however, if there's no communication between them, they can't explain the full extent of what's going on.

In Chapter 14, it was noted that there should be a process concierge. That is, any given process should have someone who knows everything about that process and can answer for where things stand at any given time. For example, since a salesperson makes an initial sale, it's probably reasonable (as an example, not the definitive and only way to handle it) to decide that the salesperson is responsible for following through with the order fulfillment until the customer is satisfied.

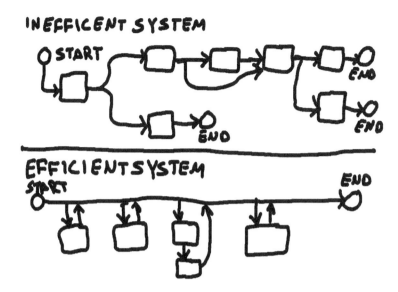

FIGURE 15.3 *Inefficient and efficient systems.*

Just like a work breakdown shows broad tasks as composed of smaller tasks, process design should take into account this interrelation of tasks. One very efficient method of structuring a system is with a central system process that is responsible for tracking all orders, clients, employees, and processes—everything else is a set of subprocesses that extend from it. This system process is too complicated for an individual to be the process concierge, which is why there are several types of programs that will do so. This type of system is called an ERP, or enterprise resource planning application.

An ERP, essentially, takes over all of the functions of an organization and begins to structure the rest of the processes around itself. This centralizes all of the information about the data and, for example, allows a salesperson to know stage of production a custom item is at. Another example of an ERP demonstrating intricate knowledge of myriad tasks is with shipping companies. Frequently, it's possible to check in with a serial number on a shipped package to see where it is, which distribution center it is at, if it's out with a delivery driver, or if it's sitting on a front porch.

ERP systems are complex systems requiring a specialty in implementation and maintenance. More than acknowledging that they exist and are frequently beneficial, a custom consultation with an ERP provider is probably a better source of how an ERP can be applied in a specific situation.

MAIN STORY: REDESIGNING HARDWARE OR PEOPLE

Returning to the seesaw model, we have stated that our goal in the model is to be balanced around the data. Typically, a system is modeled around its processes. This means that the sections on process and/or software are the easiest to change. Changing a process is as "easy" (it's not really) as changing the steps on the process design document. Changing software is as "easy" as downloading an update. But, as with all conceptual matters, it gets more complicated in the real world. Let's address each of the five areas in turn:

1. Changing hardware is typically expensive and requires manual intervention, and it frequently requires a change in software to accommodate.
2. Changing software frequently requires a minor change in how it is used but an often large change in how people perceive its user interface changes.
3. In terms of content, don't change the data. It's there to reflect a series of true facts. It may, however, be necessary to reorganize or relocate data or see the other areas.
4. Changing processes changes how people engage in the process. This is the subject of this chapter.
5. People are slow to change and update. For the most part, these changes are the province of human resources.

It is a general rule that changing hardware and software is expensive but not complex. Changing the data is rarely changing the data; it is typically the same data but either with additional attributes or different software/processes surrounding it. Changing a process is resource inexpensive and primarily bears a time cost. But people don't change easily or quickly.

The result of this is not that nothing can be done. However, it does suggest that in anything but the smallest organizations, change needs to be managed. A good start is predicting changes early and often. If a person is going to be expected to learn a new program or utilize a new interface, they should be notified, in detail, of the change as early as possible. Immediately prior to the change, the employee should be repeatedly trained on what the new expectations will be, what they will look like, and how they should utilize them. Even after the change, repeatedly affirming their positive use of the new system and documenting why their proper utilization is resulting in positive change will improve adoption rates.

SIDE QUEST: USER INPUT

Ultimately, we've established that the Information Systems Department never drives the development or direction of an organization. At best, the Information Systems Department acts as an expert advisor for what's possible and what's advisable. But, if it's not the Information Systems Department, then who is responsible for determining development or direction?

The typical answer to this is the user. Anyone who is going to be using a particular process or piece of software should be responsible for knowing how it works. The classic example is the apocryphal story of a university in Alaska. They needed to replace sidewalks due to the constant wear from the cold and warm cycles, but they wanted to make them as efficient as possible, so the planners decided to wait until winter to start planning. During the winter, when all the existing sidewalks were covered and students plowed their own ways between buildings, the planners recorded the paths students took. When spring came, those were the paths that got the sidewalks, since it was evident that those were the ones students naturally used.

This story is full of holes, but it's a nice idea in theory. It presents a couple of tenets: Process design should revolve around the users, not the designers. One very frustrating situation is when a lazy designer refuses to spend a few extra hours working toward a more efficient or effective solution that will consistently save time or frustration on the part of the user. One rule of thumb is that extra minutes from a designer are worth saving seconds for the user; and for constantly repeated tasks, extra hours from a designer are worth saving seconds for the user.

Another tenet is that a user typically does not know what they need. If the fictional university had just asked students where sidewalks should go, they would have likely gotten a different map. What a person thinks they need and what they actually need are very different. Everyone's had experience with a buffet where something looked good during the selection process but, after trying a nibble, they discovered they didn't like it. Or there's the person who thought they were going to eat a lot and piled their plate high only to leave half of it after realizing they weren't as hungry as they thought. So, direct user input is effective and nice, but it's ultimately only useful in an advisory capacity. Whenever a user says, "This is what I want to be able to do," it should always be expressed in terms of the user's stated desire, not in terms of how to accomplish the task. A systems designer should be able to articulate why there's a better way of doing things after the design phase of the SDLC.

Finally, if the design should revolve around the users, but the designer shouldn't rely on asking the users, what is the best method for rapprochement? Typically, there needs to be some form of observation. The expert should observe what the user is doing and attempt to develop a simple and effective way to improve that activity. The user is the ultimate expert in the day-to-day engagement with that activity, but the process designer should be an expert in general processes.

SIDE QUEST: DEPARTMENTAL NEEDS

One approach is to never note a problem without also expressing a possible solution to it. This allows both parties to recognize that the conversation is solution oriented rather than fixated on the problem.

The approach for determining the needs of a department is varied based on the designer's experience and the department. One approach is to begin the conversation by noting the need to reevaluate the department's needs. If the designer can produce a tentative list of what processes the department currently uses, as well as a tentative list of what processes should be revised, added, or removed based on some external factor (analysis, industry standards, consultant recommendation), then it provides a base to start the discussion.

The next step is to determine the scope of the needs analysis (i.e., how much time is going to be devoted to analysis phase of the SDLC). This process can be anything from a one-time meeting with the head of the department to a multi-week or multi-month minute-by-minute observation of every member of the team. Which end of the spectrum is standard changes by the industry and over time. For example, creative industries tend to prefer broad strokes on describing the actions of their employees. But logistics-oriented industries prefer to document every detail. Further detail on the latter can be found in ISO 9000 certification, which is beyond the scope of this chapter.

BONUS LOOT: BUSINESS FUNCTION—FACILITIES AND CONSTRUCTION

One of the most fascinating parts of information systems is seeing how tightly it needs to integrate with facilities and/or construction departments to make sure that everything works well. At the outset, the two departments utilize a surprisingly similar set of tools to accomplish their tasks (WBS and Gantt charts). To a certain extent, this eases communication, as they're both working off the same sets of expectation.

However, aside from facilities, IT tends to be the only part of an organization that actually installs infrastructure. Facilities is typically responsible for plumbing, electric, HVAC, and other building-oriented needs, but IT is responsible for cabling. They are frequently both the only two departments with comprehensive floor plans for the physical plants of an organization.

Finally, the big issue that IT faces is in access. If IT is trying to put a data cable up to the 100th floor of a skyscraper, it needs Facilities' expertise and assistance to make sure that it can get there in a reasonable and safe manner. The other big issue tends to be distance: When a campus sprawls over a large area, it's important for IT to collaborate with Facilities to be sure that the wires are laid in a location and manner that precludes them from being damaged by routine Facilities' tasks.

PART IV

Conclusion

WHERE WE'VE BEEN

The first three parts of this text defined and gave detail to the information systems business function.

LOOK AHEAD

Part IV represents the conclusion to this book. This might seem an odd statement, given that Part IV consists of nine chapters (Chapters 16–24). After considering a newer addition to the Information Systems Department—business analytics (Chapter 16)—we turn to conclusions (Chapter 17) and summary (Chapter 18). Chapters 19–21 offer various perspectives on working in an Information Systems department. Chapter 22 offers some illustrative cases that the authors have collected. Like all cases, they illustrate some things to do, some things to avoid, and a lot of things to consider. Chapter 23 offers some salient models for consideration. Finally, Chapter 24 describes some of the more important historical figures in the information systems field.

Business Analytics

VOCABULARY

> Modeling

> Business analytics

> Data analytics

CONCEPTS

> Machine learning

> Data visualization

> Artificial intelligence

MAIN STORY: DRIVING PRINCIPLES

1. Business analytics has three components: modeling, data analytics, and business analytics.
2. When business analytics isn't its own division, it tends to be part of information systems.
3. Effective business analytics requires a balance among mathematical, technical, and social aspects.

SIDE QUEST: ANALOGY—ZOOMING IN AND OUT

One of the most fascinating and enduring videos on the internet is called "Cosmic Eye." It starts centered on a woman lying on some grass and then slowly zooms out, superimposing different magnitude images one atop another.

It goes from a facial scale in the centimeter range out to the entire projected universe at tens of billions of light-years. Then, while galactic superclusters, planets, and buildings are rushing past the camera, it zooms in on the eye again superimposing different magnitude images down to the level of imagining individual quarks at the femtometer scale.

Every moment is fascinating; a huge amount of information is packed into a single 3-minute video. Between a femtometer and 10 billion light-years are over 40 orders of magnitude. Almost every second of the video presents a new scene with a new scope and a new way of looking at the universe. As the seconds tick by, Cupertino is placed within California is placed within the United States is placed on the globe. Sol is placed in relation to its star neighbors and then within its spiral arm of the galaxy. Going the other direction, blood vessels are shown with their red blood cells, white blood cells, and down to their chromosomes and DNA.

This video is a lot like how most organizations want to see the universe. The human mind is a wonderful construct that is capable of feats of intuition and insight, but it's also very easy to get stalled on specific viewpoints and approaches. There needs to be a bridge between the multifaceted, multi-scoped viewpoint that an organization wants and the narrow, intuitive scope that an individual can perform.

The bridge between these two viewpoints, in modern industry, is analytics. Analytics plays a nebulous role in businesses. On the one hand, it's largely a math function, since it's firmly in the realm of statistics. On the other hand, it fulfills a presentation role since it explains complex concepts to nonexperts. The information communicated by analytics is not technological (generally). Yet analytics requires technology to operate at large enough scales to be effective. So analytics as an industry function could be considered applied information systems (with functions as extreme expressions of process). Because it looks like programming but acts like a business role, it tends to get lumped into information systems. It will eventually develop into its own field, but in the meantime it's frequently developed and driven by the field of information systems.

Incidentally, we could have used the word *fulcrum* instead of bridge. And that would imply that the narrow and wide viewpoints need to be balanced. And further, when we consider how to balance them, we might have come up with five components arranged on a seesaw. The two extreme positions each have different approaches to a central data-oriented concept, and they need an intermediary function such as data visualization and data analytics to cooperate with each other. And if we presented the analogy in that manner, it might be apparent why business analytics aligns so nicely with information systems. However, if we did that, we'd be implying meaning to a convenient form of convergent development.

BOX 16.1   Coincidence

"Trifles light as air are to the jealous confirmations strong as proofs of holy writ."

– William Shakespeare, *Othello, Act III, sc. 3*

MAIN STORY: BUSINESS ANALYTICS

Business analytics is a strange topic to put in the beginning of the conclusion. Unfortunately, it's also an odd component of information systems. It doesn't really belong to information systems, but it doesn't belong anywhere else either. Modern business analytics is impossible to separate from machine learning, artificial intelligence, and business intelligence. They have always been academic or clandestine fields, but technology has developed enough in the last 10 years to operationalize them in a wide variety of venues.

Business intelligence is an interesting term. It sounds an awful lot like military intelligence, which is at times a euphemism for spying. And, realistically, business intelligence has been used in the past as a euphemism for corporate espionage. How does it come under the umbrella of business analytics then?

It turns out that it is easier for companies to learn more about their competitors from sheer data processing than from any amount of corporate espionage.

And that leads to why business analytics headlines the concluding section. It is the forefront of modern information systems—the various tools of machine learning and artificial intelligence programs are changing one of the fundamental models of almost all of business. The distillation model stems from the idea that good data produces good information, and good information produces good decisions. Alternately, it's always been reliable that good decisions only came from good information and that information was only as good as the data it was based on.

However, with modern analytics methods, big data, data warehouses, and other newer algorithms and automated modelers, it's become true that more data leads to good information. It doesn't matter how good the data is: If a thousand good data points lead to good information, a trillion unreliable data points lead to better information.

MAIN STORY: ANALYTIC TRIANGLES

Just as Anthony's triangle is an attempt to take a multiplicity of roles and express them as a cohesive framework for strategic analysis, business analytics can be perceived in the same way. There are three primary skill sets needed for business analytics to thrive.

First, business analytics is, at its core, a form of statistics. We won't go into too much detail on the statistics, but we do need to consider enough to know what's needed for a business analytics department to thrive in an organization. The most fundamental level of the analytics process is the modeling role. Modeling requires an in-depth understanding of how to create both descriptive and predictive models. Further, as industry standard methods of modeling data change or improve, the modeling process must be able to adapt the organization's existing models to the new methods while preserving compatibility with older methods.

Second, business analytics is, at its core, a byproduct of data. For business analytics to work, it needs data, data, and more data. This means that there is a wide range of roles from data entry to the design and implementation of data collection methods that are involved with procuring this data. We discussed in a previous chapter many ways that this data is obtained, but someone has to be responsible for actually performing the process of integrating data into the organization. This skill requires attention to detail and an ability to convert a wide variety of formats into a single unified standard provided by and required by the modeling role.

Third, business analytics is, by function, a decision support system. For business analytics to support the making and implementation of good decisions, it has to be able to communicate. This means that data has to be formed into a structure that is easily understandable by any decision makers. The information that is distilled from the data has to be some variation between what was asked for and what was actually needed. And, finally, that information has to be conveyed in a way that is accurate but condensed enough to apply to nonanalytic decision makers. This skill requires an intuitive understanding of how to communicate with people, although training both substitutes for and enhances that intuitive understanding.

These three skill sets constitute the entirety of the business analytics function. The triangle has modeling in one corner, data analytics in another, and business analytics in the third. Just like many of the other models we've covered, it doesn't have a fixed set of points. Instead, it's a three-pointed continuum, and the categories are neither distinct nor mutually exclusive. For instance, a modeling role might also spend time designing how to acquire data in a way that makes the modeling most effective. A business analyst might need to spend some time cleaning data; alternately, a data analyst might be responsible for updating and improving existing data visualizations.

In the very center of the triangle is that most woeful of positions: sole analyst for an organization. This unfortunate person has to be a jack of all trades and has to have mastered several dichotic skill sets such as technical programming, mathematical creativity, and social influencing.

SIDE QUEST: DATA VISUALIZATION

There is an important part of statistics called data visualization. This slice of the statistics pie is responsible for the charts and graphs and visual representations of the data. It is arguably the most powerful part of the analytics process since it's the representation of the department that the outside world sees. If the data is accurate and provides valuable insight, the Analytics Department will be well regarded. Similarly, if the graphs and visual elements are sloppy or boring, the Analytics Department will be poorly regarded.

This is why it's so important for the business analytics role (in its presentation layer analogue) to be a master of both the quantitative aspects of analytics and the qualitative aspects of communication. Most decision makers want a simple and clear-cut explanation. For any decision, when there's an analytical basis, they want to know that there is a justification for the conclusion. And quite possibly they will want immediate supporting images. However, a complete justification along with examination of all alternatives is neither necessary nor desired.

The analysts know that the full justification provides the entirety of the interesting story to the question being pondered. Every layer of analysis introduces a layer of abstraction, where some of the finer details are lost. So when a massive wealth of data is distilled down to a simple diagram, it's not always accurate. On the other hand, frequently decision makers have to make decisions so quickly that a simple answer is more effective than a completely accurate one. This competing set of objectives is a constant feature in the role of the analyst.

Incidentally, dynamic dashboards are becoming much more common to help address this dichotomy of simplicity and accuracy. Whereas traditionally data visualization has been focused on creating newer and more interesting ways of creating graphs, modern data visualization frequently centers around an interactive display. For example, rather than showing the breakdown of ethnicity, a modern data visualization will allow the user to determine in real time whether a graph should be broken down by ethnicity, gender, age, or even a combination of factors. This allows for decision makers to satisfy immediate quantitative questions (What percentage of a category exists as a certain kind?) and also more drawn out qualitative questions (Are there any explanatory variables for a situation of unknown cause?). Ultimately, however, the extra flexibility is no substitute for well-designed visualizations.

SIDE QUEST: MODELING

Modeling requires a certain amount of cross-brain cooperation just like the rest of analytic functions. Whereas traditional math is most closely associated with a crystalline intelligence, understanding words is most closely associated with a fluid intelligence. The modeler's role is to take some business problem like "Why do fewer customers come on Tuesdays?," figure out what the real question is, and then formulate that question into a mathematical statement.

After they have this mathematical statement, the modeler needs to design what the solution would look like. For example, the previous question really begins with "Is there a pattern of fewer customers coming on Tuesdays?" That could get quickly expanded to both "Do any of the days of the week show a different pattern than the rest?" or "What patterns exist in customer appearance rates?" Finally, the solution would look something like this: "Given the fixed set of facts we have data about, are there any patterns that look very similar to the patterns in customer appearance rates?" Alternately, their problem statement would be this: "Is there a statistically significant relationship between any of the variables in the set that we are examining?"

The complexity can increase from there since they may be using any of a wide variety of possible methods. Rather than looking at a list of complicated statistical modeling paradigms, it would be more valuable to enroll in a course on statistics and/or statistical modeling.

SIDE QUEST: DATA ANALYTICS

Data analytics is the role that's most closely aligned with the data. The business analytics role is concerned with taking finished products and describing them. The modeling role is interested in taking questions and describing what the solution would look like. But data analytics is interested in interfacing with the broader world and making measurements.

This means that a data analyst needs to be competent to acquire and process data from a variety of sources. Data can be acquired from rival companies, data warehouses, or as a result of previous analyses. But data can also be acquired in first-party sources. Typically, this is the role of researchers or marketing functions. But as the analytics field gains more self-definition, it will almost certainly be the data analytics role that provides the most comprehensive expertise on data.

The most important part of data collection is what's called RCR, the responsible conduct of research. Many industries have their own version that is catered to their specific needs. The essential understanding is that there's a difference between sensitive and nonsensitive data. Nonsensitive data still needs to be ethically collected, but aside from retention, it's just numbers.

Sensitive data typically revolves around people and their responses. Personally identifiable information (PII; much of this is a specific approach to the information security chapter) is any information that can be used in whole or part to identify someone. For research, that's okay, but only if the customer gives consent. Collecting information about people without their awareness or understanding is not necessarily illegal, but it is often considered immoral (cultural context notwithstanding). Finally, the bulk of the data needs to be stored in a manner that is secure but also separate from the PII.

SIDE QUEST: DATA CLEANING

There is one duty that is frequently performed by both data analysts and business analysts. Data cleaning is the process of taking "dirty" data and making it uniform and sensible. There are a dozen different reasons data might be considered dirty. But they can be boiled down into a couple categories. Data is dirty when it's inaccurate. Data is dirty when it's required but missing. Data is dirty when it's organized in a poor manner.

Cleaning the data refers to removing data that has a high likelihood of inaccuracy, finding some way to fill in missing values, and restructuring it into a more standard pattern. Cleaning the data is often a method of normalization for a set of data that provides any next steps with more availability.

MAIN STORY: ARTIFICIAL INTELLIGENCE

Artificial intelligence (AI) is an imprecise term. It's artificial largely because it is completely unrelated to what humans would consider true intelligence. However, AI is frequently able to act like a decision-making entity, even if it doesn't provide the follow-through. One of the reasons AI is frequently shrouded in mystery is because the algorithms that power it are typically designed such that the input and the output are reasonable. But each of the intermediate steps it takes are only meaningful (in a nonsemantic sense) to the AI itself.

AI programs are relatively simple if they're viewed as a black box. They are still just computer programs, and so they perform a task designed and implemented by a human programmer. They are also, ultimately, a process. They have input, output, and a defined series of steps (often called a heuristic) along with all of the other standard components of any other process.

Typical tasks that AI excels at are structured decision making, semistructured decision making, and pattern recognition. All three tasks require the same basic sets of input. The inputs are the algorithm designed by a human that is coded into a programming language and a large amount of training data. Training data tends to be examples of the decision that needs to be made. For example, when developing a medical expert system, the training data might be a huge list of reported symptom groups paired with the diagnoses made by medical experts. The medical expert system would process these pairings and attempt to come up with a way to convert from a new group of symptoms into an accurate diagnosis.

The accuracy of the AI tends to increase as the quantity and variety of diagnoses increases. There are two errors that tend to creep in with training data that is insufficient. Suppose that 1,000 randomly selected medical decisions are used as training data. For an ailment that only affects 1 in 100,000 people, it would be reasonable that pure chance resulted in the ailment not appearing in that training data. With 350 million people living in the United States, there would be an expectation of 3,500 people who should be diagnosed with that ailment. However, since the algorithm was never trained on how to identify that data, it would always misdiagnose every person in this group.

On the flip side, as a simplistic example, suppose there was an ailment that only affected one person in a billion. If the random selection of medical diagnosis just happened to include one of these rare cases, the AI algorithm would expect that 0.1% of the population should be diagnosed with that ailment. As a result, there would be a very substantive chance of misdiagnosis.

As noted, the output of the AI process is frequently a decision. For structured tasks, that decision is simple. But for semistructured decisions, it is very common for the output of the AI to be the constraints themselves. The input might be very unstructured data like, "Here's everything we know about our customers," and the output might be "a method of determining which customers are the most profitable." The output might look like, "If a customer has never returned a product, check how frequently they shop: Frequent shoppers who have never returned a product are profitable. If the customer has returned a product, calculate the total percentage margin of items they bought: Customers who return a product but only buy high-margin items are still profitable." There may be more detailed conclusions to be made, but the AI is typically given a level of complexity for its response and will stop at that point.

As an aside, this is actually what's happened in the past. With the introduction of some of the CRM concepts, some retail companies actually went out of their way to notify customers who were not profitable that they were no longer welcome to shop at particular stores. While this was well within the rights of the company, it did not go over well with the general public. On the other hand, this is the exact method credit card companies use to determine who should be targeted for which level of credit card.

Finally, the training data is an interesting concern. The algorithm will always attempt to duplicate the training data's conclusions. The third category that AI applications excel at is pattern matching. This typically takes the form of image recognition. When a mapping and directions website has excellent representations of roads and buildings, it's not because someone programmed in where all of the roads are. It's because the mapping company uses satellite images to try to recognize the patterns of roads within the satellite imagery. This is also the same method most tax-collecting agencies use to determine size and value of buildings: It's easier and more cost effective to be mostly right with an automated analysis and individually handle disagreements than it is to employ assessors to visit each property in a district.

This also leads to a side effect of the captcha class of authentication. Many websites will use a captcha-style method for identifying whether someone registering or logging into the site is a human or a robot. The method is relatively successful but relies on the assumption that nobody has trained artificial intelligence to beat the captcha method. Ironically, one side effect is that many captcha service providers actually use the captcha methods to provide training data for their AIs.

This is called crowdsourcing: Rather than hiring someone to do a repetitive task and deal with the job satisfaction and turnover problems that such involves (imagine the monotony of a job that required a person to spend 8 hours a day clicking on the less fuzzy of two pictures once every second), some companies turn to services that present one or two problems to a large number of people who are each paid a pittance (pennies or fractions of pennies for each problem). There is a growing service sector that looks for ways to both provide a service and use a captive audience to solve these problems. Websites looking to authenticate human users are a great cross point for that situation, and they result in training data that looks like "Out of these 100 million images, humans indicated that there was a car in these 10 million of them."

BONUS LOOT: BUSINESS FUNCTION—HOSPITALITY MANAGEMENT

One of the most common situations where analytics are used is hospitality management. Restaurants and hotels have huge markups over their fixed costs. For example, at a hotel, a room is going to be there regardless of whether it's used. So, in a certain sense, it costs the hotel nothing to have a room available for rent.

However, since restaurants and hotels are more properly considered to be service rather than retail industries, they need to provide a level of service to match their rates. This causes them to have a large amount of fluctuation and control over how they are perceived and the deals they can make with customers.

Analytics provides a great way to get closer to that holiest of grails, the satisfied customer. For example, if a hotel room typically goes for $100 a night, the hotel management knows that some times of the year are slower than others and that they'll be able to get more customers if they change the rate when it's obvious that the hotel room is going to be empty. The problem is that most humans trust their gut instinct to make these decisions. A manager might assume that the winter months are slower and that they'll get more customers by dropping the price to $50 a night 6 months ahead of time.

However, an analytics department might be able gather profit and customer data to make the decision much more objective. For example, by calculating daily values, the analytics team could make a report of exactly which days are less popular with customers.

By using a factor analysis, the Analytics Department might be able to indicate which categories of customer were more likely to rent a room at which levels of discount. For example, families might only show up on slow days when the discount was 50%, but business travelers would still show up at 0% discount. The analysis might even be able to suggest certain categories of customer who might warrant an increase in rate.

Finally, by comparing the occupancy rates with the dates of initial reservation, the analytics team might be able to come up with a predictive analysis that suggests when the best time to start worrying about empty rooms would be. Further, they might be able to make that prediction per day. They might say that the first 3 days of spring break should have advertisements sent out a month prior. But if someone spends the entire spring break at the hotel, they make that decision 6 months ahead of time and need to have advertising made at about that time period.

The ultimate goal of analytics of this nature is to provide advertising that is 100% effective to the advertiser but is also always welcomed by the customer. For example, in the previous situation, the ideal situation involves ads that are only sent to customers who rent a room at the expected time period and explicitly appreciate the reminder to make plans ahead of time for their spring break.

BONUS LOOT: RESUME BUILDERS—ONLINE TRAINING SITES

There are a number of online training sites that can provide a brush-up of skills. Collegiate and business training differs drastically in both form and function. College-level training tends to emphasize critical thinking, social interaction, and a broad base of knowledge to allow addressing novel situations. However, industry training tends to be more focused on specific job-ready skills. For example, learning how a particular industry works and gaining the breadth of base knowledge tends to be more effective at the college level.

But after a person has graduated from college, where do they go for further training? Some industries such as education and accounting require continuing education credits, so a wide variety of options is available. But, historically, if continuing education wasn't a structural part of an industry's expectations, people in that industry were left to determine their own framework for maintaining competency.

This became particularly frustrating in the IT environment, where skills became obsolete quickly and maintaining currency frequently meant learning the next popular skill set before it became popular. As a result, IT has led the way in online training sites for new skill development. A modern skills training website tends to have an interactive design that will automatically grade and correct a student. They are not as great at providing the broad base of knowledge required to learn a new skill, but expanding a given skill set is exactly what they're for.

Further, most of them provide some level of certification that indicates how much training was accomplished. They will even provide notifiers for popular social media sites. A good place to start looking into these would be LinkedIn Learning, DataCamp.com, or Codeacademy.com. Industry professional associations are also a great place to learn about sites that will allow experienced individuals to brush up their skill sets and demonstrate their currency.

BONUS LOOT: SOFT SKILLS—FINDING AN AUDIENCE

Finding an audience is a skill in itself. Everyone knows the person who walks around and tells everyone the same story, even when it's particularly inappropriate. Instead, it's important to identify with your listener and cater the story such that it involves them and makes them part of the story.

This is difficult to express but easy to see. Typically, it's possible to ask, "Who's the most entertaining guy here?" and find out how that person approaches things. Another term for this is "the gift of gab": a person who talks a lot but doesn't bother people because they always feel better after the conversation.

Not everyone is going to be able to use this skill all of the time, but it is an advantage to selectively use it when it's of the most benefit.

BONUS LOOT: CERTIFICATIONS—KHAN ACADEMY

Khan Academy is a site for learning GED-level skills. There are more and less advanced topics, but the idea was originally to provide adults with a free, web-based platform to study for the GED. It provides a number of tools and interactive reports and is generally a good utility for that purpose. Since then, it has expanded into a study and tutoring site for anyone learning the topics that it has on offer.

However, people don't retain everything they've learned. Typically, retaining 5% to 15% of a lecture is a good general expectation. A good lecturer will engage in breaks, anecdotal tangents, and general silliness to keep enough mental infrastructure hooks to keep their audience remembering. But it is important to remember that everyone forgets the majority of what they learned and that retention rate goes down even more significantly over time.

Using Khan Academy as a way to review and refresh basic skills is the smart course of action, rather than a remedial task. It may not be worth spending hours and hours, but quickly looking over their table of contents to see what's unfamiliar and taking a few minutes to refresh that knowledge is a good plan, especially for math areas. That leads into statistics, which leads into business analytics.

REFERENCES

Shakespeare, W. (1604). *Othello*. http://shakespeare.mit.edu/othello/full.html

Bringing It All Together

VOCABULARY

> Enterprise software

> BLUF

CONCEPTS

> Data silo/information silo

> Semantic web

> Big data

> Augmented reality

MAIN STORY: DRIVING PRINCIPLES

1. Information systems, like all responsible business practices, needs to consider social responsibility.
2. Information systems is a tool that helps people and society achieve impressive results.

SIDE QUEST: ANALOGY—MEGASTRUCTURES

There is a trope in sci-fi called the megastructure (or, less flatteringly, big dumb objects). In Arthur C. Clarke's classic *Rama*, an asteroid launched by an alien civilization explores and collects knowledge. A Dyson sphere, envisioned by Freeman Dyson, is a way to collect 100% of the solar energy by building a massive object around a star. *Ringworld* was Larry Niven's sci-fi world that was so huge it could fit the surface of the earth 3 million times over.

But no matter how many interesting physical structures appear in sci-fi novels and television shows, authors keep returning to the tried-and-true idea of fantasy-style artificial intelligence. Clear and accessible representations can be just as huge and epic as any of the physical structures. Dan Simmons's noosphere was a representation of all human thought in an ubiquitous atmosphere around the planet. Neal Asher's Polity is a galaxy-wide civilization of systems administered by AIs; if clubs made primitive man hit harder and cars make modern man go faster, then AIs are just tools to help humankind think better. John von Neumann's classic thought experiment was a self-replicating machine that could expand into the galaxy and develop just like humans.

The point is that while sci-fi is obviously fiction and not a clear picture of the future, the present is always the first step toward getting to those impressive future structures—the visions of the future are being assembled in miniature form right now.

SIDE QUEST: INFORMATION SILOS

There is one primary bit of warning to consider—it is less of an entrenched problem now than it has been in the past, but poor organizational structure can still result in data silos.

A data silo is, effectively, when one part of an organization has data that other parts of the organization do not. Typically, we consider information silos. An organization might structure a data silo for legal or ethical reasons: HIPAA requires that certain data not leave the physical confines of a doctor's office under certain situations, quality assurance staff shouldn't know whose work they're evaluating, and Human Resources has access to employee data that is unavailable to most employees.

When we say *information silos*, we're discussing something much more broad and far reaching. In an information silo, the seesaw model has been duplicated, in whole or in part, by one portion of an organization. As a result, that part of the organization begins to operate on a different set of information and decision support capacity than the rest of the organization. The question then becomes, "Why can't the rest of the organization access that data?" Typically, the answer lies not in a fault with the systems design but in personal or professional pettiness.

Historically, computers didn't have the technical capacity to address the entirety of the organization en masse; instead, the computerization of an organization was typically performed by lower-level staff. A help desk worker might decide that the system of written notes was clumsy and frustrating, so they'd create a small database that other workers could access to see what needed to be addressed. Or a team manager might put together a quick team spreadsheet addressing pricing or other relevant information. Over time, these tools typically developed holistically into larger and more complicated structures that required full-time oversight.

However, in the late '90s to late '00s, it became more feasible to integrate all of these structures into unified structures. Rather than having IT teams for each individual department, organizations started to enforce organization-wide departments and structures. However, the transition (requested or mandated) during which individual departments gave up their homegrown tools and worked within the larger systems was frequently met with resistance.

In a modern system, it's important to begin on a firm footing using enterprise software that addresses the needs of the entire organization in larger structures. This software is typically called enterprise resource planning (ERP) software and is used to manage the data and processes of the entire organization and to get large-scale overviews of the entire organization. Since its primary utility revolves around this high-level overview, it's important that all portions of the organization be treated equally and included in the ERP.

MAIN STORY: BIG DATA

Presume for a moment that data is a commodity. In fact, let's posit that it's a product that would work in a perfect market (that is, there's no difference between one piece of data and another). That's obviously not true, but the details are unimportant in this discussion. In fact, when "big data" comes up, the conceptualization that the details are unimportant is frequent.

Consider our analogy about wealth. Whether we're discussing money itself, power, or social responsibility, there's a whole different category of application, scope, and structure for an organization that has a trillion-dollar market cap versus one with a billion dollars, a million dollars, or one that just started. It's not just that there's more; it's that at a certain scale, quantitative differences become qualitative differences. They're all still companies and retain certain similarities, but at the same time there's a fundamental difference working at or with a trillion-dollar company compared to a million-dollar company.

Data performs similarly. When we deal with one piece of data, we're typically talking about information. When we deal with 1,000 pieces of data, we quickly want some summaries. But somewhere between a million and a trillion (or, for the largest, quadrillions and quintillions) there has to be some different approaches. A simple summary isn't enough; we need different ways to access the data and see the ways that a summary is obfuscating or enhancing the data.

One of the clearest ways to consider this is by region. Let's consider something simple like the use of the phrase *y'all*. Simple statistics would indicate that most Americans don't use the word *y'all*, but that covers over too many variations. That aggregation discounts the culture and verbal idiosyncrasies of tens of millions of people. Instead, we want to "drill down" and see that people in the North rarely say *y'all*, people in the Midwest frequently say *you all*, people in the traditional South do say *y'all*, and people in the rural South frequently say *all y'all*. Suddenly, the simple statistic that "most don't" becomes a little bit more clear. Most software for interacting with big data allows for manipulating the question and varying the output to get a good cognitive grasp of multidimensional data on a two-dimensional presentation medium.

MAIN STORY: SEMANTIC WEB

Discussion of a semantic web has been ongoing for decades (W3C, 2015). The goal is to provide a way for computers to learn or mimic the semantic understanding of humans. Earlier in the discussion on semantics, we talked about the idea that humans automatically know what a cup is. But the semantic web intends to do more than that because knowing the semantic meaning of cup suddenly pulls in other concepts.

What goes into a cup? What's a liquid? What kinds of liquids are there? Why are some liquids okay to put in a cup but not others? What is poison? Why is poison bad? What is death? Basically, it always escalates really quickly into really abstract concepts. But the semantic web wants to make associations between concepts that will allow a computer to interpret these concepts and present them in a way that makes sense. For example, rather than getting a prerecorded voice on the phone, the computer might be able to automatically understand that when you call in to report your defective drinking device, you want a refund because it doesn't adequately hold liquids upside down.

That sounds silly, but trying to explain that to a computer right now would be difficult. It's unlikely that a specifically programmed response would consider someone talking about upside-down liquids. But by providing a well-documented semantic web full of hooks for other applications to tie in with, the idea is that it will be possible for computers to make the connections needed.

MAIN STORY: AUGMENTED REALITY

Augmented reality is a layer on top of the current reality. In augmented reality, an advanced visual image processor is constantly evaluating the scenes from a camera mounted immediately over a user's eyes to determine what they're seeing. It then augments that with some form of data.

One of the easiest, current, and ubiquitous examples of this is an in-dash monitor for cars. Aside from the "augment" of playing music, it typically has a mapping function that tells the user which lane to be in, where to turn, what the current speed limit is, what their estimated time of arrival is, and so on. The next step is for some of this information to be projected onto the windshield so that it becomes a part of the actual driving experience. For example, speed limit signs might disappear in favor of heads-up data and roadside exit signs might become less necessary.

BONUS LOOT: BUSINESS FUNCTION—INFORMATION SYSTEMS

Information systems is, again, a business function. But a wide variety of roles exist within information systems. Just like every other department has administrative assistants, general purpose managers, and entry-level employees, so does information systems. What's important to remember is that this book is intended for the nontechnical manager. But information systems departments are not about technology. They're about the business function. And as we've seen, that business function is focused on strategic planning, good decision making, and promoting information flow.

In order to achieve excellence, every field requires training. Experience is only gained with time. Anyone can be successful in information systems, with experience and a learning mind-set.

One of the most frustrating aspects of being a technical employee is always "the dark side." There's an ethos that technical work is good, clean work. Programmers have a sense of camaraderie and one-upmanship. Technicians tend to appreciate the opportunity to be left alone and have a technical problem to solve. It's considered to be almost a betrayal to convert to management. This leads to situations where many (not all) supervisory employees in information systems were technical employees. It also means that an influx of good management principles from outside is resisted, but not always very strongly. It's worth considering whether you have the sound business acumen necessary to succeed; if so, there's no technical reason you can't succeed in information systems.

BONUS LOOT: RESUME BUILDERS—EXTERNAL REVIEW

Consider a foreign country, like Japan. Behavioral expectations in Japanese society are quite different than those in the United States. Nonnative speakers will say that even after decades immersed in the language, they are still constantly caught off guard by social or linguistic surprises. For an area as highly competitive as job hunting, there's an even more extreme standard of perfection. As a result, almost all Japanese resume advice ends with "but bring it to a native Japanese speaker to review," because otherwise it's almost certain that a nonnative speaker will make a mistake.

Further, most resume advice specifies bringing the resume to an experienced resume reviewer as well. Not only is it possible to make a linguistic faux pas, but presenting oneself for career review is a social function with a high level of complexity. These experienced resume reviewers can point out both better or more culturally appropriate ways to phrase things as well as specific things to avoid that might not be immediately apparent.

The next question is "Why is all of this advice appropriate to Japan but not the United States?" Japanese culture is not any more culture-y than the United States. English is one of the most complex languages in human history, so there's no reason not to have a second set of eyes look at a resume. The cultural situation of hiring is also tied up in incredibly nitpicky rules, and even minor things can have a reviewer (correctly or incorrectly) rolling their eyes. In short, there is no shame in asking someone to review a resume both grammatically and professionally.

BONUS LOOT: SOFT SKILLS—SUMMARY AND BLUF

One of the hardest things to realize is that most people don't care what you're going to say. For example, if an employee spends 40 hours per week performing a specific operational task for an organization, that task is likely at the forefront of the employee's mind. They could probably talk about it for hours. It seems relatively anti-climactic for it to be summarized as a three-sentence status report during an end-of-week meeting.

The full report is important; however, it is helpful if it is written in a more context-sensitive matter. Bullet point summaries are a good tool. Being able to relate concepts in a hierarchical set of sentence fragments, each consisting of three to eight words, is a good skill to master. Someone will read the highlights of a full report when they're formatted in three-to-eight-word chunks, because that's easy to read.

Another consideration is that most people don't want to be led down a path to an inevitable conclusion. The reality is that employees are hired for a job, and at a certain level most managers trust that the person is doing that job satisfactorily. The more appropriate paradigm is bottom line up front (BLUF): Give the conclusion and then support that conclusion. This is a harder skill to master than it sounds, but most supervisors will recognize a BLUF master as the person they paradoxically want to hear more from.

REFERENCES

W3C. (2015). Semantic web. https://www.w3.org/standards/semanticweb/

■ **CHAPTER 18**

Driving Principles

PRE-READING CHECKLIST

VOCABULARY

> Strategic

> Managerial

> Operational

CONCEPTS

> Enterprise system

> Decision makers

> General principles

MAIN STORY: DRIVING PRINCIPLES

1. Information systems is a reflection of a universal form.
2. Every system should be considered a cycle, never a singular pass.
3. It's okay to look at other functions and see the only-the-good-parts version.

SIDE QUEST: ANALOGY—BLOOD AND THE VASCULAR SYSTEM

We've already used the human body in an analogy. Since everyone has a body, it's immediately comprehensible. Consider the parts of the vascular system that transfer blood from the heart to the brain and extremities and back again. Starting with the heart providing pressure, the blood flows out along major

197

arteries, then to minor arteries, and then to the capillary level. It's fascinating to consider how one central hub can manage to provide blood to each of the trillions of cells in the body. And here's the most important part: Every single cell in the body needs that blood to survive. That means that every biological structure has managed to organize a system that vastly overwhelms any human social organization in terms of complexity and by orders of magnitude!

But the system doesn't stop there. The blood comes back from the capillaries, back through the minor veins, the major veins, and then back to the heart. Not only does the heart distribute blood to each of those trillions of cells, but the guiding pressure of the singular organ also compels each of those cells to transfer the blood back to the heart. The cycle only works if it is a cycle. There are any number of medical traumas that occur when the heart is pumping the blood but not receiving it back. Similarly, if the heart can't push the blood out but is able to receive it, things go wrong in a hurry.

Finally, it's important to remember that everything has a vascular analogue: a pet dog, a milking cow, one of those lizards on the picture of every postcard from the Cayman Islands, bird or fish, reptile or amphibian. They all have vascular systems. Insects don't have direct vascular systems, but they do have an analogue that takes its place. Even abstract concepts have vascular systems. Rome's vascular system was its roads. A technical skill like carpentry's vascular system is the give and take of knowledge between masters and their peers and apprentices. This form of branching into the infinitesimal and then returning back to the singular is universal and worth contemplating in its own right. But here, the pertinent argument for information systems is that analogy.

This chapter will not introduce anything new. This chapter is devoted to a bare-bones, stripped-away view of information systems. Some people call it the 100-mile viewpoint. We just call it a highly abstracted description. We'll revisit information systems in a very broad and generalized description and then reiterate the important part of each of the previous chapters. This book is intended to leave you with a broad understanding of how to interact with or to be reported to by an information systems department. We'll end with the S. Morgenstern approach.

MAIN STORY: *ABSTRACTIO AD ABSURDUM*

The analogy discussion eventually presents the vascular system as representative of a universal form. In a nutshell, that's what information systems is. Some people say that the entire field of economics is just two graphs that come from one theory, and everything else can be derived from there. It might be a little presumptuous to assume that the functioning of quantum computers or machine learning can be derived from a single principle. But, with regard to the management functions of information systems, it's probably a fair statement to say that everything can be derived from the universal form.

Beginning with the primary enterprise system for an organization, the functioning of a system should be organized around that point. This is why information systems can't lead an organization; while all the other business functions are equal in the topological hierarchy, information systems presumes to be more central. This makes information systems the medium for modern business, not the method or the message.

Each organizational function shares data with the others through the central hub of information systems. From those functional areas, the information flows down to departments and teams and individuals. This only works when information is shared. Individuals must share information about their work with their team. Teams share within the functional area and back up the hierarchy to the central information store within the Information Systems Department.

Almost every proper functioning or competitive advantage derives from that sharing concept. Information technology develops its technologies to allow strategic decision makers to make good decisions, and those decisions inform the practices of managers who train the performance of frontline employees. But then those employees' performances need to be measured and responded to by the managerial decision makers. The managerial decision makers in turn provide aggregated data on performance to the strategic decision makers. The strategic decision makers then feed responses on success rates back to the Information Technology Department.

Similarly, unstructured decisions lead to the formulation of policies that allow structured decision makers to make their decisions. Those decisions, in turn, produce or eliminate possibilities for future unstructured decisions, and the cycle continues.

We can even introduce a completely new concept and immediately see how it fits into this cycle of major artery down through capillary and back up. One form of analytics is called data mining. We can do large-scale unsupervised data mining, which will produce results that need to be investigated further with more targeted yet still unsupervised data mining. The results of these operations need to be explored to determine whether they're interesting and valid through the use of a supervised data mining technique. And the results of that data mining then need to be empirically verified by the frontline operations. Whether or not the new findings result in an improvement in efficiency or effectiveness will help the supervised data mining team refine their results, which in turn will help provide better constraint and validity analyses for the unsupervised data mining employees. The whole process is constantly producing more data that then gets funneled right back into the large-scale unsupervised data mining. This paragraph may or may not have made sense, but it should be clear that the form was still there even if the specifics weren't.

This is one reason a good information systems manager tends to be a bit nosy. Being skilled at information systems requires a broad range of skills. Hardware requires a certain mechanical-mindedness. Software is a very logical, attention-to-detail field. Data revolves around mathematical relationships. Processes are one part human resources, one part programming, and one part sociology. And like all management functions, the person still has to have the social skills needed to interact with their peers. Armed with these broad skill sets and the understanding of the universal form, an information systems specialist frequently feels competent to speak on a wide range of matters. That feeling is equal parts contextual expertise and unfounded bravado.

MAIN STORY: GENERAL PRINCIPLES

Information systems is a business function just like any other. Every individual member of every business function operates better as they understand both the specific details of the other functions and the philosophical intentions. For example, much of the process section of this text was informed by borrowing some of the philosophy of accounting's structures and controls. What follows is an attempt to produce short, pithy statements that can act as guiding principles. The ultimate goal of this book is to be valuable enough that the instruction provided so far allows this page to serve as a printed and posted guide for every student.

- Guiding principles: Now is always too late.
  - You should always be working toward specific long-term goals in the context of what the environment will look like in the future.
  - Eventually everything available now will be free in the future.
  - Data is key.
- Information technology: Technology is only a tool.
  - Let computers calculate and remember, but let humans think.
- People and processes.
  - People are adaptable; they just require early and consistent changes.
  - People are the part of the system with agency to affect the real world.
- Hardware and software: Framing any problem appropriately aids in solving it.
  - Break problems down into smaller pieces.
  - Determine what you can get for what you budget; don't budget for what you want to get.
  - Learn just enough to be able to trust the expert.
- Communication: Communication is the primary way we affect the world around us.
  - Not saying the wrong thing is more important than saying the right thing.
  - Words in the modern era are always permanent.
- Data: Remember the broader reasons to do something.
  - Quantity is better than not.
  - Quality is better than quantity.
  - A responsible purpose is better than quality.
- Decision making: Organizational position doesn't equate to intrinsic value.
  - All employees are decision makers; place the right decision in front of the right decision maker.
  - For complicated questions, don't pursue the best solution; pursue a sufficient solution.
  - Over time, attempt more strategic decisions, but try to make more decisions operational.

- Process: Nobody can read your mind. Explicitly state everything.
  - Processes should be designed; they should not just happen.
  - Having a shared statement of purpose reduces confusion.

- Systems design: Find problems sooner rather than later.
  - Every activity benefits from having a planning phase.
  - Remember that 90% of any activity or role is routine maintenance.
  - Succeeding at routine maintenance is still succeeding.

- Information security: Every function requires a security mind-set.
  - It's always better to outsource specialized functions.
  - Some tasks are eventually going to fail; always have a recovery strategy.

- Business analytics: Asking the right questions leads to better decisions.
  - Some models should be a stacked model, and some should be an egalitarian model.
  - Complex subjects need to be communicated to nonexperts.
  - If the input is good and the output is good, anything with a confusing middle section shouldn't be scary.

- Information systems: Good managers give information and receive information.
  - Everyone exists as part of the organizational structure.
  - The universal form has application everywhere. All processes are cycles.

CHAPTER 19

So You Want to Work in IT?

Q: Can you give us your job title, a brief description of your role, and what it took for you to get to this point in your career?

A:

- Official title: Senior analyst
- Effective title: Linux Solutions architect

Q: How do you see your role fitting into the larger organization?

A:

- Goal: Make everything I am responsible for (Linux servers) as easy to use as possible for my customers and for me.

Q: What do your routine interactions with other departments in the organization look like?
A:

- Provisioning new servers on request.
- Building automation tools: Why do the same thing five times when you can have more fun making a robot do it for you?
- Figuring out how people are using my servers: Application A lives on Server B that needs to talk to Application C on Server D (more complicated than it sounds and the people using it often don't know).
- Maintaining limited privileges for security and sanity: Everyone's job would be easier without any limitations, but if we're going to play together in the same sandbox there have to be some ground rules.
- Assisting application migration between environments (dev, test, qa, staging, prod).
- Recovering files or servers from backups.
- Providing on-the-spot basic Linux training as needed.

Author's note: This interview is short, but please do not consider that to be a negative. Significant conversation was had with Mr. Alston, who decided that further questions that were asked were outside of the scope of his current position. That's reflective of the position, as someone within the operational level of decision making should be able to recognize that. Otherwise, notice that the scope of most of the job responsibilities is task focused and related to the successful accomplishment of a known goal through a known process.

CHAPTER 20

So You Want to Manage IT?

Q: Can you give us your job title, a brief description of your role, and what it took for you to get to this point in your career?

A:

- I am a program manager for Nationstar Mortgage.
- Nationstar Mortgage grew into the largest nonbank servicing shop for residential mortgage loans through a series of acquisitions. These acquisitions brought with them a bulk of loan document data, most of which is in the form of single and multi-page PDFs and TIFFs, about five billion pages worth. The company received this data from prior servicers and has little understanding of what types of documents are in those image files, let alone what information is contained within each type of document. The program I lead is charged with properly classifying each imaged page and extracting the data from within. Leveraging cutting-edge AI technologies, we are working toward this goal in an iterative (agile) fashion. My role as program lead is to

prioritize the specific business problems we are working to solve, ensuring a solid understanding of those problems in the team, taking the team through a series of activities that break the problems apart and align the right talent to the work items best suited for their skill set, and then tracking that through to completion.

▪ Curiosity and a willingness to evolve has led to a variety of experiences and now provides me a broad base of understanding for the business problems we are solving. Thirteen years in technology, several years in Lean Six Sigma process engineering, and another several years leading projects have helped me understand the variety of perspectives and technologies that I come into contact with. None of this would have happened though if I didn't have a desire to understand how things worked and why organizations do what they do and to remain open to repeatedly being stretched out of my comfort zone.

Q: How do you see your role fitting into the larger organization?
A:

▪ Program management is a pretty general term and could fit into a number of different areas within the business. I find that at any given time it is synonymous with being a collaborator, coach, scapegoat, mentor, scrum master, strategist, technologist, designer, or the guy who brought the donuts ... whatever it takes to keep the team focused on the goal and moving toward it. And while I may be at the front of the room, it's important to never make it about me; I always focus on the team around the table and what we're doing together. Anywhere the business has an opportunity to improve, there is a chance they could use me.

Q: What do your routine interactions with other departments in the organization look like?
A:

▪ Organizations range pretty dramatically in culture and norms. The way a business operates and the talent that it attracts will mean everything in how I engage with folks. My current organization is on the forefront of a rebrand; they have declared an intent to become more collaborative and more technology-minded. I align to this way of thinking and try to bring an element of these intentions into my meetings with others throughout the business. Using active listening or design thinking or some other technique, I try to keep the meeting I'm running as positive and collaborative a space as possible. It's often just the old adage of "you have two ears and one mouth, use them proportionately" that sets folks at ease and promotes a willingness on their parts to help and participate. Sometimes this means pushing back hard on the natural inclination of some to go negative. From a technology perspective, it's often about educating folks, not in a condescending way but in a "being the tide that lifts all boats" kind of mentality. People are far more apt to buy into what you're doing if they feel they are being heard and understand the concepts and ideas being discussed.

Q: What advice would you give to someone who wanted to switch from their current field to a more technically oriented role? What's their best approach?

A:

- Over the last 25 years there has been an evolution in how business relates to technology. There are lots of good resources out there that track this evolution, and I won't try to restate those concepts here. I'm also speaking more broadly here, not so much about my current organization but organizations in general, because different companies are in very different places with respect to their own journey in this evolution. So as I think about industry in terms of business operations and technology, I see the two as approaching a state of complete integration, where you can't distinguish (from a distance) between a technologist and an associate in operations. The approaches of agile (or agility), CI/CD, and particularly DevOps promotes these concepts and has begun to really take hold across a number of industries. Clearly, there will always be a need for specific skill sets and no one person can ever be all things at a deep level, so realistically we will always see distinct roles. However, a trend has begun in organizations that are taking the long view, where individual associates possess a greater awareness of both business and technical concepts.

- Staying curious and humble will drive one to continually seek to improve and educate themselves; just accept that learning is lifelong and is ideally a love and not a chore. A chore is not the same thing as hard work. With that in mind, if learning is not a love and doesn't require hard work, then it's probably time to revisit your "why" and push to challenge yourself further. Strategically speaking, I try to apply some structure and order to the way I approach continued education. There are so many avenues to follow and invest one's time that it takes some discernment. I like the ideas promoted by Simon Sinek and Dan Pink on the topics of "why" and motivation. When mentoring folks who are struggling with wanting to learn or are having problems staying engaged, I take them through a protracted conversation of self-examination that leverages the concepts from these guys. Tactically speaking, it's all about self-education. Fortunately, once a person decides where to spend their time, there are tons of good resources out there; many are free or inexpensive. Early in my career I did not spend much energy on certifications and such, but I have come to realize over time that they are valuable in building one's brand and opening doors that might not ordinarily have been there. Once I got my PMP and Lean Six Sigma certifications, folks just started assuming—mistakenly or not— that I knew what I was talking about.

Q: What advice would you give to a nontechnical professional who suddenly found themselves managing a team of technical employees?

A:

- I feel like I am this person on a nearly daily basis. Don't feel bad about it. Everyone has their skill sets to contribute to the overall success of the effort. Enjoy the ride and learn as much as possible along the way. Like speaking to stakeholders and sponsors in the business units, build a brand of listening actively and showing a desire to learn, so the technical teams know they are being heard in their own way and that you are invested in what they are spending their 40-plus hours per week doing. When I came into my current program midstream, the team had already formed and was storming through the early design work. The technology involves a lot of artificial intelligence work—what I like to call augmented intelligence, to position the technology as more supplementary and less usurping of the business associates' roles. I found a few members of the technical and analyst teams who were willing to participate in what I dubbed "train the dummy" sessions. They had a heart for teaching and were willing to exercise patience, taking me through enough material that I became effective at leading a technical huddle or bridging the gap between business and technology associates. I also find it helpful to maintain a strategic view of the work and feel free to ask what I call "dumb questions." Often the simplest (or dumbest) questions will uncover some nuance or aspect that hasn't been considered because so many folks stay in the tactical space.

Q: What should a nontechnical executive do to help their company succeed from a technical perspective?

A:

- Like leading a technical team, admit that you don't have all the answers and work hard to get educated. As an executive, there will be availability to resources—internally and externally—that you might struggle to gain access to at a lower level. Look to leaders of other companies who are doing aspirational things in their own industries and who have made the journey themselves. Mentorship should continue indefinitely, especially as one climbs the senior leadership ranks. The thought processes are going to be far more strategic than before and, again leveraging the material produced by Sinek and Pink, being intentional about developing a culture of collaboration and learning, giving people room to take risks, and demonstrating authentic leadership will cultivate the kind of culture that you can be proud of. In the end, despite how technologically centered a company is in its solutioning, the conversation should always come back to the "why" and the customer.

Q: What lessons have you learned, or what advice would you give, based on your experience to someone outside your field?

A:

- Always assume positive intent but not much else. There's a good chance you don't understand the perspective of the person opposite you and vice versa. If you can both come at things with those table stakes, it's going to be a productive conversation.

Q: What things do you wish that people outside your field understood about your role?

A:

- That the problems they cause today—wittingly or otherwise—are probably my "to-do" items tomorrow. It is astounding to me how careless some people can be and often without regard for what might happen next or, more importantly, to whom it may happen.

Q: How can others in an organization help you succeed, personally or professionally?

A:

- The relationships we cultivate are our greatest assets in life. Be it personal or professional, there is no escaping the fact that we live in a space where people influence our lives and vice versa. The mistake we too often make is to believe that we are building actual relationships when we're not. Similar to George Shaw's statement that "the problem with communication is the illusion that it has taken place," we count our relationships by measure of frequency or volume but not depth. Clicking "like" is not going to get it done.

- So if this is where we admit to finding ourselves, what next? The first step I have found to be most effective in garnering help from others is to help them first. Achieving success can be accomplished any number of ways but, strategically speaking, that success will likely be a derivative of either pushing everyone around you down or lifting them up. To me the most gratifying and authentic way is by lifting those around you up, but I'm not one who wants to reach the top only to feel alone.

- In business, I like to often repeat a phrase that I learned from a very successful CEO who I admire, and that is "one team." Influence for others and they will usually influence for you. It's really that simple. And if this isn't working for you, if this isn't resonating with those around you, it's probably time to reconsider where you find yourself.

Q: Do you have any other advice for a student in business school?

A:

- "Life is what happens to you while you're busy making other plans."
- Never mistake knowledge for wisdom or experience.
- Learn to be comfortable (but not complacent) not knowing.
- Set your boundaries and keep your scruples.
- "Wear sunscreen."

Author's note: IT management certainly falls square within the realm of managerial decision making. This is a good place to overview the fact that there is room for making creative decisions, but that the overall goal is typically specified. There is a comparatively larger amount of interaction with others and much of the focus of the position itself relates to interacting with people.

CHAPTER 21

So You Want to Be a CIO?

Q: Can you give us your job title, a brief description of your role, and what it took for you to get to this point in your career?

A:

- I am a project information manager. I work for a company that specializes in the design of oil and gas facilities (refineries, chemical plants, offshore platforms, etc.). I have worked in this industry for over 30 years.
- The first 10 years of my career, I had roles in information technology, including IT manager, application development lead, business analyst, software developer, and network administrator.
- For the past 20 years, I have held roles that are considered functional and business roles in information management. In this industry, the definition for information systems primarily applies to the software tools used by an organization. The term *information management* in this engineering firm applies to the timely and efficient delivery of

information that is used to design, build, commission, start up, and later operate a facility. This includes documentation, tag data, and 3-D models. My role is to pull from millions of bits of data and transform it into meaningful information that feeds the business processes and multiple stakeholders.

Q: How do you see your role fitting into the larger organization?
A:

- A key success factor in information management is the effective organization of information that is generated, collected, classified, grouped, quality checked, and provided to the consumers or owners of the information. To perform this role well, the information required to meet the organization's business needs should be identified and classified. Information is required by different stakeholders at different phases of an information life cycle. An information management plan is created for each project. The information management plan includes identification and classification of documents, data and 3-D model deliverables, performance tracking/reporting, data maturity, delivery milestones, software tool implementation activities, and business processes for gathering the right information during day-to-day business processes.

Q: What do your routine interactions with other departments in the organization look like?
A:

- To ensure that business information meets company needs, key stakeholders are regularly engaged to identify the information for their particular function. This information is categorized, data sources for the information are documented (a functional data matrix is maintained), and ownership of the information is identified and applied in the business processes.
- Regular meetings with stakeholders and consumers of the information are essential. Typically, new data is often identified and added to the functional class library (i.e., data matrix), information management plan, and business processes. The goal is to ensure that valuable data is added and made available in an easy-to-use and accessible format. Conversely, the data with little or no business value is eliminated from scope to prevent data overload.

Q: What advice would you give to someone who wanted to switch from their current field to a more technically oriented role? What's their best approach?
A:

- If a person has a desire to be technical, they can achieve this simply by attending training and applying the learnings in an area they have interest in. Personal observation: Not all people fit well into technical roles. Education alone does not make a person successful in a technical role. For example, a person with low attention to detail is not likely to succeed in a technical position.

Q: What advice would you give to a nontechnical professional who suddenly found themselves managing a team of technical employees?

A:

- Ensure the nontechnical professional meets with the technical team routinely to understand their roles, tools, deliverables, and processes. Implement measurements and tracking so that the work products from the technical team are visible and validated. If required, set up a peer review or audit process amongst the technical team members. This will ensure technical issues are identified and addressed.

Q: What should a nontechnical executive do to help their company succeed from a technical perspective?

A:

- A nontechnical executive should utilize internal or external technical resources to advise them on the current technical options available to the organization. Often an external consultant can advise on the best practices, tools, and processes that are currently in use in a specific industry.

Q: What lessons have you learned, or what advice would you give, based on your experience to someone outside your field?

A:

- Do not assume the information currently tracked is correct. Identify the source and validate the information.
- Eliminate unnecessary or redundant creation and reporting of information (e.g., How many spreadsheets are generated each day in a company that contain the same information from different sources with different results?).
- "Big data" is not necessarily "good data." If data is being gathered that has no practical use, eliminate it.
- Do not count on software tools to solve a company problem. Do not implement tools without first defining the business "processes."
- Identify and document the office of record for information sources.

Q: What things do you wish that people outside your field understood about your role?

A:

- Information is powerful. It can save a company money, improve efficiency, ensure sound decisions are made, reduce rework, and make a company successful.
- If invalid information is used, it will cost a company money and ensure inefficiency, poor decisions will be made, rework will occur, and a company will not be as successful as it could have been.

Q: How can others in an organization help you succeed personally or professionally?

A:

- An organization should identify information silos. These silos are areas where information may be kept and used only by one team member or a small team. An organization should seek to eliminate information hoarding.
- Organizations should identify the sources of business information and the *owners* of the information. There is often a lack of data ownership and a lack of accountability for the integrity of the information.

Q: Do you have any other advice for a student in business school?

A:

- Intern at more than one organization while attending school. Working in different industries will enable practical application of the college learning in a business environment.

Author's note: Ms. Byrnes's answers to the questions should seem a little more vague than in the previous two chapters. This is exactly what would be expected of a strategic-level decision maker. Rather than accomplishing specific goals, her responsibility to is to ensure the continuing operation of her organization. This is difficult to delineate in an itemized fashion, so many of the answers are more fully answered.

■ CHAPTER 22

Cases

OVERVIEW

It is useful to have real-life examples of the use and perception of information systems. Consider these cases and extend some suggestions on what the potential underlying problems might be and how those problems might be solved.

CASE 1: LA SUPERIOR

These cases were developed from the author's experience teaching in the executive MBA program at Instituto Technologico de Monterrey, Chihuahua Campus.[1]

Chihuahua is the name of both a state and a city in Mexico. The state is situated at the northern end of Mexico. It borders the United States on its north and northeast sides. The state of Sonora borders its western and southern sides. The state of Sinaloa borders its southeastern side. Chihuahua is the

---

1   Cases 1 and 2 originally appeared in the article, "Chihuahua Cases," (pp. 104–116) by Daniel D. Friesen, Rocio Marcela Ramirez Rubio, Liliana Molina Chavez (2005), published in *Business Journal for Entrepreneurs*, no. 4. Copyright © 2005 by Franklin Publishing Company. Reprinted with permission.

largest state in Mexico. The city of Chihuahua is home to approximately 500,000 people; it is the second largest city in the state. Approximately 2.9% of Mexico's gross national product comes from Chihuahua. Manufacturing (cellulose, wood moldings, beer), agriculture (apples, nuts, tree, sheep, and cattle), and mining (nonferrous materials, zinc, and silver) are important economic activities. Higher education outlets and well-equipped industrial parks are available throughout the region.

Chihuahua City is located 372 kilometers from Juarez (El Paso, Texas), 494 kilometers from Monterrey, 920 kilometers from Guadalajara, and 1,455 kilometers from Mexico City. It is located at the intersection of the Chuviscar and Sacramento Rivers. The railroad that connects Chihuahua City to the Pacific coast has been called "the most scenic engineering work of Mexico."

"La Superior" is a small convenience store located in Chihuahua City at the intersection of 37th and Ojinaga Streets. Mr. José Rubén Contreras Delgado (Rubén) has owned and operated La Superior for 20 years. The original business was founded in 1960 by Mrs. María José Delgado, the mother of the current owner. Rubén's store is actually one of the three La Superior convenience stores that are owned by the Delgado family. The sign above Rubén's door reads, "*Abarrotes La Superior.*" Rubén's sister owns and operates one of the stores located 10 blocks away. A cousin owns and operates the other store located approximately seven blocks away. The sister's and cousin's La Superior stores have a cooperative arrangement whereby items unavailable in one store are sold from the other store. This transfer is accomplished by messenger. Rubén does not participate in the cooperative arrangement.

The neighborhood is middle-class urban residential; that is, most of the buildings are dwellings and there is little space between them. Small convenience stores like La Superior are interspersed among the residences with some frequency.

The floor plan of La Superior is small, approximately 15 feet wide and 40 feet long. A schematic of the floor plan appears in Exhibit 1. An array of food, toys, and household items are available for sale; although, as one might imagine, the selection is generally limited (single brand, single size, etc.). The products with the highest turnover include milk, sodas, bread, tortillas, fruits and vegetables, beer, snacks, and cigars. Freshly baked breads and tortillas—purchased from a bakery and a tortilla maker, respectively—are kept in a humidor. The fresh items are more popular than the processed breads that are also available. Other important inventory items include flour, cleaning products, canned products, dry beans, general medicines (aspirin, antacids, bandages, etc.), and candy. A refrigerator case with milk, beer, cheese, and other perishables occupies a wall (a license to sell beer is required).

The store also sells products with little turnover. Rubén feels that these products help attract the clients and maintain their trust, ensuring that they will find what they need at any time. Low turnover products include small toys, envelopes, wrapping paper for presents, candles, and magazines.

Obviously, the neighborhood convenience store concept has a different implementation in Mexico than in the United States. Smaller sizes are the norm among the neighborhood stores in Mexico. A higher level of congeniality is present in the Mexican counterpart: Generally, the owners recognize their clientele and know most of them by name. Such is the case at La Superior. Rubén knows his clients pretty well: He knows where they live, their names, and their familial connections. Sometimes when his favorite clients—older ladies mainly—call him, he collects the items they request and delivers them to their homes. Telephone calls to determine item availability are common. Customer traffic arrives mostly by foot. Larger, more formal convenience store chains exist; for example, there is a Mexican version of 7-Eleven named Oxxo. These stores tend to be located in commercial areas rather than residential neighborhoods.

La Superior's hours of operation are 7:30 a.m. to 10:00 p.m., 7 days per week. The majority of time, the store is attended by Rubén; occasionally, Rubén's nephew Caleb attends the store. These occasions occur mainly on Saturdays, Sundays, and Monday mornings.

Rubén relates the following problems:

- As the principal employee, he feels that he has little free time outside of the store. He would like to have a person help him, but he would not trust just anyone. After all, the business is small and his reputation is at stake.
- When he closes the store, even for a short duration, his clients get very upset. This reaction is so extreme that there are times when he cannot go to the general market to replenish his inventory. Fresh vegetables and fruits (avocados, tomatoes, onions, etc.) are problematic because of high turnover on an inventory purposely kept small to avoid spoilage.
- According to Mexican tax law, all businesses must present a list of what they have sold during the quarterly reporting period. This is difficult for Rubén to do accurately because he records his list in a notebook, by hand. He gives this notebook to an accountant who makes the tax declaration for him. Sometimes his handwriting is misunderstood; fines have resulted from this situation. Furthermore, when there are a lot of customers in the store, accurate recordkeeping becomes difficult.
- Sometimes Rubén will extend credit to trusted customers. Sometimes he takes losses on this credit because his notebook-based accounting system generates many annotations that become confusing.

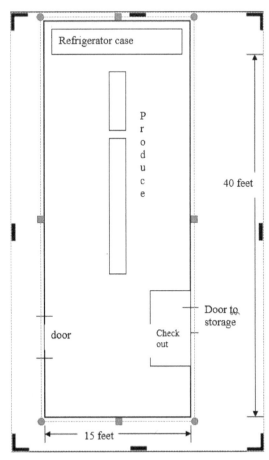

FIGURE 22.1 *Case study door-to-storage produce 15' × 40' refrigerator case to check out.*

- Approximately 1 year ago, Rubén tried using a computer, both to manage the inventory and to track sales. This attempt was unsuccessful for several reasons. First, he lacks computer skills. As a result, he felt frustrated by the procedure. Second, implementing the product bar code system caused some consternation among the customers. The computer he used was an older, hand-me-down model obtained from a family member.

CASE 2: D'ANSA JAZZ STAGE

D'ansa Jazz Stage (DJS) is a dance school located in Hacienda de la Esperanza in Chihuahua. DJS was founded in 1997 by Liliana Molina Chávez and her sister. The initial enrollment was 15 girls. At that time, DJS was managed using a single computer. Today, DJS's enrollment is approximately 500 students. There are 27 employees and DJS is organized into the following four departments:

1. Academia: Organizes the students' and instructors' schedules. Disciplines, courses of study, and student progress are tracked.
2. Administrative: Manages the collection and distribution of funds, including student tuition and billing, paying DJS's bills, and instructor compensation.
3. Events: Responsible for all aspects of school events, other events, and participation, including shows, recitals, competitions, trips to conventions, costumes, scheduling venues, tickets, and so on.
4. General Coordination: Responsible for coordinating the departments, ensuring that information exchanges are timely and correct, and creating cordial relationships with other schools.

Each department has a computer with internet access via telephone line and modem. Enrollment management is accomplished using small database management systems for each department. Information sharing between departments is accomplished via physical document exchange (i.e., paper or portable computer media). For example, when a student goes to the Academic Department to add a class to their schedule, the Academic Department notifies the Administrative Department of the schedule changes using the appropriate form.

DJS is the largest competitor in the market, although the second largest competitor is comparable in size. The other dance schools in Chihuahua really do not compete with DJS because (a) they are much smaller and (b) the dance classes are not the main activity offered (e.g., fitness clubs that also offer dance classes).

Finding teachers for DJS has not been difficult; DJS subscribes to the "grow your own" plan. Most of the teachers are former students who have been preparing for teaching at DJS for years. When an interested student acquires the necessary age and experience, they are given small groups of beginner students in order to hone their teaching skills. New teachers are assigned progressively more advanced students, larger classes, and increasing responsibilities. Occasionally a teacher from outside DJS is required. This situation requires interviews, a resume, and a demonstration class to assess technical and pedagogical skills.

As mentioned, DJS has a large enrollment. The building was designed and built for DJS; however, the purchase was financed by a local bank and that mortgage is still being paid. DJS has enough space to accommodate 1,200 students. At this point, there is unused capacity. To use the building at its maximum capacity, classes would have to be conducted continuously throughout the day. Afternoon classes are almost at maximum capacity in terms of ability to accommodate students. Morning classes are a different story: There are very few dance classes held in the morning due to low demand.

Liliana's second concern is the lack of efficiency that the current information-sharing system possesses. Transforming student records to paper in order to transfer them between departments seems to cause much loss of time.

CASE 3: MANAGEMENT OF TECHNICAL PEOPLE

Will has worked in information technology for close to 40 years. His latest position was working for one of the top technology providers in the country. His job title was principal security engineer, but he works in development and development operations. I've seen him create a decision support system running on Visual Basic, using Excel as both storage and functionality. I asked him about his best manager. Here is his description:

> My last manager, Brent, was by far the best manager I've ever worked with. I'm disappointed I only had a year to work with him. His management style seemed, from my perspective at least, to (a) collect only quality talent and remove those who weren't qualified (bad teammates are at least as terrible as a bad manager) and (b) throw new people at as many different projects and at as many differing technical "slots" as he could, and (c) take the results of the latter and then assign accordingly. I'm not kidding when I say I learned more in the first 4 months working in technology development than I had in the previous 4 years in CSO. Yeah, it was being thrown in the deep end and stressful as all hell, but he always made sure it wasn't too much—frequent check-ins; letting me know I really could say, "I've already got too much," and actually asking my opinion on how much (get this) *fun* I was having with it. As I settled into a slot, it felt like I had picked the best place for me, but really it was both of us working together to find the place where I could do my best because it actually was the best.

Compare that to his answer about his worst manager:

> Previous "manager" (team lead, technically we were peers on the organization chart) was the worst. He would assign a task; then 90% through my completion, he would say, "Why didn't you do it with xyz technology. ... Never mind, I'll just do it myself." He'd micromanaged my process up to that point, so he knew what I was doing all along, but he waited until I'd spent days or weeks on something to effectively steal it from me and do it his own way. It got to the point where I just wouldn't do anything at all. I would just

wait for him to do it. Why waste all that effort? He wanted everything to be done his way, and he would argue for days (literally) until you either gave in or he would just do it himself. It was terrible.

CASE 4: THOUGHTS ON MANAGING TECHNICAL PEOPLE

This case was reported by an associate director for administration, information technology services, at a small midwestern private college. He had been working in technical fields at academic institutions for 21 years. The majority of his time was spent on procurement, strategic communication, collaborating with peer groups, inventory management, vendor relations, budgeting, and basic departmental management.

> The most effective thing that I've ever seen my manager do is prove his intellectual agility. In so doing, he completely turned our departmental expectations (and those of the campus) around. In February 2008 we had already planned a 6-month rollout of Google apps. We had already dealt with much faculty reluctance, especially from the moron who was our CAO/ provost at the time. Then a server disaster forced us to cram that migration into 3 weeks. We did it, and within a couple months we had changed nearly everything we did. We could begin decommissioning and clearing out much of our old data center equipment; our documentation writer was freed up to do one-on-one training sessions rather than group classes; since Google Docs included effectively limitless space, our network people were able to abandon a clumsy network file sharing system that had rigid, too-small storage limits; and since the system was pretty much completely reliable, all of us were able to actually do our damn jobs for a change.
>
> I found out later that the president of the college, not a very IT-savvy person and not a patient person either, had a short private conversation with our CIO just days before the disaster. He said something like, "What would you say if I directed you to immediately buy and implement Microsoft Outlook and be done with it?" My manager gently replied (he never raised his voice, ever), "I would say, sir, that you need to find another CIO if you did that. I and my people are preparing to implement what the college has publicly chosen over the past year. If you choose to override that, I won't be a party to it."

This case points out some important ideas. You pay for technical expertise. The technical experts went through an arduous process of vetting ideas and balancing needs. It would take the most extreme situation to consider second-guessing them. In addition to being borderline unethical behavior, the president's actions violate some of the most reliable principles of project management. Another interesting idea is software by service.

CHAPTER 23

Models

Information systems and management science share a fascination with conceptual models. It is not always fashionable in current business programs to include a model-based approach to management. However, many of these models are widely recognized in the field of information systems. As a result, this is a list of one model for each chapter, along with a short description, a reference for online study, and the original source where possible. Accessing and at least perusing the original source is a good practice. There's a difference in authority between someone who says "I learned about this in class" and "When I read the original article …" while talking comfortably about the material.

CHAPTER 1 MODEL: OPTIMIZATION

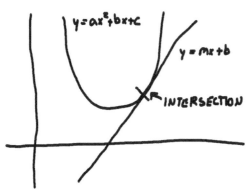

FIGURE 23.1 *Optimization example.*

A lot of management science is related to math. As a result, many of the basic models for approaching management from a quantitative point of view are really just a rehash of basic math. In an optimization problem, there tends to be an assumption that two different forces are working at odds. Typically it's some variation of production versus some variation of consumption. One common example of this is a supply/demand curve from economics. Other examples might be production versus time or variable cost per unit.

The two things that are necessary are a rate that is the result of two measurements and the two measurements themselves. It's possible to increase this to three or four or five measurements. At that point, the easiest solution is called linear algebra. For an overview of linear algebra, Khan Academy (n.d.) has an excellent series of videos.

CHAPTER 2 MODEL: SWOT ANALYSIS

FIGURE 23.2 *SWOT matrix.*

A SWOT matrix can be a simple tool for evaluating the efficacy of new ventures or when deciding on how to continue an existing venture. It can also become very detailed and technical when used as a primary evaluative mechanism. However, this description will just apply to its use as a relatively subjective brainstorming tool.

The idea is to create four spaces. In these four spaces, list the possible strengths of a particular approach, weaknesses of that approach, opportunities that might come as a result of that approach, and threats that may be related to that approach. These last two can be seen as possible or probable positive or negative situations that could arise. In each of the four spaces, the lists should be ranked in order of importance, and then only the top three to five should be used.

Next, a 2 × 2 grid is drawn (sometimes called a TOWS matrix), with strengths as the top row, weaknesses as the bottom row, opportunities as the left column, and threats as the right column. The idea is to then come up with strategies in each respective cell whereby each strength could be used to maximize each opportunity, each strength could be used to neutralize each threat, each weakness should be addressed to avoid missing out on each opportunity, and each weakness should be coupled with each threat to identify situations that should be avoided at all costs.

Used this way, a SWOT analysis has the potential to identify a number of possibilities. It was developed by a researcher named Albert Humphrey at the Stanford Research Institute. Unfortunately, primary sources on the material are scarce, but secondary articles are numerous.

CHAPTER 3 MODEL: CIA MODEL

In information security, one ubiquitous model is the CIA model, which stands for confidentiality, integrity, and availability. These three attributes are the broad target for information security decisions. Confidentiality refers to the idea that only people who should see the data can see the data. Integrity refers to the idea that the data only changes in ways that are intended and part of the normal operation of the organization. Availability refers to the idea that when appropriate people need access to the data, it's available.

The most ideal use for the CIA model is to understand that any security decision is going to be a tension between all three of these areas. For example, posting confidential information on a bulletin board is going to be great for avail-

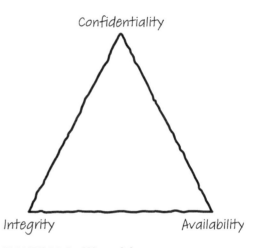

FIGURE 23.3 *CIA model.*

ability but ridiculously bad for confidentiality (anyone can see it) and integrity (a little whiteout and a steady hand could change it). Good information security decisions try to balance all three of these areas without falling between a minimum appropriate threshold in any of them.

There is not a good, referential source. However, it is part of the CISSP certification material for (ISC)[2], the International Information System Security Certification Consortium.

CHAPTER 4 MODEL: REVENUE MODEL (P = R – C)

An organization needs to know the relative value of any of their activities. A company should make money on most of its activities or there's little purpose in it doing that activity. As a result, probably every business function needs to remember that it is responsible for how it spends its money and what it's getting in return. This isn't always in real dollars, as larger organizations also use internal accounting metrics to identify value.

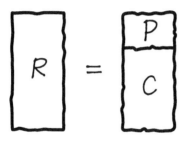

FIGURE 23.4 *P = R – C.*

However, the basic revenue model is further valuable. Every activity's benefit is directly equitable to how much it makes minus how much it costs, or profit is equal to revenue minus cost. As a result, as long as the units are the same, it's a useful metric. It's used in information technology to project whether there's a relative value in hardware upgrades; it's used in time management to determine how much preparation is valuable. There are a large number of more advanced models that build off of this basic one.

CHAPTER 5 MODEL: C = VC + FC

FIGURE 23.5 *Costing.*

Another fundamental business function is understanding how much something costs. The problem is that cost is not normally a strict matter of "go to the store, buy a thing, and it costs what it costs." Instead, there are a number of ancillary costs that are involved in every decision. For example, going to the store costs gas, it causes some wear on a vehicle, it costs time that could be spent doing something else, it uses up some durability on clothing, wallet, and so on.

As a result, there are two kinds of costs: fixed costs and variable costs. Fixed costs are easiest to conceptualize as costs that will have to be paid regardless of what happens. A factory costs the same amount in rent and taxes regardless of whether it's working 24 hours a day, 8 hours a day, or sitting idle. A computer that's purchased to work from home costs the same amount whether it's being used for 30 minutes or 8 hours. Variable costs are the costs that are directly related to a specific item. In the factory, using the equipment for an hour costs an hour's worth of electricity, costs an hour's worth of raw material for the manufacturing process, and costs wages for the workers.

This cost is not always in dollars. Opportunity costs might be measured in people not met by attending one event instead of another. Many projects are costed by the number of hours employees put into them. However, because these are put into numbers, they're easy to massage into a specific model for determining optimization under the optimization process.

CHAPTER 6 MODEL: THEORY OF TRANSPORTATION

One of the first academic logistics models was actually produced by sociologist Charles Cooley. Cooley believed that the process of transportation was a function of society. As a result, it was possible to analyze the distribution and layout of cities by looking for certain key factors. His model predicts that "wealth and population will accrue in areas where there is a break in transportation." Breaking that down, it suggests that in many situations it's possible to look at some value getting bigger when there is a break in some process.

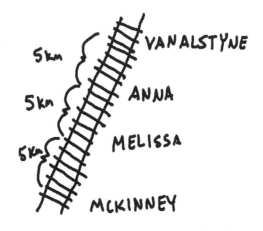

FIGURE 23.6 *Theory of transportation diagram.*

This is important, because it explains things like why insurance companies make money even though they don't produce anything; why the Medicis were such a powerful family in medieval Italy; or even why Amazon is such a large company in the current era. Breaking the theory of transportation down into a model provides a good overview of where some of the problems or successes in an organization are.

Charles Cooley's *The Theory of Transportation* was published in 1894. Parts of it have aged very well, and parts of it have not. It is, however, worth looking through to see how many of the patterns of development and business have changed or stayed the same over the last century and a half.

CHAPTER 7 MODEL: CLASSICAL ECONOMICS

There are a number of modern economics theories. However, one of the basics of classical economics is still a good broad-strokes approach to evaluating decisions. Adam Smith suggested that all production comes down to the use of capital (that is, machinery, equipment, or tools), land, and labor. The economic environment has changed substantively since Adam Smith formulated his theory. In an effort to unify the theory across many different cultural conceptions of the rights of landowners, and because land is purchased in a manner similar

FIGURE 23.7 *K Versus L.*

to capital, the theory can be simplified to capital versus labor (K versus L). Economists use this as a simplistic measure of whether it is easier in a given region to buy a machine to perform a task or hire someone to do the task.

In a more applied business scale, K versus L has a more direct approach. Essentially, it asks "Does capital make the overall process go faster?" Only, in this case, capital is something like designing a spreadsheet that automatically calculates certain values. If those values need to be known routinely and the spreadsheet reduces the time from hours to seconds, it is likely a good trade-off. On the other hand, if someone could hand calculate the value in a few minutes, the spreadsheet took hours to make, and it only needs to be known once, it's probably not a good idea. The anecdotal story relates a man running down the street next to his bike. When someone asks why he doesn't get on, he says, "I can't! I'm running late, and I don't have time to stop and get on my bike!"

Adam Smith's (1776) *The Wealth of Nations* is part of the canon of both business and economics. It was written in 1776 Britain, so the language has not aged well; however, both the book and a number of summaries are available on open source book repositories like Project Gutenberg.

CHAPTER 8 MODEL: FIVE FORCES

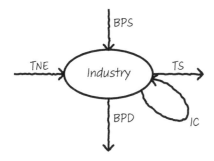

FIGURE 23.8 *Five forces diagram*.

Porter's five forces model is one of the cornerstones of strategic business. It is less helpful for low-level decisions that need more precise numbers; however, for brainstorming and broad thinking, it is one of the most useful tools available. Almost every business professional should be able to recognize it, and it is very much in the common lexicon.

Porter proposed that one method of evaluating the healthiness of competition in an industry (and therefore whether it was an industry worth entering) could be evaluated in five parts. Each of these five parts could easily be covered in a chapter on its own, even one that specialized in information systems—especially in information systems:

- Bargaining power of suppliers is the relative ability of suppliers to dictate terms (e.g., if only one company in the area sells a particular raw resource or there are legal protections on price).
- Bargaining power of distributors is the relative ability of distributors to dictate terms. For example, a franchise can't dictate terms to the corporate office but a company that has a legally protected monopoly probably can.
- Threat of new entrants refers to the difficulty new competitors encounter when entering the industry. If a particular market requires billions of dollars in factories, there is less competition compared with one that just requires printing business cards.
- Threat of substitution is the difficulty consumers encounter when they attempt to replace a product with a substitution. For example, there is no practical difference in many areas between bottled and tap water, which is why bottled water is so heavily marketed.

- Internal competition is the relative fierceness of competition in an industry. Some industries are cooperative (e.g., one company will send clients to the other company if it's a better fit). Others are not.

Michael Porter is typically worth reading, and his models are widely used. His original article is titled "How Competitive Forces Shape Strategy" from *Harvard Business Review* in 1979. However, he immediately followed it up with a book titled *Competitive Strategy* (1980) that goes into broader detail and depth.

CHAPTER 9 MODEL: THEORY X VERSUS THEORY Y (THEORY Z)

Douglas McGregor developed a theory of motivation centered on expected results. In theory X management, an employee expects to get punished for not completing a task properly. In theory Y management, the employee expects to get a reward for completing a task properly. This basic push and pull of managerial responses both informs about a company's culture and provides a predictive model for how to capitalize on certain approaches.

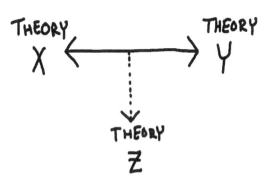

FIGURE 23.9 *Theory X/Y/Z diagram.*

There is a third approach, theory Z, that is intended to be a counterpoint to both X and Y. In theory Z, the reward or punishment of an employee is immaterial; the employee performs a task properly due to corporate loyalty.

The original sources are a journal article by Douglas McGregor and a book, *Theory Z: How American Business Can Meet the Japanese Challenge*, by William Ouchi (1981). However, McGregor's two books, *The Human Side of Enterprise* (1960) and *The Professional Manager* (1967) are more interesting.

CHAPTER 10 MODEL: PLUTCHIK'S WHEEL OF EMOTION AND SENTIMENT LEXICONS

One of the things that business is well known for is pulling theories and models from a wide variety of fields. Because large-scale data analysis is so new and the application of traditionally qualitative forms of management to quantitative functions is still novel, their data analysis has some staple models and references that are further afield than standard business.

Robert Plutchik was a relatively obscure researcher for the business field until analysts needed a simple framework to define emotive structures. Plutchik's full model is

FIGURE 23.10 *Plutchik's wheel.*

complex, but it reduces every human emotion into a variation on one of eight: joy, trust, fear, surprise, sadness, disgust, anger, or anticipation. This is useful for data analysts because it means that they can categorize words or phrases into just one of those eight emotions rather than the thousands of similar emotive words in the English language. As a result, Saif Mohammad developed the NRC emotion lexicon, which uses a broad survey of users to attempt to categorize as many words as possible into one of those eight emotions.

This means that when analyzing text, rather than having to understand the material semantically, an analysis can simply count up the number of words that correspond to emotions in the lexicon and respond accordingly. But if dropping down to eight is a good idea, how about further? Bing's lexicon reduces words to either having a positive or a negative connotation, meaning that entire text sources can be reduced to aggregate analyses of positivity or negativity.

Dr. Plutchik's (1991) book is just called *Emotions*, and it realistically is only going to be attractive to some people. More interesting and applicable to information systems is the NRC lexicon can be found at Dr. Mohammad's website (www.saifmohammad.com), and the Bing lexicon can be found at Dr. Bing Liu's website (www.cs.uic.edu/~liub/).

CHAPTER 11 MODEL: RATIOS

Finance is, at its core, about ratios. In another sense, finance is about measuring efficiency. Remember that efficiency is, at its core, a measure for all processes. So, in another sense, finance can be reduced ad absurdum to a measure of ROI: both the expected rate of return for investment in a certain course of action as well as the historical rate of output given a certain investment of input. There are too many ratios to go over each of them. However, for information systems, the wide range of investment and finance ratios are an excellent source in looking for more ways to evaluate the efficiency of a process.

Here's one easy ratio to consider: Current ratio is current assets divided by current liabilities. One example of this might be for a process that repeatedly fails. If current assets are equated to what was accomplished and current liabilities are equated to what was promised but undelivered, then it may be an indicator that the process will eventually begin to succeed if that current ratio improves each time.

This is a bit of a stretch, but it is one way of transferring from expertise in finance to information systems or alternately pulling useful approaches from outside information systems.

CHAPTER 12 MODEL: DEMING (PDCA) CYCLE

Lean processes, PMI, and Six Sigma are all methodologies related to the improvement of current processes by identifying areas where the quality is in a nonideal situation. But where did they get their methodology from? The most popular, early model is the Deming cycle. He proposed that the cycle be related to plan, do, study, act. Like many of the other cycles discussed, it is intended to feed into itself in an iterative cycle.

Plan means documenting the current situation and identifying which areas need to be observed in better detail. *Do* implies the actual development of the better process, likely in some form of prototyping situation. Study is to go back and make sure that the do phase was actually producing the desired results or to determine whether there's now evidence of a better approach. The *Act* phase is then to implement the solution across the board. But the entire approach can be expanded with much greater detail.

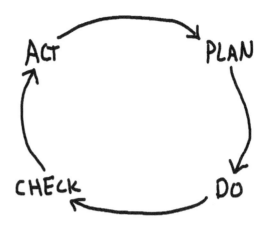

FIGURE 23.12 *Deming cycle.*

The Deming cycle is referred to throughout literature, and there are several widely endorsed variations that are also worth looking at. Unfortunately, most of his works are out of print.

CHAPTER 13 MODEL: MASLOW'S HIERARCHY OF NEEDS

Abraham Maslow presented a hierarchy of needs as a fundamental force that drives humans toward the attainment of goals. It is a difficult concept for a business person to talk about (and this goes for many field-specific theories). While two business people can talk about the theory in a broad and applied way, when they present their conclusions to a psychologist, the psychologist will explain that they don't really fully understand what's going on. Typically, businesspeople continue on with their presuppositions.

FIGURE 23.13 *Maslow's hierarchy of needs.*

Maslow's hierarchy of needs is a pyramid design. People seek to fulfill needs lower on the pyramid before the needs that are higher on the pyramid. For example, on the bottom are physical needs like food and sleep. Above that are things that extend the ability of the physical needs to continue to be met (clothing, a place to sleep, etc.). Only after those needs are met is a person going to try to find friendship or love. The next level is focused on nontangible rewards like fame and praise. At the top of the pyramid are spiritual needs such as understanding and a sense of having given back to the community.

Maslow's hierarchy of needs is published in a number of places, but the original paper is called "A Theory of Human Motivation," (1943). This is available at a number of places online.

CHAPTER 14 MODEL: ACCOUNTING MODEL (A = L + E)

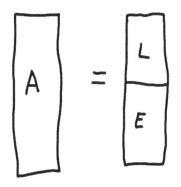

FIGURE 23.14 *Accounting model.*

In accounting, there is a basic model: An organization's assets are equal to liabilities plus equity. Assets are the accountable items of value that belong to an organization. The liabilities are promises made in order to get those things, and equity is essentially a variation of promises fulfilled. This is not how an accountant would represent these concepts.

These concepts have two important factors. The first is that it's a fundamental aspect of corporate accounting. Every manager should be familiar with these basic concepts and understand how they apply to both departmental and organizational budgets. This directly impacts the ability of any given process to function. In addition, understanding that the basic accounting practices are lingua franca in business and allow for representing technical or complex internal workings of a process or a system into a basic set of terms that will allow at least a broad understanding of what is happening.

CHAPTER 15 MODEL: SIMON'S MODEL OF DECISION MAKING

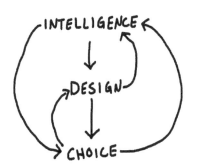

FIGURE 23.15 *Model of decision making.*

Herbert Simon's model for decision making rested around what he called an ideal administrator. How does the ideal administrator make a decision? This introduces his model of choice. It is a separate model, but it is easy to see how it bears a striking resemblance to the software development life cycle. But while the SDLC is related to the design of something, Simon's model is related to decisions of all kinds. In his ideology, it was possible to abstract the idea of what the decision-making process was, regardless of whether the actual decision was related to something simple and basic like shampoo selection or something huge like whether to invade another country.

The first step is the intelligence phase where the ideal administrator knows and can gather all of the information or data needed in order to make a rational choice. This leads to the design phase, where the ideal administrator is able to detail every possible solution to the problem, resulting in a listing of many alternatives. Finally, the choice phase is where the ideal administrator is able to make a valid decision based on the options. It's important to note that there is a fallback option of going back to the intelligence phase from the design phase and to the design phase from the choice phase, as it's possible that something was missed in a nonideal implementation of this model.

Simon's (1947) model is detailed in *Administrative Behavior*, which is one of his earlier works. Like many of the academic areas, this should lead into a wide range of follow-up works that extrapolate on the original model.

CHAPTER 16 MODEL: CLUSTER ANALYSIS

Cluster analysis is a statistical analysis technique. It has been around since the first half of the 20th century, originating in psychology as a way to objectively group complex phenomena (like personality). In a cluster analysis, the analyst is essentially attempting to take a group and divide it into two or more subgroups where each element is more similar to the other elements in its subgroup than it is different to those not in its subgroup.

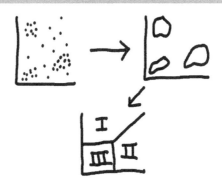

Performing a cluster analysis in a modern, data-rich environment is a computationally intense process that definitely requires all of the variations

FIGURE 23.16 *Cluster analysis example.*

on business analytics. However, since most people outside of business analytics are not familiar with business analytics methodology, it's a good gateway. It is a common situation for an analyst to want to be helpful but not be able to open a coherent dialogue with their clients (internal or external). As a result, the expertise of the analyst is wasted as they produce technically correct graphs or models that are not what the viewer requested.

Learning about the broad spectrum of analytics techniques, what they can do, and how to read their output graphs is becoming a more valuable skill. Many analysts are pleased to have a request come to them along the lines of "I think this data would benefit from a cluster analysis. Can you look at a rough outline of what I want and either confirm it empirically or improve it?"

O'Reilly has an excellent series of books called In a Nutshell. These texts are intended to provide either the first steps in learning a new skill or a concise reference for someone trying to remember specific task details. They are a good source to learn just enough about analytics to be able to communicate with analysts.

CHAPTER 17 MODEL: PORTER'S GENERIC STRATEGIES

Michael Porter's competitive strategies model suggests that there are only two effective ways to compete in a market-driven economy. The two poles in this model are the cost method, where a company tries to compete on the basis of low-cost alone regardless of quality, and the differentiation model, where a company

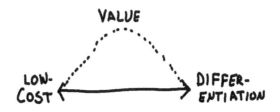

FIGURE 23.17 *Porter's generic strategies.*

trades based on the perceived quality of their product regardless of cost. The model tries to demonstrate that this is not a spectrum, since competitors operating at the edges will always outcompete those in the center.

The competitive strategy model also allows for a second dimension of competition. Competitors can seek to be operative across the entire industry or they can choose a narrow scope within the industry. This is why, for example, regional ice cream, local fast-food chains, and local convenience stores will frequently survive in a specific region alongside widespread nationwide competitors.

Porter's generic strategies are detailed in the same text as his five forces model.

CHAPTER 18 MODEL: PRISONER'S DILEMMA

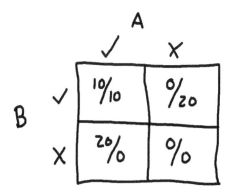

FIGURE 23.18 *Prisoner's dilemma.*

The last model isn't fully a model. It is a representation of an entire field of study, one that is easy to lay out and consider the implications of. Game theory is not a theory about playing games, per se. Instead, it is a field of information sciences that is concerned with making logically and/or provably correct decisions based on a variety of situations in which symmetric or asymmetric information is available. For example, in chess there is symmetric information since everyone knows every possible move both sides can make. In poker there is asymmetric information since each player only knows their own hand, not the others. Advanced game theory is an absolutely vital source of learning for managers to more fully understand their own and others' decision making.

The prisoner's dilemma is any situation where the best move for each person is to each trust the other not to betray them, but both will betray the other regardless. The set-up is typically that a crime is committed and two conspirators are arrested and locked in separate cells without the ability to communicate. Each prisoner knows the following:

- If neither confesses, they'll each get off completely free.
- If both confess, they'll get a normal sentence of around 10 years.
- If one confesses but not the other, the confessor will only be charged with a minor crime and get a 2-year sentence but the other will be charged and get a stiff sentence of 20 years.

Obviously, the best solution is for both prisoners to keep their mouths shut. However, the expectation is that both parties will inevitably confess for fear that the other will confess. They see the "reward" of only a 2-year sentence and the "punishment" of a 20-year sentence, and so they ignore the 0- and 10-year sentences as factors.

There are a number of variations: The amount of symmetry of information that is available, how the responses change based on the ratios of sentence, how the responses change based on the units used (e.g., money or reputation instead of sentences). The original formulation for the prisoner's dilemma was put together by Albert Tucker, but so many variations and extrapolations have been developed that an introduction to the field is more useful. *Prisoners of Reason* by S. M. Amadae (2016) is a good overview.

REFERENCES

Amadae, S.M. (2016). *Prisoners of reason*. Cambridge University Press.

Cooley, C. (1894). *The theory of transportation*. Publications of the American Economic Association.

Khan Academy. (n.d.). Linear algebra. https://www.khanacademy.org/math/linear-algebra

MacGregor, D. (1960). *The human side of enterprise*. McGraw-Hill.

MacGregor, D. (1967). *The professional manager*. McGraw-Hill.

Maslow, A. (1943). A theory of human motivation. *Psychological Review* 50(4).

Ouchi, W. (1981). *Theory Z: How American business can meet the Japanese challenge*. Addison-Wesley.

Plutchik, R. (1991). *Emotions*. University Press of America.

Porter, M. (1978). How competitive forces shape strategy. *Harvard Business Review*.

Porter. M. (1980). *Competitive strategy*. Free Press.

Simon, H. (1947). *Administrative behavior*. Macmillan.

Smith, A. (1776). *On the wealth of nations*. W. Strahan and T. Cadell.

CHAPTER 24

Historical Figures

In biology education, most students are exposed to the lives and contributions of famous figures within and outside of the biology field. In mathematics education, most students learn the names of some salient figures and about many of the men and women that the various theories are named after. In history education, biography of historical figures is self-evident. It is a shame that in business education the various important figures of the fields are not always considered. Many fundamental precepts of business are the same, as human nature doesn't change quickly. As a result, this is a varied and eclectic list of historical figures with some relevance to information systems, including a quick biography, their contributions, and why they appear on this list.

One very valuable resource for business professionals is reading biographies. These are people who have developed a career worth having a biography written about them. They tend to have insight that is either valuable to emulate or valuable to know about because others find it worth emulating. Either way, a broad and eclectic mix of biographic reading is a good investment in yourself.

CHAPTER 1 FIGURE: HERBERT SIMON

Herbert Simon was an expert at the science of making decisions. He was an economist and a computer scientist who won awards in both fields in the 1970s. He is interesting as he is one of the last generations of pre-computer-ubiquity academics. Computers existed, but they weren't the driving force that they are now. Instead, he conceptualized a sort of ideal administrator who always made the right decisions. The vast majority of his career was describing how this ideal person made those decisions in a rational, fair, and implementable manner.

What's fascinating is how thoroughly this ideal administrator represents, but still predates, computers. As a result, many of his concepts and theories apply to modern decision sciences in a relatively close approach. His book, *A Behavioral Model of Rational Choice* (1955), could be considered a required text for understanding what constitutes a proper management information system (MIS).

CHAPTER 2 FIGURE: MICHAEL PORTER

Michael Porter is an interesting figure in the strategic management industry. He is still active as a researcher and consultant in the field. He represents a common sequence of roles (within the confines of survivorship bias) in the academic world. He started in a practical field, engineering, and then proceeded to a business focus. From there, he established his research and teaching agenda at Harvard Business School. After he gained tenure, he began to expand his influence to broader fields in an effort to demonstrate how his theories had a wider impact in more fields than just strict business (e.g., health care and international politics). At a certain point, however, there tends to be a drive to establish a longer-lasting legacy than just a few theories. So, for the last 10 or so years, he has been focusing more roundly on social issues and encouraging social responsibility in organizations.

There aren't any good biographical books on Michael Porter. However, his book *On Competition* (1998) could be read as a progression of his ideas on the subject. Otherwise, there are also a number of articles available on the internet documenting his perspectives in bits and pieces (for example, Colvin, 2012).

CHAPTER 3 FIGURE: BRIAN KREBS

Identifying information security experts is a little difficult. There are three reasons for this (that are related):

1. Successful security experts tend to value their privacy and are therefore hard to identify.
2. Information security is, in many ways, measured by how much a person doesn't know.
3. Information security experts have almost all had major failures, and these failures tend to gain the spotlight more than their successes, which can ideally be described as "nothing happened."

Rather than identify information security experts, it is possibly more valuable to identify a reference on information security. Brian Krebs is a well-respected journalist who specializes in information security issues. He, himself, is not a security expert. However, he routinely interviews experts and highlights specific areas of concern.

Krebs on Security is an excellent website to use as a springboard to understanding the current issues in the information security world and for discovering more resources to brush up on specific issues.

CHAPTER 4 FIGURE: MICHAEL DELL

Michael Dell is a classic story in the field of technology. He started Dell Computers in his apartment, put together computers, and built a business into a global brand name that was one of the leaders in the PC sales field. As the company grew, it issued stock and became publicly traded. As part of this process, Dell lost some of the control over the company that he might have otherwise had. The details are murky, but the outcome was clear that, over the course of a decade or so, the company's name became synonymous with poorly made computers.

This was not an ideal situation for Michael Dell, since the company was literally giving him a bad name all over the world, so he proceeded with a fascinating financing arrangement to buy Dell back and turn it back into a private company, thereby providing him with much greater control. Since then, he's done an excellent job improving the quality of the computers his company produces. His story is an insight into the inner workings of the hardware industry as well as the motivations of what drives a high-level CEO.

Dell's (1999) autobiography is called *Direct From Dell: Strategies That Revolutionized an Industry*. However, the book was written during his earlier wave of success. A more recent biography is worth watching for, otherwise more surface-level articles are relatively common (e.g., Bort, 2018).

CHAPTER 5 FIGURE: ADA LOVELACE

Ada Lovelace is one of the most fascinating and anachronistic figures in history. She could, unchanged, star in a Victorian steampunk novel. Her biggest claim to fame was being a computer programmer before computers existed. Otherwise, she was a mathematician in a time when women weren't considered even-keeled enough to learn mathematics. She was an English countess who was also the daughter of a Romantic poet.

Charles Babbage was one of her contemporaries, and he proposed the analytical engine— what someone from the modern era would recognize as a computer. Ada's response was to conceptualize that this analytical engine didn't just add; it could be programmed. A historically important programming language, Ada, was named after her as a result of this.

There are a number of resources on Ada Lovelace, but two of the most interesting are *Ada Lovelace Cracks the Code* (*Rebel Girls Chapter Books*) (2019) and *The Thrilling Adventures of Lovelace and Babbage: The (Mostly) True Story of the First Computer* (2015).

CHAPTER 6 FIGURE: VINT CERF AND TIM BERNERS-LEE

The internet originated as a technical problem for the Defense Advanced Research Projects Agency (DARPA). Their Cold War–era task was to design a system that protected the communications infrastructure of the country against the loss of a central communication hub. Their solution (ARPANET) was a packet-based network of redundant nodes and backbones that allowed for a "self-healing" routing system. That is, even if the shortest distance was normally to go from California to DC through Chicago, it would be able to detect if the Chicago node were slow or down and reroute through, say, Dallas. This was the direct precursor to the internet. Vint Cerf was one of the researchers involved in this process and has taken the larger part of the public spotlight since then.

Sir Tim Berners-Lee, on the other hand, is the "inventor" of the internet. While ARPANET was the structure and back end of the internet, Berners-Lee is responsible for the "http" (hypertext transfer protocol) at the beginning of every Web link. The idea of adding "depth" to a text article by allowing a user to click on a link to open a deeper layer of the article was novel and ultimately incredibly successful. Berners-Lee continues as the director of the World Wide Web Consortium, which is one of the organizations that defines standards for web-based technologies.

Interestingly, both of these researchers view the modern internet as ultimately self-destructive. They have both proposed solutions that are radically different from each other's, and neither solution has gained substantive traction in the face of monetization and short-term interests. Their biographies aren't interesting, but their proposals for the future can be read: Wolverton (2019) and McKendrick (2019).

CHAPTER 7 FIGURE: RICHARD STALLMAN

Richard Stallman is the quintessential 1980s hippy software hacker. He got his start as a researcher at MIT and eventually developed into the principal proponent for the modern free software movement. One of his original projects in that arena was the GNU project (GNU stands for GNU's Not Unix!; the acronym refers back to itself). He eventually moved on to a broader conceptualization of the Free Software Foundation, which provides tools and support for the production and distribution of free software. His positions are worth reading, as they are substantively different from the majority of pro-business positions on security, software, and copyright.

One of Stallman's famous quotes is, "Think free as in free beer, not free speech," which has led to a common clarification of stating something is free (as in beer) or free (as in speech), the distinction being that one is a statement of monetary value and the other is a statement on human rights.

Stallman's website is a panoply of modern digital civil rights calls to action. His GNU manifesto is an interesting piece of technology history, providing insight into the motivation and rationale behind producing a product and giving it away for free (Free Software Foundation, 2015). Sam Williams (2002) has a biography of Richard Stallman called *Free as in Freedom* that is most interesting for its interviews and quotations from others. Interestingly, because it's published under Stallman's GNU free documentation license, it's easily obtainable from public sources as well as for purchase from booksellers.

CHAPTER 8 FIGURE: DONALD KNUTH

Donald Knuth is one of the greatest programmers of the modern era. What has he programmed? Probably nothing of any common recognition. However, his life goal is to complete *The Art of Computer Programming*, which is the final word in computer science. Knuth begins by defining his nomenclature, moving on to defining every operator he uses and then proceeding to develop the entirety of computer-based math.

The first volume of *The Art of Computer Programming* was published in 1968. It has been slated for seven volumes, and he is currently about halfway through writing the fourth volume. The fascinating part of this text, from an outside perspective, is that the entirety of it is still as valid as when it was originally written. Each volume builds on the one before, expanding the function of computer science from a mathematical foundation.

The *Art of Computer Programming* is worth flipping through. However, it is a patently difficult text to follow. Much of Donald Knuth's correspondence is publicly available and worth reading. His *Things a Computer Scientist Rarely Talks About* (2001) is of particular interest.

CHAPTER 9 FIGURE: JOHN MCAFEE

McAfee Antivirus is one of the world's leading antivirus programs. It's also a scam, according to John McAfee, the founder of its owner company. Many security experts agree that antivirus programs are ineffective at protecting against viruses (or rather, they're effective at protecting against the very small percentage of viruses they are designed for). This is not a uniform opinion, but it is a commonly held one.

However, McAfee draws particular attention for being willing to state publicly that the company he founded and built is not effective. In response, of course, McAfee Associates has disavowed his opinion on the matter. He also draws particular attention for a variety of bizarre and ostentatious positions and escapades: from seeking the Libertarian nomination for U.S. president to living on the lam claiming that government operatives were hunting him because of his knowledge of illegal activities.

McAfee has a large number of public position statements available based on his previous presidential campaign and his upcoming 2020 primary run. They may or may not be of value to review, but frankly with anything related to McAfee it is difficult to separate fact from fiction.

CHAPTER 10 FIGURE: NOAM CHOMSKY

Noam Chomsky is one of the most brilliant men alive. He is a linguist who was so frustrated with the process of cataloguing the English language in a systematic process that he developed a branch of mathematics to aid in his proofs. This process of normalization has led to a fundamental process in database design. Chomsky's normal forms go from 1 through 4 in routine database operations (CNF3 is a standard expectation for a properly designed database) but then go through higher numbers and across specialized paths depending on the application.

Reading Noam Chomsky's works is a little different, since he's operating from the perspective of a linguist. However, the fact that it is so substantively different from the commonality of business perspectives is precisely what makes it worth reading. In addition, some of his later work presents a more political science orientation that presumes concepts of game theory that are useful to a business professional. The key to understanding his work is to understand that his word choice is based on the word's most technical denotation, even for words that most people use in a sloppier, more connotative form.

Chomsky's website is https://chomsky.info. It would be worthwhile to have a broad understanding of most of his books, but also take time to read his biography, *Noam Chomsky: A Life of Dissent* by Robert Barsky (1997).

CHAPTER 11 FIGURE: ELON MUSK

Elon Musk is a cautionary tale. He is a relatively intelligent person. He is not always a very smart person. There are different kinds of intelligence, and it's possible to excel in some and not others. In Musk's case, he has a tendency to promise too big, and he has a tendency to say things he shouldn't say. Neither of these are unforgivable; however, he also has a marked inability to back down from the trouble that either of those put him in.

Elon Musk made his largest windfall from his involvement with PayPal in the early 2000s. (This is interesting in itself, since there are parallels to be made between the suddenly rich in the technology industry, the suddenly rich in sports, and lottery winners. They all have a tendency to self-destruct.) He's leveraged that windfall into more money, largely emphasizing a data-oriented approach deriding the government and others as being unable to accurately assess a given industry or technical problem. He is consistently panned for his inappropriate and insulting conduct toward others.

Doing a search for news about Elon Musk will prove valuable to glean examples of what not to say, what not to do, and how not to act. Elon Musk may make valuable contributions in several industries, but it will be by luck and despite himself.

CHAPTER 12 FIGURE: JACK MA AND JEFF BEZOS

Jack Ma and Jeff Bezos are both fascinating individuals. They are both more and less than human from the perspective of the majority of people. A lot of the stories about them devolve into Hellenistic stories about betrayals or epic divorces or the lavishness of their lifestyles. On the other hand, the rest of the stories are very impersonal, detailing their actions without going into their motivations at all. They're just shells for their business interests. It's important to remember that these are people with personal, human motivations behind their actions. They are able to make true philanthropic decisions as well as succumb to narcissistic impulses.

But what's interesting is that in the United States the discussion about either the downfall of stores or the novelty of modern commerce tends to rest around Amazon (and all those other guys). But to a certain extent, in China and parts of Asia, the conversation revolves similarly around Alibaba (and all those other guys). Amazon and Alibaba are two major international companies, both of them relatively unknown and unused in the other's sphere of influence, and they're in direct competition with each other. Jeff Bezos and Jack Ma are the respective CEOs and driving personalities behind the companies, respectively. Understanding how they got to the point they're at and why they make the decisions they do is an excellent exercise.

Two biographies that are fascinating to read are *Alibaba: The House That Jack Ma Built* by Duncan Clark (2016) and *The Everything Store: Jeff Bezos and the Age of Amazon* by Brad Stone (2013). These are best consumed while keeping in mind that they are very heavily massaged into a specific shape by PR teams. Similarly, that shape is the same; Samson, Gilgamesh, Thor, and Hercules all represent the same cultural aggregate persona, and Ma and Bezos try to cast themselves in an eerily similar light.

CHAPTER 13 FIGURE: LINUS TORVALDS

Linus Torvalds is the originator of the Linux operating system. This is interesting because his original release was in 1991, about 3 decades ago. For that entire time, he has been the principal and primary developer behind the operating system. Granted, it isn't the exact same role, and he's changed and matured along with it, but he still maintains day-to-day control over every aspect of the development of the main Linux kernel.

Whereas that position was originally almost entirely a computer science–focused programming role, it has developed through phases into one more oriented toward software development, then project management and team lead, and now through strategic planning and development. Torvalds likely still does some programming, but realistically it would only be at a hobbyist level. The vast majority of the programming is done by the widespread volunteer base of the open source community, and he serves as the final project manager. That doesn't mean he doesn't still have the programming expertise, but it does mean that it has changed. And tracking that change is very interesting.

Torvalds's correspondence is frequently profane and impolite. It is frequently very technical, and his tirades are about small things. As interesting as reading a person's own words might be, it is not necessarily fruitful in this case. However, comparing a curated interview from relatively early in Linux's history (Moody, 1997) with a more recent one (Young, 2019) is of value.

CHAPTER 14 FIGURE: BILL GATES

Calling Bill Gates a cautionary tale would be too strong a phrase. However, he does represent a certain almost mythological quality in his role at Microsoft. He started the company in the mid-70s. It was the standard nerd in a garage mythos that has been the "official" story for almost every tech company started around the same time. While he had help and a lot of luck, he did have an expertise and knack for programming that allowed him to build the first couple of convenient and easy-to-use operating systems for PCs and lay the framework for the mega-company Microsoft eventually became.

However, the interesting part is in the running of Microsoft. Gates turned out to have a certain business acumen as well. His interactions with other companies are all common examples that are referred to in a variety of situations. However, in retrospect, he takes a bit of flak for his ruthlessness and the fact that many of his decisions were good for Microsoft but not necessarily good for the industry. For example, one generally accepted interpretation of events is that Microsoft Office's dominance stems from Microsoft purchasing the parent companies of all competing products solely to shut the companies down. Even further, it turned out that Gates was good at running a smaller company, but as Microsoft grew, he wasn't trained or equipped for the larger corporate leadership role.

Regardless, Bill Gates's (1999) autobiography is called *Business @ the Speed of Thought: Succeeding at the Digital Economy*. For more recent thoughts and biographical notes, Gates's website is www.gatesnotes.com.

CHAPTER 15 FIGURE: STEVE JOBS

Steve Jobs is a fascinating counterpoint to other technology leaders of the same class. However, where they focused on business or the technical aspects and had a certain amount of give and compromise, Jobs was always focused on the user experience. There are dozens of stories about products that were never launched because of a minor design imperfection or products getting stuck in the development area for decades before Jobs felt that they had been refined enough to be palatable to the public. He has a fascinating story: His harsh obsession with perfection essentially got him fired from his own company, and then when the company started dying without him got him hired back.

Jobs's most important contribution to the world of business and information systems is not the specific technologies he pioneered or supervised. Instead, he redesigned the landscape of product improvement. Prior to the release of the iPhone, products would compete with each other and release a new version when the old version stopped selling well. After the release of the iPhone, products needed to compete with themselves, release on a more fixed schedule, and offer tangible benefits toward replacement.

There are dozens of biographical books and movies on Steve Jobs, and they're worth reading (given that he was somewhat idolized). However, also interesting are the careers and biographies of his contemporaries, such as Jony Ive, Steve Wozniak, and Tim Cook.

CHAPTER 16 FIGURE: BARACK OBAMA AND DONALD TRUMP

The nature of politics was changed worldwide with the 2012 and 2016 U.S. presidential elections. Regardless of whether President Obama would have won the 2012 election without it, his team's use of data-mining techniques ensured victory and definitely excited the scope of his victory. A good article to read about it, with a number of secondary references to follow, is Szkolar's (2013). However, the team was stymied by its own success. Essentially, there was a disagreement within the Democratic Convention about what to do with the tools. One side suggested that the data would be valuable to the DNC only if it were openly made available for improvements before the next midterm elections. The other side was worried that it would lose it advantage by releasing it.

The tools were not released publicly; as a result they were not developed until just before the 2016 election. President Trump's team looked at the approach that the 2012 democratic team used and realized that it could make anyone win an election. As a result, they doubled down on the mechanism. Again, regardless of whether President Trump would have won the 2016 election without it, his team's use of data-mining techniques ensured victory and definitely excited the scope of his victory. Finding a summary of this effect is difficult, as it's much more politicized than the data-mining aspect of the 2012 election, even at the time. The most authoritative and objective documentation is likely the Mueller Report, which is extremely long and detailed. Otherwise, more readable sources will develop over time and they will hopefully become less partisan. Search for news related to Cambridge Analytica.

CHAPTER 17 FIGURE: JOHN VON NEUMANN

John von Neumann is a different historical figure from the rest. Chapter 17 is a bit of a visionary chapter, and von Neumann was definitely visionary. He developed theories and ideas that are still being used by a variety of fields as, variously, idealistic targets, presuppositions, or working theories.

Two basic structures from von Neumann of specific interest to information systems are the von Neumann architecture and the von Neumann machine. The von Neumann architecture is the source of the four-component model this text used earlier. All modern computers and almost all computers through history have followed the von Neumann architecture (input, output, story, with processing split into an arithmetic/logic unit and a control unit). A von Neumann machine is a theoretical concept for a future wave of industrialization. Essentially, a robot is given a program that instructs it to build an exact copy of itself and then to program that copy exactly the same as its own program. This is envisioned as a way to, for example, completely mine out an asteroid or develop medical robots that replicate like human cells.

John von Neumann's various theories are well worth reading. They are technical, but most have layman summations available. Another option is *John von Neumann: Selected Letters*, edited by Miklos Redei (2006).

Finally, remember to consider the impact that short, pithy statements have. Sun Tzu (2017), for example, famously collected many verses that are used as mantra in *The Art of War*. Many businessmen would consider it a requirement to read and contemplate each mantra. The reality is that different people will take many different things out of them, and they largely only serve as a focus for consideration. It's served well for thousands of years as such, so it is probably worth at least a review.

There are other examples that have historically been used as representative of human society. Zen Koans, self-help gurus in modern times, and specific industries' codes of ethics are all common examples. Others consider a classic literary education as being vital: Plato, Aristotle, Homer, Virgil, Shakespeare, are all classics of Western education. Pairing them with an expository description of what should be taken from them on the nature of men and their decision making is also useful. If nothing else, having read them is useful for pulling out pithy quotes in business settings to seem wise.

The key, though, is that all of these biographies and classic texts expound on human behavior. Information systems may deal with information and have a large technical component, but it's still largely a field about humans and how they make decisions.

REFERENCES

Barsky, R. F. (1997). *Noam Chomsky: A life of dissent*. ECW Press.

Bort, J. (2018, November 18). The fabulous life of billionaire Michael Dell, who is once again fighting with Carl Ichan over the future of his company. *Business Insider*. https://www.business insider.com/life-of-michael-dell-2016-9

Clark, D. (2016). *Alibaba: The house that Jack Ma built*. Ecco.

Colvin, G. (2012, October 15). There's no quit in Michael Porter. *Fortune*. https://fortune.com/2012/10/15/theres-no-quit-in-michael-porter/

Dell, M. (1999). *Direct from Dell: Strategies that revolutionized an industry*. HarperCollns.

Free Software Foundation. (2015). The GNU manifesto. https://www.gnu.org/gnu/manifesto.en.html

Gates, B. (1999). *Business @ the speed of thought: Succeeding in the digital economy*. Grand Central Publishing.

Knuth, D. (1968). *The art of computer programming*. Addison-Wesley.

Knuth, D. (2001). *Things a computer scientist rarely talks about*. CSLI Publications.

McKendrick, J. (2019, July 15). World Wide Web inventor Tim Berners-Lee pushes for a better Web. *Forbes*. https://www.forbes.com/sites/joemckendrick/2019/07/15/world-wide-web-inventor-tim-berners-lee-pushes-for-a-better-web/#4af82082c762

Moody, G. (1997, August 1). The greatest OS that (n)ever was. *Wired*. https://www.wired.com/1997/08/linux-5/

Padua, S. (2015). *The thrilling adventures of Lovelace and Babbage: The (mostly) true story of the first computer*. Pantheon.

Porter, M. (1998). *On competition*. Harvard Business School Pr.

Rebel Girls (2019). *Ada Lovelace cracks the code* (A Good Night Stories for Rebel Girls Chapter Book). Simon and Schuster.

Redei, M. (2006). *John Von Neumann: Selected letters*. American Mathematical Society, London Mathematical Society.

Simon, H. (1955, February). A behavioral mode of rational choice. *The Quarterly Journal of Economics*, 69(1).

Stone, B. (2013). *The everything store: Jeff Bezos and the age of Amazon*. Little, Brown and Company.

Szkolar, D. (2013, January 24). Data mining in Obama's 2012 victory. Syracuse University. https://ischool.syr.edu/infospace/2013/01/24/data-mining-in-obamas-2012-victory/

Tzu, S. (2007). *The art of war*. LSC Communications.

Williams, S. (2002). *Free as in freedom*. O'Reilly Media.

Wolverton, T. (2019. January 20). The internet's "father" says it was born with two big flaws. *Business Insider*. https://www.businessinsider.com/google-vint-cerf-explains-why-early-internet-lacked-security-and-room-2019-1

Young, R. (2019, April 2). 25 years later: Interview with Linus Torvalds. *Linux Journals*. https://www.linux-journal.com/content/25-years-later-interview-linus-torvalds

Conclusion

W here should you go from here? That's always a good question after completing a text of this sort. The authors included a large series of recommended readings and further topics for study in the appendices. Those are certainly worth exploring. They were intended to be of value regardless of specialty. Further, independent study on these matters is also useful. Remembering that collegiate-level study is not intended to provide absolute knowledge on all things, it's up to the individual to determine their own course of study from that point.

For nontechnical managers, the best place to go from here would be to ensure that the topics presented in this class are taken into consideration as they either pursue further study or practice their own specialty. Most of the topics covered in this text are intended to be reexamined over time.

For others who may decide they want to explore adding to their technical repertoire, here are some options:

1. A class in visualization: Visualization falls largely in the technical areas but it is definitely a human endeavor. Computers are not yet at the point that they can design or add clarity without a human director.
2. A class in statistics or analytics: Learning just enough analytics to understand what a statistical analysis means is useful. Most people can't understand the specifics of a detailed analysis, and as a result they frequently make wrong decisions based on a misunderstanding. Being the person at an organization who can understand and simplify these outputs is a valuable skill.
3. A programming class: Programming in any language is a specific skill. But there is also a meta–skill set behind it that is involved with analytical thinking, clinical troubleshooting, problem solving, iteration, and several other thought patterns. Those skills are general and are valuable in almost any industry.

CPSIA information can be obtained
at www.ICGtesting.com
Printed in the USA
LVHW062006140922
728392LV00001B/6